Special Edition
Using
Storage
Area
Networks

NIIT

201 W. 103rd Street
Indianapolis, Indiana 46290

D1475438

SPECIAL EDITION USING STORAGE AREA NETWORKS

Copyright © 2002 by Que

International Standard Book Number: 0-7897-2574-6

Library of Congress Catalog Card Number: 20-01096112

Printed in the United States of America

First Printing: November 2001

04   03   02   01   4   3   2   1

Trademarks

Warning and Disclaimer

Associate Publisher
Dean Miller

Acquisitions Editor
Candy Hall

Development Editor
Sean Dixon

Managing Editor
Thomas Hayes

Project Editor
Tricia Liebig

Copy Editor
Sean Dixon

Indexer
Bill Meyers

Proofreader
Melissa Lynch

Technical Editor
Aaron Rogers

Team Coordinator
Cindy Teeters

Interior Designer
Ruth Harvey

Cover Designer
Dan Armstrong
Ruth Harvey

Page Layout
Susan Geiselman

CONTENTS

About NIIT

NIIT is a global IT services and IT training corporation. NIIT has over 4,900 employees spread across 37 countries and generated over $270 million in revenue in the financial year 2000.

NIIT is actively involved in creating software solutions and learning solutions for markets worldwide. NIIT's software development procedure is controlled and managed through processes that are 100% ISO 9001-certified and assessed at SEI-CMM Level 5 for the maturity of our software processes ensuring high-quality solutions which are delivered on-time and on-budget. NIIT's client list includes Hewlett-Packard, IBM, Microsoft, NETg, AT&T, Hitachi, Computer Associates, Red Hat, Oracle, Sony, Sun Microsystems, and Toshiba.

NIIT pioneered IT education and training in 1982. NIIT trains over 350,000 career IT professionals through its network of over 2000 training centers in over 26 countries. NIIT has an alumni base of over 1.5 million IT professionals.

NIIT has one of the world's largest learning content development facilities staffed with over 900 learning content development professionals. Over the years NIIT has developed a range of curricula for people with diverse requirements—from students seeking careers in computers, to IT professionals needing advanced training, to global corporate enterprises like Microsoft, Arthur Andersen, PeopleSoft, Computer Associates, Tivoli Systems, Sun Microsystems, The World Bank, Thomson Learning, Pearson Education, and Oracle who require end-to-end learning solutions.

DEDICATION

To all the folks at home for bearing with our frequent disappearances.

—Pooja Sachdev

—Rajiv S. Arunkundram

ACKNOWLEDGMENTS

Writing this book has required a great deal of hard work and focus. To help us maintain this and encourage us through the temporary phases of writers block were a number of people whom we would like to thank.

None of this would have ever happened but for Kumar, who pushed us into writing this book and allowing us explore our way around. His encouragement and faith in us and of course the constant urging (and sometimes pestering!) saw us through the completion of this book.

Anu, who gave us valuable insights on presentation strategies. We are also grateful to her for having reviewed many of our chapters and making them more readable.

Jaishree, Mani, Nivedita, Bharathi, and Swapna for the time they spent looking at these chapters and helping us to make them better.

Karpagam, for contributing to some sections of this book. Our special thanks to her.

Sindhu, who created all those amazing graphics you get to see in the book. In trying to design the figures, she gave us a completely new perspective to the way the content could be handled.

Our special thanks to Shantanu, who coordinated the reviews for this book, and to Aaron Rogers, Sean Dixon, and Gayle Johnson for their technical and editorial guidance.

And how could the acknowledgement be complete without mentioning all our colleagues for their constant support and blind faith in us and for all those jokes and coffees. Thanks a lot!

TELL US WHAT YOU THINK!

As the reader of this book, *you* are our most important critic and commentator. We value your opinion and want to know what we're doing right, what we could do better, what areas you'd like to see us publish in, and any other words of wisdom you're willing to pass our way.

As an Associate Publisher for Que, I welcome your comments. You can fax, e-mail, or write me directly to let me know what you did or didn't like about this book—as well as what we can do to make our books stronger.

Please note that I cannot help you with technical problems related to the topic of this book, and that due to the high volume of mail I receive, I might not be able to reply to every message.

When you write, please be sure to include this book's title and author as well as your name and phone or fax number. I will carefully review your comments and share them with the author and editors who worked on the book.

Fax: 317-581-4666

E-mail: feedback@quepublishing.com

Mail: Dean Miller
           Que
           201 West 103rd Street
           Indianapolis, IN 46290 USA

INTRODUCTION

In this introduction

That you are reading this introduction is proof enough that SANs are becoming the latest buzzword in the storage sector.

A SAN is a server-to-storage network that offers a highly scalable and manageable setup. It can offer gigabit speed connectivity with a comprehensive fault-tolerance system and low ownership costs. All these features and a whole lot more have led to the increase in the market share of SANs.

We welcome you to the world of storage area networks!

THIS BOOK IS FOR YOU

This book is targeted at both network administrators and planners who are looking for an efficient way to scale the storage systems in their networks. Even if you are new to the world of storage management, this book will provide you with the basic knowledge of storage systems. This book does assume that you are familiar with the setup and working of simple networks. However, you will find that we have not assumed any prerequisite familiarity with storage networks.

HOW THIS BOOK IS ORGANIZED

This book is divided into three parts. Each part covers a specific topic that you will need to know in order to use Storage Area Networks in your network. Part I gives you a basic introduction to the features of storage area networks. Part II walks you through the different components of storage area networks. Part III deals with the concepts of designing, implementing, and managing storage area networks in your network.

At the end of the every chapter, you will find a "Products Arena" section. This section exposes you to the latest SAN products from different companies. We have tried to ensure that products from different companies are projected in a manner that will help you select a suitable product for your network.

Part I, "Basics of Networking and Data Storage," introduces you to storage area networks.

Chapter 1, "The Evolution of Storage Area Networks," introduces you to the world of SAN. You will learn about the evolution of SANs; how the storage networking concepts moved from DAS to NAS and finally to SANs. This chapter also gives you a brief overview of the different computing models that most networks follow. This chapter serves as a roadmap to the rest of the book. It introduces you to the different terms that you will find commonly used in the world of SANs.

Chapter 2, "Externalizing Storage Using Storage Area Networks," introduces you to the most forceful feature of SANs, the externalization of storage. This chapter familiarizes you with the different components of a SAN and the way data transfers take place in SANs.

Part II, "Storage Area Networks and Their Components," takes you through a detailed study of the different components of SAN. The two distinctive highlights of this section are the coverage of Fibre Channels and the explanation on how to select the right components for your SAN.

In Chapter 3, "Storage Area Network Interfaces," you will learn about the concepts of Serial and Parallel interfaces. The different types of interfaces that are used in SANs are demystified in this chapter and you will be given detailed explanations about the advantages and disadvantages of each interface. This knowledge will equip you with the know-how to decide on the right interface for your SAN.

In Chapter 4, "Storage Area Network Interconnects," you will be introduced to the devices that make SAN possible. From a simple modem to a complicated director, we take you through all of it. The combination of these interconnects is what will determine the interoperability of your SAN. This chapter will explain how each of these devices works and what advantages and restrictions it will impose on your SANs.

In Chapter 5, "Fibre Channel," you will be introduced to the world of Fibre Channel. In this chapter, we tell you all about Fibre Channel   What is it, why is it important, what is its architecture, and what are its advantages and disadvantages. We will also tell you about the different classes of services offered by Fibre Channels. And not to forget, this chapter has a section on the different topologies that you can design using Fibre Channels.

In Chapter 6, "Storage Area Network Fabrics," you will be introduced to the advantages of using fabrics in your network. This chapter will explain about the advantages of using switching in your SANs. In addition, it explains switching in SANs by comparing it with the all too familiar LANs. In addition, this chapter carries a section on storage consolidation.

Part III, "Designing, Managing, and Implementing Storage Area Networks," takes you through the most critical functions of any network   design, implementation, and management. This part aims to equip you with enough knowledge to objectively evaluate your SAN and how well it suits your requirements.

In Chapter 7, "Designing Storage Area Networks," you will be introduced to the basic concepts in the designing of SANs. This chapter provides you with the different topology combinations that you can use in your SAN. The chapter also includes some fictitious case studies that will provide you insights on how to apply the concepts covered in this part.

In Chapter 8, "Implementing Storage Area Networks," you will be introduced to the different guidelines to be followed in the implementation of SANs. This chapter will explain how to configure your SAN for backup operations. Also included is a detailed section on positioning your SAN for high availability. This chapter introduces you to the implementation of LUNs.

In Chapter 9, "Managing Storage Area Networks," you will learn about how SAN management affects the implementation of SAN. You will be introduced to the different strategies and stages in SAN management. This chapter also includes sections on zoning and the use of SNMP in SAN management. The case studies introduced in Chapter 7 are taken through Chapters 7, 8, and 9 and all concepts are explained in relation to these case studies.

In Chapter 10, "The Future of Storage Area Networks," you will be introduced to what the future has in store in the world of SANs. In this chapter, you will be introduced to Virtual Interface Architecture, which holds the promise to change the way our networks communicate. You will also be introduced to the effects of using SAN in the web scenario.

The appendixes in this book contain an advanced study of VI, quick reference information about SAN, and a detailed listing of the different SAN products. Finally, this book provides you with an appendix that contains a glossary of all the terms used in SAN.

CONVENTIONS USED IN THIS BOOK

This book uses various stylistic and typographic conventions to make it easier to use.

Note

When you see a note in this book, it indicates additional information that can help you better understand a topic or avoid problems related to the subject at hand.

Tip

Tips introduce techniques applied by experienced developers to simplify a task or to produce a better design. The goal of a tip is to help you apply standard practices that lead to robust and maintainable applications.

Caution

Cautions warn you of hazardous procedures (for example, actions that have the potential to compromise the security of a system).

Cross-references are used throughout the book to help you quickly access related information in other chapters.

→ To learn more about XYZ.com, **see** "Case Study 1," **p. 162**

Basics of Networking and Data Storage

CHAPTER 1

THE EVOLUTION OF STORAGE AREA NETWORKS

In this chapter

INTRODUCING STORAGE AREA NETWORKS

Storage area networks (SAN) are a mass storage solution for providing fast and instantaneous access to the storage in an enterprise network. SAN refers to the network infrastructure that is used to connect the computers and devices on the LAN to a separate network containing storage devices.

SAN provides a reliable and highly scalable system for the storage of enormous amounts of data. The key point that distinguishes a storage area network from other storage arrangements is that the storage resides behind the servers and not on the LAN.

SANs are used typically in enterprise networks where the storage requirements are in the range of multiple terabytes. The storage area network provides an ideal solution to networks that require a scalable and robust system. The disaster recovery features and zero downtime are key features of most SAN setups. Any organization that requires a huge storage capacity coupled with a highly reliable and scalable system and has the money to afford it should employ a SAN solution.

This chapter gives you a brief history of storage area networks and an overview of their major features.

A PARADIGM SHIFT IN NETWORKING MODELS

The storage of large volumes of data is always an area of concern in organizations and enterprises, whether big or small. With the tremendous increase in the need to store data and avoid data mishandling or data corruption, research companies and vendors are looking forward to a means that provides an effective solution for the organizations. Storage area network (SAN) is the technology being pursued as an answer to storage management and many organizations are implementing SANs as their storage system.

Storage area networks are a network architecture that has its origin in the centralized storage model. However, SANs are not just a variation of the centralized storage model. SANs can be thought of as a new networking model that has its roots in the centralized storage model. To put it very simply, a storage area network is a dedicated network for centrally monitoring the storage network. The centralized storage model and its impact on storage area networks is discussed in detail in later sections of this chapter.

In the SAN architecture, the backup process ensues without affecting the working of the existing network. The advantage of a centralized type of storage is that all the clients in a network can access the data stored from one location. The best thing about SANs is that they leverage the advantages of all the networking models. The SAN architecture is now even viewed as a networking model specialized to suit storage networks. To understand the paradigm shift in storage network management, let us look at the different network models in detail and see how SANs emerged.

The Computing Models

A storage system is a combination of hardware and software. Before getting into the details of the different storage systems, take a look at the three different computing models used for networks: centralized, distributive, and collaborative. Any network is based on one of these networking models. To understand the paradigm shift, you will see how storage management is handled in each of these models.

The Centralized Computing Model

The *centralized* computing model is a mainframe environment in which a number of dumb terminals are connected to a mainframe. The mainframe is in turn connected to shared resources. The mainframe performs all the processing activities. The terminals serve as devices that accept commands as input and display results as output.

The advantage of this model is that you can control and manage the network centrally. However, the costs associated with the centralized computing model are high, because the model requires servers that can offer high storage capacities as well as take care of all the processing.

Consider a fictitious company, Westside Inc., which creates a wide gamut of software products. The company is spread over four locations in the United States with 20 branches. The central office of the company is located in Dallas. Westside Inc. has 10 other branch offices in Texas out of which three are in Dallas. The other offices are located in New York, Seattle, and California.

Assume that the company was founded in 1976 (when the Internet was not as popular as it is today!) in Dallas and began with 40 employees. It is unlikely that a new company starts with an enterprise network, and the fictitious Westside Inc. definitely did not need one for 40 employees. Therefore, the company began with a simple 10Base-T network in which all the terminals are connected through a set of hubs, as shown in Figure 1.1.

10Base-T refers to a type of transmission medium, the twisted-pair coaxial cable, used in Ethernet networks, such as LANs. This kind of network is still commonly in use in most places, especially when the number of systems that you want to connect is limited. This is the primary reason why Westside Inc. picked 10Base-T over other networks, such as 10Base-2. The other major advantage of picking a 10Base-T network is that it is scalable and can be converted into an internetwork as the network expands.

→ To learn more about hubs, **see** "Hubs," **p. 101**

Now assume that Westside Inc. has expanded to three different offices: the documentation center, the finance center, and the software development center. The finance center is located in Seattle, the documentation center is in California, and the development center is in New York. Westside Inc. built its network in the finance center based on the centralized computing model. In the setup shown in Figure 1.2, a number of thin clients are connected to the server. The accounting application resides on the server. The clients connect to the server and execute the required component of the application. The processing for the component is done on the server and the result is either updated on the database or is sent to the client for display.

Figure 1.1
The network design of Westside Inc. is based on a 10Base-T network, in which hubs connect the terminals to the server.

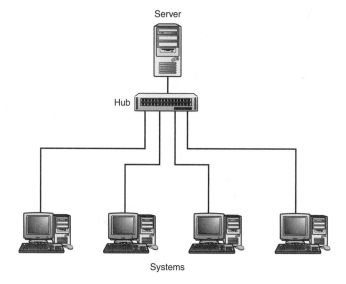

Figure 1.2
In a centralized computing model, the server is shared among thin clients.

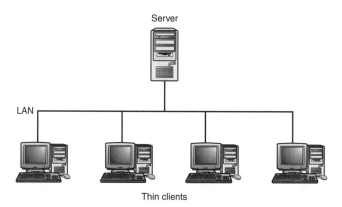

> **Note**
> A diskless network computer is also known as a *thin client*, in contrast to a *fat client*, which includes a disk drive.

The thin clients in the finance center are used for data entry. These thin clients can be referred to as *dumb terminals*, because these systems do not perform any operation other than accepting the input and displaying the output. As stated earlier, the centralized computing model proves to be expensive but Westside Inc., being a large organization, can afford this expensive computing model.

The disadvantage of the current setup in the finance center is that if the server fails, data processing stops. Server failures will eventually lead to high downtimes. As you will see later, these are the precise problems that SANs overcome by using a different networking model for storage.

Westside Inc. adopted the centralized computing model for the finance center for security purposes. Because the data processing happens at the server end alone, it becomes easier to implement checks and constraints on the data. However, if you are familiar with the implementation of security on centralized networks, you might think otherwise. It's like this: You put all your eggs in one basket so that you can guard it against all odds. However, in practice, it is more of a risk protecting them; even if one of the eggs is endangered, in effect all of them are endangered!

Any storage network needs to have security, and SANs promise you exactly that. Because a storage area network is a separate network, it can implement security across the network without combining it with the LAN security settings. Because the storage in a storage area network is not a part of the normal LAN or WAN, the security settings on the LAN need not be applicable to the storage devices. The use of a separate network enables the SAN to segment the existing LAN to suit the existing security needs. For example, in a SAN it is possible to segment the LAN users across domains. Storage area networks also use LUN masking to segregate different platforms to share a single storage device.

→ To learn more about SAN Security and LUNs, **see** "LUN Host Masking," **p. 226**

HOST-CENTRIC AND DATA-CENTRIC COMPUTING MODELS

The centralized computing model is categorized into two types of computing models: host-centric and data-centric. In a *host-centric* setup, as the name implies, the host is in the center of the network and is connected to a set of thin clients. The host-centric model is also known as the *time-sharing* model. The terminals are allotted a certain time period to access the host, ensuring that there are no bottlenecks when more than one terminal accesses the host. This model is not suitable for critical applications, because allotting time to clients implies that the clients must wait until they can access the server. The clients, being thin clients, cannot process anything during the time spent waiting for their turn. Although the wait period will only be a few milliseconds, it can have a huge impact when you need to transmit a lot of data in a small period of time.

In the *data-centric* model a number of servers are connected to clients and the servers are classified on the basis of the information that they store. The advantage of this model is that the load is shared or balanced among the servers; therefore, multiple operations can be processed simultaneously. The data-centric model offers the benefit of reducing traffic congestion in a network. This setup is timesaving and economical as long as not many servers are used.

Let's assume that Westside is setting up a documentation center in 1997. The network administrator in Austin (let's call him James Wright) has to choose between the host-centric and data-centric models. In a host-centric model, when multiple terminals try to access the host, the bandwidth is choked. Therefore, the entire process slows down. The host-centric model is not suitable for the documentation center because allotting time to clients implies that the clients must wait until they can access the server. In this manner, while one client accesses the server, the other clients remain idle.

James chose to implement the data-centric model. As stated earlier, in the data-centric model, the information is categorized and stored across different servers. The documentation center had four servers running on different operating systems. These servers were used to store information, such as the data related to the type of software products being developed, white papers, and other technical specifications of the products. A client requested the one of the servers for the required information. This server, in turn, could get the data from other servers. Therefore, the processing time was not affected and multiple operations could be performed simultaneously. However, this process was transparent to the clients.

THE DISTRIBUTIVE COMPUTING MODEL

In a centralized computing model, the host performs the processing; the terminals are thin clients. In the *distributive* computing model, by contrast, the client terminals, which are fat clients, perform a part of the data processing at their end. The server must still handle a major portion of the processing.

This computing model is less expensive than the centralized computing model and is more efficient. This is because each client is responsible for some processing on its own and does not depend completely on the mainframe computer.

Let's say the finance center of Westside Inc. wants to expand. Given the disadvantages of the centralized computing model, the branch office wanted to overcome them. Therefore, the center switched to the distributive computing model. In this model, the terminals are fat clients. These terminals are equipped with finance software and have the capacity to perform at least 25% of the operations. The remaining processing is carried out by a mainframe computer, which is connected to these terminals.

Before arriving at the decision to implement the distributed model, the finance center considered the cost of implementing the network and later costs in possible upgrades. In the case of a centralized network, the upgrades will cost you an arm and a leg, because you will also have to upgrade the main server, apart from acquiring additional systems. In a distributed model, the additional systems would cost you a little more than the thin clients. However, the total cost of expansion would be less than that of a centralized system and the downtime of the network would be minimal as against the centralized model.

Because of the change in the model, the way storage was handled also changed. In the distributed model, storage was partly held in the workstations and among the servers. The implementations of file servers are an example of this. Storage management in such cases could be a problem because of the distributed nature of the data. The other problem with storage management would be that it would take a sizeable chunk of LAN bandwidth for management routines.

THE COOPERATIVE COMPUTING MODEL

The third computing model is the *cooperative* or *collaborative computing* model. In this model, each client is equipped with equal processing power. These clients are interconnected. The clients share the processing capabilities with one another. This sharing of processing power can be in the form of clients running programs on other client computers, or the processes can be designed in such a way that they can be distributed across various clients.

A familiar example of a collaborative model is the process of browsing the Internet. Web servers on the Internet use resources to inform your computer about how the elements of a particular Web page should be displayed, such as the graphics, font style size, and colors. Your computer then interprets this information by using its processing power and displays the Web page in the format required.

Consider that the software development center of Westside Inc. has 30 employees. In this center, each computer on the network has equal processing power and is interconnected. The reason behind interconnecting these computers is that each computer has its own set of resources, in terms of different software, which it shares with the other computers. These computers are also connected to the servers, as shown in Figure 1.3.

Figure 1.3
The cooperative computing model has computers inter-connected and linked to the servers to enable the servers to take care of specialized tasks.

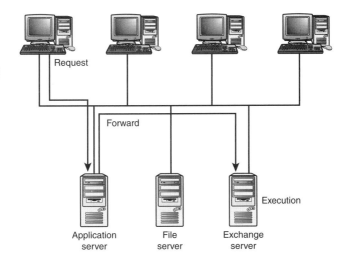

In the preceding example, the application server receives the requests and forwards them to the respective servers for execution. In most cases, the application server will receive all requests and forward them to other servers. For example, if the user wants to access a certain file in the file server, the request sent by the user is received by the application server and then forwarded to the file server for execution.

Each of these models attempts to improve on the general working of the network. However, adapting storage management in such a network is bound to have some problems. SANs, instead of building on existing systems and adapting them to existing networks, represented a shift in approach. In SANs, a separate network is created for storage management, which provides you with many additional features when compared to any adaptation of storage management. This shift in paradigm is a key point that makes SAN different from other storage systems, such as Direct Attached Storage (DAS) or Network Attached Storage (NAS). These storage systems and how they compare with SANs are covered in a later section of this chapter.

DATA STORAGE SYSTEMS IN A NETWORK

A company or enterprise that deploys a network and works on any type of data requires a suitable storage system. Does this mean that you will have to discard your existing storage devices? Well, the answer to that question would depend on the extent to which the current storage devices are compatible with SANs. In the following sections, you will learn about how to evaluate storage devices, new or old.

FACTORS TO BE CONSIDERED FOR A DATA STORAGE SYSTEM

You should keep several factors in mind while selecting the method of storage required for your company or enterprise. These factors are

- The techniques involved are cost-effective.
- The storage capacity is scalable.
- The access to data is instant and reliable.
- The data is secure and data loss is avoided.
- The maintenance system can be designed to prevent breakages in performance.

Although there is no rigid order in the factors to be considered, the order mentioned above is based on the relative importance of the factors mentioned. The relative importance could vary from enterprise to enterprise. Cost has been placed at the top of the list for the simple reason that in more cases than not it plays a very important role in the final decision. Moreover, this factor would also justify the move to a SAN. You can and should vary the order on the basis of the relative importance of the factors. For example, if cost were not a prohibitive concern, then that would be the last factor to be considered in determining the choice of storage device.

THE COST FACTOR

Regardless of the business you are in, the amount of money that can and should be spent on data storage equipment is always a major concern for the company. When you buy the hardware and software required for storage, you need to keep in mind the cost factor. First, you must calculate the purchase cost of hardware and software that is initially required. Then, calculate and consider the cost of maintaining all this hardware and software. You also need to take into account in the budget the fact that human effort, in the form of network administrators or technicians, is essential and needs money.

STORAGE CAPACITY WITH SCALABILITY

You can identify the type of storage system required for your company after allocating the money for a storage system. Of course, if cost is not a prohibitive concern, this step would go in parallel with the determination of cost. You need to give a lot of forethought prior to deciding the appropriate storage system. You must carry out a detailed analysis of the current storage requirements and the expected growth. An organization is never stagnant. As the organization grows, the amount of data the company handles also grows. If data grows, so does the need for data storage.

> **Note**
>
> A storage system can be said to be scalable if it can retain its performance levels when the storage volume increases. It should also be able to take advantage of the new scenario and produce higher performance levels. For example, if a storage system currently returns data in time x, it should continue to do so even after additional storage capacity is added, as well as handle the storage space more effectively.

In most real-life situations, each of these factors figures in the final decision on the storage system to be used. Therefore, you must be able to objectively look and assess each factor separately. This would enable you to make a decision on which storage system to use, without any unnecessary constraints on the decision. In fact, it would be advisable that you evaluate the different parameters separately, even if, say, cost was a prohibitive factor.

Ensure that the components of the storage system you purchase are scalable to accommodate a sizeable amount of data in the future, with little or no modifications. The technology you adopt for the organization must possess the potential to accommodate any unexpected changes in the company. You must employ a storage system that requires minimal upgrades when the company grows.

The simplest way to assess scalability is to check on the number of expansion slots available in the device. You might also want to check the compatibility issues with devices and parts from other manufacturers. An assessment of the technology used in the product, in terms of how old and reliable the technology is, is also important. Also, find out about the maximum theoretical limit stated for the device and the maximum practical limit to scalability. You will be able to get information about the latter from dealers and from performance trials that have been conducted by different groups, including researchers and industry magazines.

THE PERFORMANCE FACTOR

The storage technology that your company adopts must have the capability to deliver information swiftly and continuously whenever required. It is simpler to design a storage system for a small network than for a large enterprise network. If a small number of users are linked to the storage system, the system remains efficient. A challenge arises when the number of users increases. The storage system must be able to provide instantaneous access even under this condition.

The capability of storage systems to provide instantaneous connections depends on the number of channels supported by the device, the number of physical links (bus slots) supported, and so on. The performance of the storage system is actually an accumulation of the topology used and the maximum achievable speeds of the devices.

THE SYSTEM RELIABILITY FACTOR

Any product, regardless of the hardware employed, has a specific lifetime. Some products do not last for the specified lifetime and break down unexpectedly. Each type of storage system comprises hardware and software. These hardware and software products can break down. If a breakdown occurs in a small-scale network, it is possible to retrieve the lost data, because the volume of data is very small. In contrast, it is difficult to retrieve the data lost in a large network because of the volume of the data and the vastness of the network. More than the actual difficulty in the data retrieval process, the downtime and loss would be at near unacceptable levels. An administrator needs to design the storage system so that the system can create a backup from which data can be retrieved.

→ To learn more about disaster recovery, **see** "Storage Area Networks for Backup," **p. 194**

THE MAINTENANCE FACTOR

After the storage system is designed and ready to be implemented, the maintenance aspect of the system gains importance. A large amount of time, money, and effort is involved in the designing of the storage system. Therefore, an experienced group of administrators must be employed to handle technical difficulties that might occur. The administrator must constantly monitor the functioning and the usage of each component of the storage system and check regularly whether the company's storage requirements are being met.

Here, the intent is to evaluate how maintenance-intensive the product is and what amount of normal maintenance would be required. As opposed to the performance reliability factor, the maintenance factor is concerned with keeping the system performing at its current level. While evaluating this factor, keep in mind that the purpose of the maintenance factor is not to identify areas of improvement. However, there is a fine line between the two, and because of that both factors tend to go hand in hand during evaluation.

DIRECT ATTACHED STORAGE

Direct attached storage (DAS) contains storage devices, such as JBODs or disk arrays, attached directly to the server. The setup of DAS is shown in Figure 1.4.

Note

Just a bunch of disks (JBOD) refers to the hard disk drives connected to a computer by using multiple slots. In a JBOD, a number of drives (which are not partitioned) are grouped together to form a single large logical volume. This enables the user to make optimum utilization of the capacity of the disk drives, because it combines the storage capacity of multiple drives.

Figure 1.4
In the storage model, the storage medium is represented by the disk arrays attached to the server.

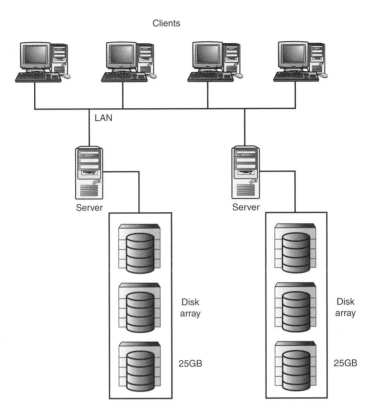

In this storage architecture, it is possible to add storage devices to increase the storage capacity to 25GB.

When there is a need to increase the storage capacity, disk arrays are added. This type of storage not only proves to be expensive but also causes problems in terms of network traffic by choking the bandwidth. The clients (user machines) might not be able to access the server quickly for data. The main problem that is evident in this kind of a storage system is that if the server attached to a specific storage device malfunctions, the data stored in that device cannot be accessed, thus indicating a single point of failure.

Note

A *single point of failure* refers to a situation where when one of the devices on the network fails, the entire network goes down for the task concerned.

To ensure that there is no single point of failure, you can have a storage system that is common among servers. This strategy, which is an improvement on DAS, is known as *direct attached shared storage*. Here, the storage device is shared between servers to ensure that there is no single point of failure, as shown in Figure 1.5.

Figure 1.5
In the direct attached shared storage architecture, the storage device is shared between servers.

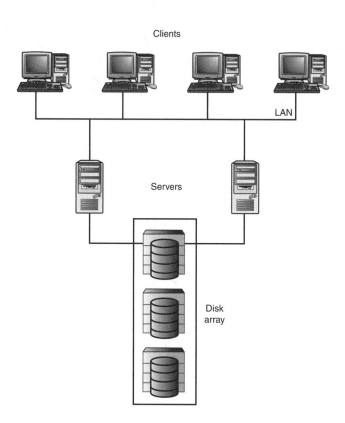

However, in direct attached shared storage architecture, a problem arises when you need to expand the network by adding servers. The problem can be like a double-edged sword. If servers are added to the existing network, you could have a situation were all the servers try to access the existing storage device. Therefore, bandwidth congestion might occur. On the other hand, if you decide to add a new storage device for the new server, the costs incurred are high.

DAS was the first type of network storage system to be used. It has been (and still is) very popular in the PC and LAN segment. It is ideally suited when the storage requirements are not too high. To cope with huge storage requirements, other storage systems, such as NAS and SAN, have emerged.

NETWORK ATTACHED STORAGE

To overcome the problems of DAS architectures, there was a need for a storage architecture that could perform storage without consuming the bandwidth significantly. The solution was to implement an architecture in the network that performs only the file input/output operations. The network attached storage (NAS) strategy includes NAS elements, such as file server and storage device, in the network, as shown in Figure 1.6. A NAS element need not be a single device; it can be a group of network devices.

Figure 1.6
This network contains storage in the form of NAS elements attached directly to the network.

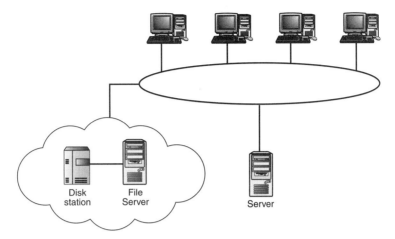

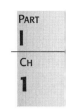

NAS elements do not perform any other task apart from sharing files. NAS is assigned a unique network address. The NAS element offloads the task of storing data from the main server and allows it to be dedicated solely to processing. Offloading eliminates bandwidth bottlenecks in the network. It also ensures that the entire network is not shut down when the storage device must be replaced or upgraded.

The clients might need to access the files that are on the main servers. If the NAS elements are included in the network, the main server is relieved from input/output operations. Therefore, the clients can retrieve data from the NAS elements directly. The clients issue file access commands by using file access protocols such as Common Internet File System (CIFS) and Network File System (NFS). The NAS elements in the network can receive and provide files to the clients, on request, with a very high rate of performance. NAS owes its high performance to the dedicated processor it contains. This processor works on specifically designed operating systems along with a special file system.

The NAS operating system is optimized to cater to file I/O and file serving activities. Because of the optimization, the performance of the NAS operating system is better than a normal multi-purpose OS. The NAS OS is relatively smaller and less resource-intensive than the normal multi-purpose OS, and the result is evident in the improved data access times for the clients. In NAS, unlike other storage systems, the NAS server manages the file system used. An industry standard file system, such as NFS or CIFS, is used to store data.

The setup and design of NAS has a number of benefits. The NAS setup has a simple configuration that makes it easier for the network administrator to install NAS on the network. The probability of downtime in NAS is significantly lower than that of DAS. NAS offers higher rates of data availability to the clients over the network.

Even if the NAS devices malfunction, the remaining operations in the network that involve the main server are unaffected. In case the main server crashes, the clients can continue to request and retrieve data from the NAS devices. The reliability of the main server is higher because NAS offloads the task of input/output and data storage from the main server.

NAS offers improvements in terms of backup and security of data. This is because the backup of data takes place from one device on the network and not from all the servers connected to the network. In cases where the storage capacity of NAS elements is low, it is possible to add more tape backups to the NAS setup effectively without hindering the processing operations on the network. The NAS setup also offers the benefit of allowing data to be shared across heterogeneous platforms.

DATA SHARING IN NAS

A NAS setup permits different clients, such as Windows NT and UNIX, to share the same file. NAS employs industry standard file sharing methods to allow users to access data. Because the file system is at the storage end, NAS employs standard file sharing protocols to serve the requests of the different servers in the heterogeneous network.

Files can be shared using two networking models, peer-to-peer and client/server. If these two networking models are compared in terms of how they share data, the client/server model is more appropriate because it provides a central warehouse for files that all users can access. This method also allows an administrator to centrally control and maintain all operations. A common example of the client/server architecture is a general-purpose server that shares files with clients over the network.

Note

A *peer-to-peer* network consists of multiple PCs where each PC is a peer in that there is no applicable hierarchy. There is no dedicated server involved in this type of a network. Each PC or peer performs its own set of services. This kind of a networking model is applicable for companies that require a small-scale network.

Note

In a client/server networking model, there is one computer that performs the role of a server and the other computers on the network act as clients. This networking model follows a many-to-one relationship where all the clients send requests to a server to carry out services. The server performs the function of supervising and processing the requests made by the client.

Client PCs can access shared files if they have the required client software to connect with the relevant server. In addition, this type of an arrangement also builds pressure on the administrator to ensure that the client is updated when the server is updated. This is necessary to ensure that client has the same version of the software as the server, in order to ensure proper communication.

The solution is to provide a file server to support the heterogeneous clients, as shown in Figure 1.7.

Figure 1.7
Data sharing
implemented in a
NAS setup by using a
file server.

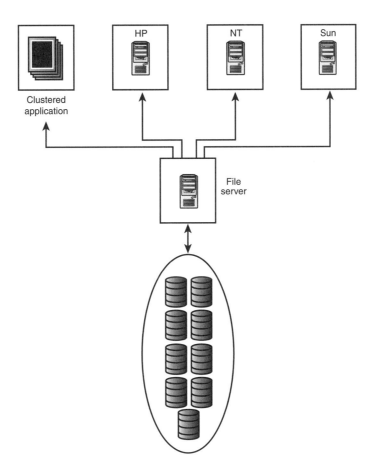

WHY STORAGE AREA NETWORKS?

Overall, NAS paints a rosy picture; it is economical, promises reliability and security, but it has a few drawbacks.

Let's go back to our fictitious company, Westside Inc., which grew over the years and expanded. With the expansion, the volume of data that needs to be stored also rose. The NAS model was useful as long as the volume of data was lesser than terabytes. This increase in the volume of data was a problem because it was not feasible to add innumerable tape backups to increase storage capacity. A system that can back up terabytes of data without causing any bandwidth bottlenecks in the network was required. Storage area networks then gained recognition as a storage system that offered a solution to this requirement.

Again, the advantage that the storage area networks offered over the other systems, such as NAS or DAS, is that all the processing happens behind the servers. Of course, if your network were properly designed then you would be able to get the system going as in most companies not currently implementing SANs. However, this poses its own set of problems;

in a complex network, the performance is going to be far less than that offered by a SAN setup. In a NAS setup, the transfer of data is going to happen over the existing network. This adds a considerable overhead on your LAN, which is typically suited for short bursts of transmission. On the other hand, in a SAN setup, the entire transfer happens over a dedicated network capable of high-speed, high-bandwidth transfers. The bottom line is that if you can afford it and performance and reliability are your prime concerns in handling multiple terabytes of information, SANs are the solution for you.

SAN is a technology that comprises a high-speed network of storage devices, interconnects, and interfaces. SAN is a group of components designed to form a transparent link between the servers and the storage devices. SAN reduces traffic congestion in a network by providing a strategy different from the conventional means of storage. SAN is a storage network that increases scalability and efficiency by setting apart consolidation of storage from the main network.

Implementing a storage area network does not require the replacement of the existing network. A SAN can be easily implemented to work on the existing network with a few modifications, the details of which are explained in Chapter 7, "Designing Storage Area Networks."

In terms of cabling, a general opinion is that SAN works only with fiber optic cables or Fibre Channel, which is not the case. This kind of opinion exists because most SAN devices come with a lot of information and advertising about compatibility with Fibre Channel and the speeds it can reach are also measured with Fibre Channel connections. It is possible to build SAN by using the cables existing in a local or wide area network. The next section discusses a few of the cable types used in the existing networks, which can also be used in SANs.

Note

Fibre Channel is a technology standard that enables data transfers between systems at very high speeds. Fibre Channel is a type of interface that works on both fiber optic as well as copper cables. More about Fibre Channel can be found in Chapter 5, "Fibre Channel."

TYPES OF PRIMARY CABLES

The various types of cables that connect the computers on a network serve as a medium to transfer data in the form of signals. The use of a particular cable depends on the size and requirement of the network. The choice of cables in SAN is quite similar to that required for a normal LAN. The most preferred cable in SAN is fiber optic cable for the sheer transmission speeds supported by them; however, other copper cables can also be used.

Selecting an appropriate cable for a network can be a difficult task. Three commonly used types of cables for connecting computers in a network are

- Coaxial
- Twisted-pair
- Fiber optic

The following sections describe each of these cable types and their relative advantages and disadvantages. This will help you decide the ideal connection interface to link the systems and devices on your network and give you an idea as to what will be useful for a storage area network.

COAXIAL CABLES

The *coaxial* cable is the commonly used connection cable mainly due to the benefits it offers, such as being fairly inexpensive, flexible, easy to install and use, and lightweight. The coaxial cable comprises three internal layers. The innermost layer consists of a core made of solid copper, the second layer is an insulation layer, and the third layer is an outer cover (see Figure 1.8). The function of the core is to transmit the electronic signals containing data. The insulation layer is a braided metal shielding, which is a woven or stranded metal mesh. The types of shielding available in coaxial cables are dual (two-layer) and quad (four-layer). The purpose of the metal mesh is to absorb stray electronic signals so that they do not enter the cable and distort the data being transmitted.

Note

The dual shielding system consists of two metal tapes. The shield interfaces are flooded with an adhesive compound to provide a moisture barrier and inhibit corrosion. These cables are very flexible and are used for internal wiring.

A quad shielding is a type of shielding used in coaxial cables which has an extra layer of braid added to the cable for additional strength. These cables are typically used for drop lines from the pole to the house.

Figure 1.8
The internal layers of a coaxial cable.

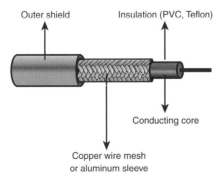

Outer shield   Insulation (PVC, Teflon)

Conducting core

Copper wire mesh
or aluminum sleeve

The two types of coaxial cables available are thicknets and thinnets. As the names suggest, *thicknets* are larger cables and *thinnets* are smaller cables. Thinnets are used in Ethernet networks. Backbone networks usually employ thicknets. The distance to which the signal can travel varies proportionately with the thickness of the cables. The main feature of coaxial cables is that they are highly resistant to attenuation and interference. The shield used in the coaxial cable helps to protect the signal from interferences and this makes the cable resistant to attenuation. Coaxial cables are safe and well protected from attenuation. The protection from attenuation makes the coaxial cable the cheapest and the preferred cable for long-distance communications.

Note

Attenuation refers to the loss or deterioration of signals as they traverse the length of the wire.

In SANs, coaxial cables are not very popular because of the slow transmission speeds. However, some storage networks use these cables because of their relative cost advantages and compatibility with various devices. Coaxial cables support a bandwidth ranging from 2.5Mbps to 10Mbps whereas the bandwidth supported by thicknet cables is higher. If security is a primary concern, you should not use coaxial cables because these cables are susceptible to EMI (electromagnetic interference). Coaxial cables radiate a portion of the signals that can be picked up by sophisticated eavesdropping equipment.

TWISTED-PAIR CABLES

A *twisted-pair* cable, in general, comprises two insulated strands of copper wire. These wires are twisted around each other for protecting the signal from disturbances. These noises are released from external sources. The two types of twisted-pair cables available are Unshielded twisted-pair (UTP) and Shielded twisted-pair (STP).

The unshielded twisted-pair cable consists of two insulated copper wires twisted around each other with no shielding used between the cables, as shown in Figure 1.9. A UTP cable does not have the shielding layer of the STP cable. Therefore, the signals passing through the UTP cables are prone to radiations emitted from other cables.

Figure 1.9
A simple unshielded twisted-pair cable is color-coded to distinguish between the pairs.

On the other hand, the shielded twisted-pair cable (STP) uses a woven copper braid jacket, which provides higher quality and more protection than the jacket contained in the UTP cable. The STP cable also uses a foil wrap between and around the wire pairs and internal twisting of the pairs. This gives STP excellent insulation to protect the transmitted data from external intervention.

Both varieties of twisted pair cables are used in normal networks. They are easy to install and are very cost effective. For the same reason, SAN also provides support for the usage of twisted-pair cables.

The Electronic Industries Association and Telecommunications Industries Association (EIA/TIA) 568 Commercial Building Wiring Standard has specified standards for UTP cabling. The UTP cables are classified into different categories (see Table 1.1) based on their applications and properties.

TABLE 1.1   LIST OF CATEGORIES OF UTP CABLE

Category	Description
Category 1	Can transmit voice but is restricted in terms of transmitting data. Most conventional telephone cables are Category 1 cables.
Category 2	Supports data transmission at speeds up to 4Mbps.
Category 3	Supports data transmission at speeds up to 10Mbps.
Category 4	Supports data transmission at speeds up to 16Mbps.
Category 5	Supports data transmission at speeds up to 100Mbps.
Category 5e	Supports data transmission at speeds up to 300Mbps.
Category 6	Supports data transmission at speeds up to 1,000Mbps.
Category 7	Cables are expected with performance speeds that go beyond the 1,000Mbps mark.

UTP cables are very popular, because many buildings are proactively wired for twisted-pair telephone systems. Extra UTP cables are often installed to meet future cabling needs. If preinstalled, twisted-pair cables are of standard specifications (Categories mentioned previously) that facilitate data transmission. However, common telephone wires might not have the required characteristics for secure data transmission so extra care must be taken to ensure that the cables used are compatible for high-speed data transmission supported by SANs. The type of cable used in your local network would determine the effectiveness of SAN because if the data cannot reach the client as fast as the SAN systems can send them, you will have a slow network. In SAN, the best kind of UTP cables to be used are category 5 and above cables for the transmission speeds supported by them.

Note

To ensure secure data transmission, the cables used must offer the least attenuation and interference. The impedance mismatches must also be low to ensure that performance of the systems is not affected because of the cables.

FIBER OPTIC CABLES

Fiber optic cables transmit data in digital form. The data signals are transmitted in the form of light pulses through a medium that might be plastic, glass, or fiber.

Optical fibers mainly comprise two layers, core and cladding. The core is a very thin cylinder of glass or plastic that is enclosed by a concentric layer of glass called *cladding*, as shown in Figure 1.10.

Figure 1.10
A thin cylinder of glass forms the internal layers of a fiber optic cable.

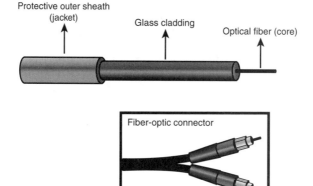

Each glass strand is capable of transmitting signals in one direction only. Therefore, a cable requires two strands of glass for the transmission and reception of signals. These glass strands are enclosed in separate jackets. Each glass strand is enclosed within a reinforcing layer of plastic.

The method of transmitting data by fiber optics is a better option, in terms of data security, when compared to coaxial or twisted-pair cables. Data transferred using fiber optics is secure because these cables do not use electrical impulses that are prone to interference. In this manner, the data cannot be tapped or tampered with, which is possible in copper-based cables transmitting data. When the fibers are made of plastic, it is easier to attach the cable.

The fiber optic cable is best suited for high-speed and high-capacity data transmission due to the lack of attenuation and the purity of signals. The purity of these signals is unaffected because they are passed through a medium that is covered by a protective layer.

Fiber optic cables are a preferred choice for SANs due to their superior features. Fibre Channel can be used over fiber optic cables to derive the maximum advantage out of SAN. The use of Fibre Channel over optical cables is recommended because it helps leverage both the fast transmission systems.

→ To learn more about Fibre Channel, **see** "Fibre Channel," **p. 109**

Going back to our fictitious example, assume that a branch office at New York introduced the SAN architecture in Westside Inc. In this SAN environment, the clients access the storage devices indirectly through the server. Here, the clients interact only with those servers that process data requests. The SAN setup of this center is shown in Figure 1.11.

PART

I

CH

1

Figure 1.11
SAN acts as a bridge to connect the servers and storage devices and to separate the storage from the network.

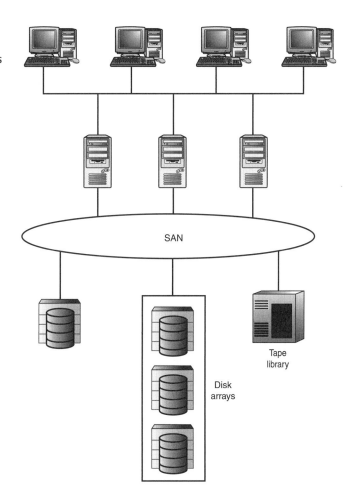

SAN is a network on its own, although it works as a part of the existing network. The storage devices are not directly connected or attached to the servers as they are in DAS, which is where SAN comes in. With SANs, the connections between the servers and storage devices are controlled by the storage area network.

STORAGE PARTITIONING IN SANs

In a SAN, storage systems are shared instead of the data. The storage systems are shared at the cabinet level, that is, the storage device is shared as if they were different sets of devices. This is made possible by partitioning the physical storage devices. Then, logical volumes are created on the server, as shown in Figure 1.12.

Figure 1.12
Partitioning of the storage space enables the allocation of the storage space to different entities on the network, such as servers.

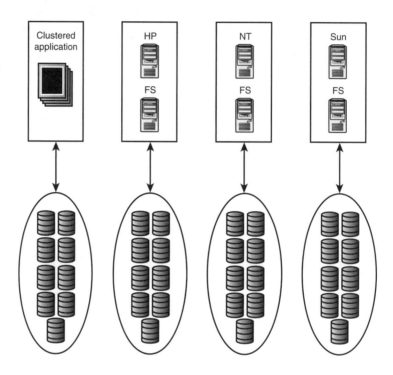

COMPARISON BETWEEN NAS AND SAN

SAN and NAS differ in few aspects. SAN is a storage network consisting of storage devices, interconnects (which include HIPPI, SCSI, and Fibre Channel), and interfaces (which include hubs, switches, repeaters, and directors). NAS is a group of devices that mainly involve a specialized file server. Of course, NAS also consists of SCSI or Fibre Channel. However, in most NAS these components are not distinct, it is in the form of an integrated system. The center of SAN is around the storage devices, interconnects, and interfaces. However, in NAS storage management tends to be around the storage device and the controlling server.

→ To learn more about the interfaces used in storage area networks, **see** "Storage Area Networks Interfaces," **p. 63**

→ To learn more about the interconnects used in storage area networks, **see** "Storage Area Networks Interconnects," **p. 87**

NAS transfers data by using protocols, such as TCP/IP over Ethernet, token ring, and ATM, whereas SAN uses Fibre Channel. Next, NAS uses standard file sharing protocols, such as CIFS and NCP. In SAN, the data requests are sent directly to the disk drive. During data sharing, SAN requires software on every node so that heterogeneous nodes can share files. In NAS, there is true data sharing among the heterogeneous clients because the file system is located at the storage section and data is transferred to the client by using file sharing protocols.

Finally, the NAS setup is inexpensive because it requires only a few devices and can be installed as a plug-and-play device. However, the SAN setup requires a number of devices, which makes it difficult to install and equally expensive. For this reason, SAN is more suitable for an enterprise network. NAS is suitable for small-scale as well as large-scale enterprises.

Some storage vendors advertise that SAN is better than NAS, whereas a few vendors argue than NAS is a better choice than SAN. The SAN and NAS architectures can be suitably designed so that they are compatible with each other. Several NAS devices and functions are likely to coexist with SAN for sometime to come. More about designing a Storage Area Network compatible with NAS is covered in Chapter 7.

SUMMARY

Today, organizations and companies are using different networking models. The three networking models are centralized, distributed, and collaborative. The centralized computing model can be either a host-centric or data-centric. In the host-centric computing model, the host carries out the processing. In the data-centric computing model, different applications are run on different servers. In the distributed computing model, individual computers perform their own processing. The collaborative or cooperative computing model is a type of networking in which computers share their processing power.

Different types of storage technologies are used in companies: direct attached storage, network attached storage, and storage area networks. The data storage in a heterogeneous environment is made possible using SAN and NAS elements.

PRODUCTS ARENA

In this section, we will look at some products, currently available, with reference to some of the components discussed in the chapter so far. In the current section, we will look at some storage systems.

A well-known organization, MTI Technology Corp., has introduced the Gladiator 6700 storage system. The Gladiator 6700 storage system offers the feature of Volume Mapping to bring data together from different places and also facilitate the redeployment of data to different storage devices on different servers. The design of this storage system is compatible with the online transaction processing (OLTP) environment. The OLTP environment needs a high rate of random access data requests. The Gladiator 6700 storage system promises a transfer rate of 100MB/s. Its average seek time is calculated to be 7.1ms to 7.8ms. It has an on-drive cache capacity of 1,024KB.

Another well-known organization, Veritas Software Corp., provides a set of heterogeneous storage management tools. These management tools are required for the management of SAN environments. Cross-platform storage area networking management and administration are facilitated by Veritas Volume Manager (GUI interface) and Veritas File System Products. Based on the study of SAN product vendors, the existing partnerships, and those that are being formed between the various SAN component vendors (platform, storage, fabric, interface, and software), aim at swiftly making storage area networking the future's foremost server-to-storage architecture.

CHAPTER 2

EXTERNALIZING STORAGE USING STORAGE AREA NETWORKS

In this chapter

COMPONENTS OF STORAGE AREA NETWORKS

SANs provide a solution for a mass storage system where data reliability and storage scalability are the main requirements. The different components of storage area networkss fulfill these requirements. They also do away with the common difficulties that arise in a heterogeneous network environment, such as the difficulty of accessing shared data across varied platforms. When you have varied platforms on your network, the file systems each uses of them can be different, and the resulting incompatibilities can lead to problems in sharing data. Later parts of this book discuss the difficulties involved in a heterogeneous environment in more detail.

→ To learn more about how to design SAN solutions in a heterogeneous environment, **see** "Design Considerations for Storage Area Networks," **p. 160**

The primary advantage of a storage area network is that it externalizes storage from the rest of the network. This advantage is leveraged in a heterogeneous environment because of the separation of the different components of a SAN. In any network, the different components, such as servers, storage devices, and interconnects are integrated. When you use different servers, compatibility issues arise. If you are using a NAS setup for your storage requirements, then to ensure interoperability you might have to use additional equipment (such as bridges) or make some configuration modifications to the storage devices. With SAN, it is a lot easier to achieve interoperability. The SAN architecture by itself is supposed to support heterogeneous environments, because the externalization of storage in a storage area network make it independent of the networking environment. You will have a better understanding of how SANs externalize storage if you look at their architecture. The SAN architecture is divided into four layers:

- Infrastructure
- Servers
- Storage systems
- Software

The SAN infrastructure, in turn, comprises interfaces, interconnects, and fabrics. Figure 2.1 shows the different layers of the SAN architecture.

The SAN architecture consists of separate layers. Each layer controls a specific task. This is the biggest advantage of a SAN. In DAS or NAS, you could not separate the storage from the device controlling the storage (the file server). In DAS, even the connection systems were native to the servers. The advantage of a SAN is that each layer has been separated, thus enabling the externalization of storage. You can now customize your SAN solution to cater to almost any kind of network.

Figure 2.1
The four layers of the SAN architecture enable the externalization of storage.

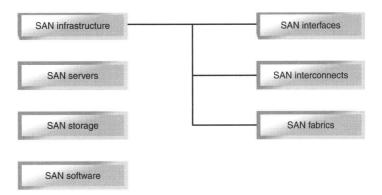

SAN INFRASTRUCTURE

The SAN infrastructure is composed of three components: interfaces, interconnects, and fabrics.

SAN INTERFACES

SAN *interfaces* are physical components that serve as a means of communication between the storage devices and the servers or interconnects they connect. They allow SAN servers to connect to the storage devices.

There are two kinds of interfaces, *parallel* and *serial*. The parallel interface transmits more than one packet of data at the same time. The serial interface transmits data one packet at a time. SAN interfaces provide a common methodology for the storage of data. The common methodology refers to the way the interface transmits data regardless of the devices at either end. This allows systems on various platforms to access data from a centralized group of storage devices. The interface ensures that the format in which the data is stored is transparent to the server. To the servers, the data is in a format that is understood by the operating system. Each type of interface has its advantages and disadvantages, and the methodology followed by the interface varies.

SAN INTERCONNECTS

SAN interconnects are physical devices that connect the servers to the storage devices. They can also act as intermediary devices connecting the fabrics and interfaces. The functions of interconnects are the same as that of extenders, such as routers and hubs, in a LAN setup. The extenders in a LAN are used to ensure that devices can communicate with each other. They ensure that the signals from one device reach the intended recipient without any loss in the quality of the signals. SAN interconnects include physical devices such as hubs, switches, routers, gateways, and bridges. Figure 2.2 shows how an interconnect works.

Figure 2.2
The SAN interconnect connects the file server to the various storage devices.

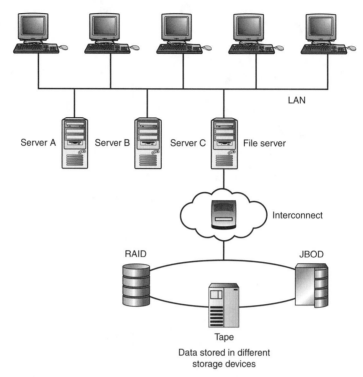

Figure 2.2 illustrates an example of a simple SAN setup where the file server alone is connected to the storage network through an interconnect. The other servers are not connected to the storage network directly and perform dedicated management of the local area network. The interconnect is used to connect multiple storage devices to the file server and create a storage network.

SAN FABRICS

In simple terms, switched network connections are called SAN *fabrics*. These are physical components that connect the various interconnects with each other. They are similar to interfaces, except that fabrics connect interconnects with each other, whereas the interfaces connect devices to the interconnects. Switched SCSI, switched SSA, and switched Fibre Channel are some examples of SAN fabrics. Figure 2.3 shows a SAN infrastructure where two switches are connected by means of a fabric.

Figure 2.3 shows the different components of a storage area network. All the connections in the storage network are based on Fibre Channel connections (represented as "FC"). In this setup, all the servers are connected to a switch, which in turn is connected to another switch hosting a number of storage devices. This kind of a SAN setup is highly scalable, and the use of the switched network over Fibre Channel makes it fast too.

Figure 2.3
The SAN network infrastructure has fabrics connecting two switches.

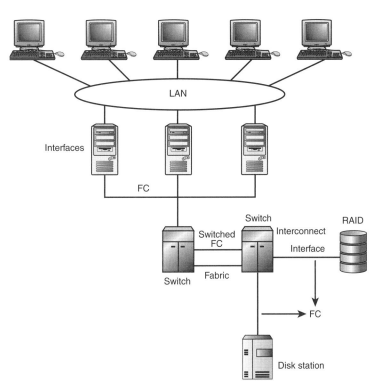

SAN SERVERS

Servers in storage area networks are connected to the storage devices by means of interfaces. At the time of this writing, no specialized SAN servers are being used in enterprises. However, considering the rate at which storage area networks are growing, you are soon likely to find specialized SAN servers in the market that cater to the needs of SAN applications. Until the market provides these servers, however; you must continue to use NAS servers. You can also use any server on the network and load the necessary software to manage the storage area network. Figure 2.4 shows how servers and storage devices are connected in a SAN environment.

The servers are connected to the storage devices through interconnects, which serve to externalize the storage. A cloud represents the actual connection, because this connection could be through any of the topologies supported by SANs. More about the different topologies is covered in Chapter 7, "Designing Storage Area Networks."

To understand how heterogeneous environments affect the storage function, consider the example of the fictitious software development center, Westside Inc., which is located in New York. Originally this center had three servers running Windows NT, UNIX, and OS/400. Each one of these was designed to control a section of the network. Each server held data specific to the section of the network that it controlled. This resulted in the servers not being able to access data residing on servers in other sections of the network. To solve this problem, copies of shared data were made on each server so that data was made available to all servers. Figure 2.5 shows how data is present in formats specific to the different platforms on which data resides.

Figure 2.4
The SAN environment connects servers to storage devices through Fibre Channel.

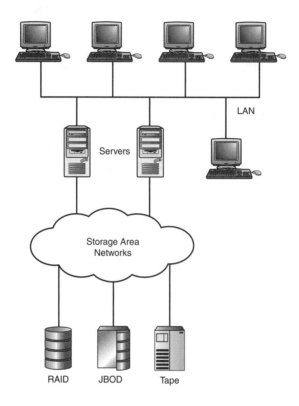

The problem with this kind of arrangement is that it would be difficult to maintain updated copies of the shared data across different platforms. To maintain a copy of the data present in the Windows server, it would have to be read and converted into a format understandable by the UNIX or OS/400 server. To accomplish this, you would have to run some intermediary utility, which would slow the performance of the server. Moreover, as the software development center of Westside Inc. in New York developed more applications, its storage requirements grew immensely. Because of this, the manager of the software development center of Westside Inc. decided to shift to a consolidated storage environment. Therefore, a storage area network was implemented in the software development center of Westside Inc.

The new environment is designed to provide a single repository of data that can be managed from a central location. In this model, all the data is stored in one set of storage devices, which are partitioned in such a manner that each platform has a certain space allotted to it. If the total storage capacity is three terabytes, one terabyte of storage space is allotted to each server. The server will be able to use that space as if it is internal to the server. In this model, any server can access the shared data directly from the storage device without the need to duplicate the data. This is possible because the data is stored in a common format and served to each platform through a standard interface. However, each platform has different data storage and retrieval methods. Moreover, data is managed differently in the different levels of the system architecture. Therefore, when you are designing the SAN solution, you should take care that the storage devices support the interfaces supported by the specific servers. In the following sections, some servers and the interfaces supported by them are discussed.

Figure 2.5
The network design of Westside Inc. has its data spread across different platforms, which is combined to form a consolidated storage on a SAN setup.

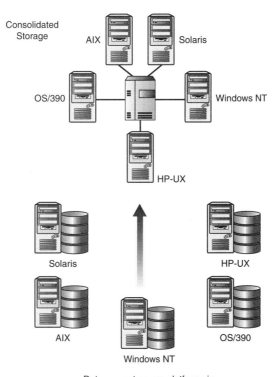

Data present across platforms in
formats specific to the different platforms

SYSTEM/390 SERVERS

System/390 is commonly known as S/390 and refers to both the processor and operating system. Initially, the processor was connected to the storage devices through a Bus and Tag interface, a very simple interface to connect storage with the processor. Later Enterprise System Connect (ESCON) channels, a proprietary interface developed by IBM, replaced the Bus and Tag interface. The ESCON channels were much superior to the Bus and Tag interface in speed and reliability. However, not many storage devices provided native support for ESCON owing to its proprietary nature. The latest technology to be implemented as an interface on the S/390 system is Fibre connectivity (FICON) channels.

S/390 systems provide a ready base for switching over to SANs because they use FICON as the connection system, which is also a kind of Fibre Channel connection used in SANs. With the use of FICON, it is possible to connect storage devices using Fibre Channel interfaces and derive the maximum advantage.

Figure 2.6 shows the architectural design of S/390 servers.

→ To learn more about ESCON, FICON, and their applications, **see** "Storage Area Network Interfaces,"
   p. 63

Figure 2.6
The S/390 processor is connected to the storage devices through bus and tag cables, ESCON Director, and a switch.

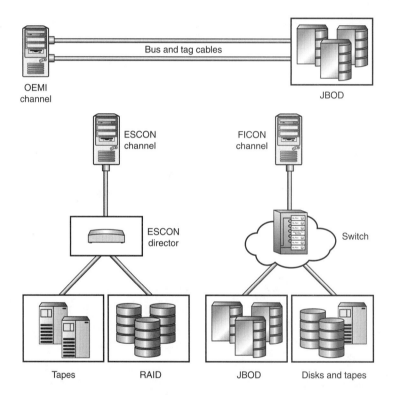

A bus and tag connection is used to connect individual devices using OEM Interface (OEMI). The problem with this kind of system is that the interface is specific to each vendor. Therefore, scalability might be a problem, as the devices would have to be vendor specific. The S/390 system also supports ESCON, which you can use to either directly connect devices or use ESCON directors to expand the number of devices. Support for the FICON channel is also provided in S/390. This can be used to directly connect devices over Fibre Channel connections. Alternatively, you can use this to connect to any SAN interconnect or even ESCON directors and expand the storage capacity.

RS/6000 AND UNIX SERVERS

The RS/6000 range of servers is from IBM. They typically run on a version of UNIX called AIX, which is an open-source operating system from IBM. These servers support a number of connection systems or interfaces to connect the processors to the storage systems. The interfaces that are commonly used in RS/6000 are SCSI, SSA, and FC-Al.

The various connection options between the processor and the storage devices are depicted in Figure 2.7. The server is directly attached to the storage device by using a SCSI bus. In the case of multiple storage devices, a linked SCSI bus connects the devices to the SCSI adapter. All the devices connected to a single SCSI adapter must be of the same kind. A single SCSI adapter would be sufficient to attach multiple hard disks. However, if you want to connect a hard disk and a tape drive, you need at least two SCSI adapters.

Figure 2.7
The RS/6000 processor is connected to storage devices by means of a SCSI bus, loop, and hub.

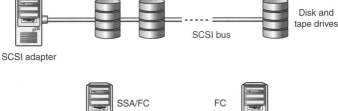
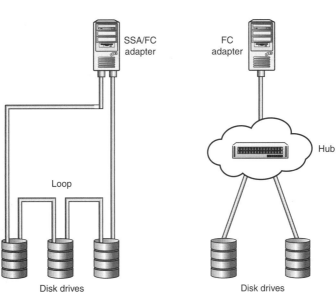

In a SCSI adapter, only similar devices can be connected and the connection has to be on a bus. This could pose problems when a large number of devices are connected. In addition, the bus system would have to be designed in a manner that all the storage devices can be accessed even if an intermediary device fails. If you are using a SSA or Fibre Channel adapter, you can connect the disk drives in loops. This configuration is a lot more scalable and easier to manage. If you need to connect different types of storage devices, RS/6000 provides support for Fibre Channel adapters that can be connected to a SAN interconnect. You can connect various types of SAN storage devices to the interconnect depending on their compatibility; more about this is covered in Chapter 5, "Fibre Channel."

The data is stored differently in different file systems. For instance, consolidation of data storage is very complex in a UNIX environment. This is because different vendors follow different file systems. In the case of UNIX, the file systems are Journal File System (JFS) and Andrew File System (AFS). The implementation of the interfaces on UNIX systems is similar to the way they are implemented on RS/6000. The interface implementation helps to abstract the differences in the file systems and ensure interoperability.

AS/400 SERVERS

An interface called Technology Independent Machine Interface (TIMI) plays a major role in the architecture of AS/400. It is a high-level machine interface. TIMI helps to isolate applications from the system hardware and hide much of the OS from the hardware.

In this type of server, the main processor is linked to the input/output operations by using a bus.

AS/400 systems also include implementation for input/output processors designed for end-user technologies, such as Windows NT and Novell.

In an AS/400 system, all the different I/O processors are connected to the main processor through a system bus. The use of the system bus enables AS/400 to consolidate and manage all I/O operations effectively. The advantage in the use of the system bus is evident in single-level storage (SLS), one of the features of the AS/400 design.

Apart from being defined by a TIMI, the single-level storage of AS/400 makes the implementation of storage area networks on an AS/400 platform different from other systems, such as OS/390, UNIX, or Windows NT. In SLS, the memory and disks are treated as one virtual space. SLS allows the processor to process jobs efficiently, because it can address the entire storage capacity across all the connected storage devices.

When you compare a system running on UNIX or Windows NT with a system that runs on AS/400, you will find there is more addressable storage in AS/400 and that because of this the processing speed of the system is increased. A system running on UNIX or Window NT uses a 32 bit-addressing scheme. In such systems, each process can have 4GB as the maximum addressable area. However, AS/400 makes use of a 64-bit SLS addressing scheme that allows the system to have over 18 exabytes of addressable memory, as shown in Figure 2.8.

Note   One exabyte is equal to one million terabytes.

Switching between processes is efficient as the whole area is mapped as a single addressable page. SLS also eliminates the need for address translation.

Figure 2.8
The AS/400 operating system has a single large unit of addressable area, unlike the Windows NT or UNIX operating systems.

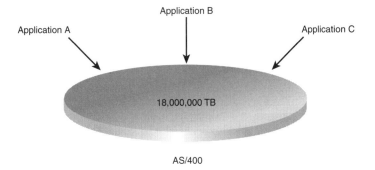

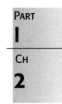

PART

I

CH

2

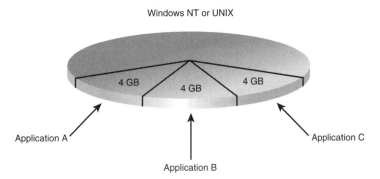

STORAGE SYSTEMS

Another factor to be considered when externalizing storage is the storage device itself. A number of storage systems can be used in storage area networks. Two commonly used disk systems are Redundant Array of Inexpensive Disks (RAID) and Just a Bunch of Disks (JBOD). Disk array systems have proved to be best suited for the type of storage needs that SANs address. The disk arrays are popular in storage area networks because they provide a fast and extremely reliable method of storing and retrieving information.

Assume that the software development center of Westside Inc received an online bookstore project from one of its clients. The bookstore stocks books and magazines related to computers. The software development for the online bookstore project was complete and had reached a stage when it was ready to go live.

Considering the fact that a number of users might access the Web site at the same time, the network administrator of the software development center of Westside Inc. needed to decide on a suitable storage system that was fast, responsive, expandable, and reliable.

Considering all these factors, the network administrator decided to choose a disk array system. Another factor the administrator took into consideration was that disk array systems, which existed in the software development center of Westside Inc., support Fibre Channel connections. Therefore, migration to the SAN environment was possible without doing away with the storage devices that existed earlier.

Note

> If the devices in your current setup do not support Fibre Channel connections, do not worry. Most storage device manufacturers have announced plans to shift their storage device interfaces to Fibre Channel. How to connect your existing devices to storage area networks by using interconnects is explained in Chapter 6, "Storage Area Network Fabrics" and Chapter 9, "Managing Storage Area Networks."

REDUNDANT ARRAY OF INEXPENSIVE DISK DRIVES

Redundant Array of Inexpensive Disk (RAID) is a technology that can quickly share and store data. RAID is a disk array system that is a cluster of disk drives. The cluster is created by combining the capacity of several disk drives. This provides you with consolidated storage space that can be managed as a single unit.

The characteristics of RAID are indicated by its name. It is a set of independent arrays of disk drives. These disks are stacked together in a physical enclosure to form a single virtual disk. The term "redundant" in the name indicates that the same data is stored on different disks. The basic purpose of RAID is to prevent data loss and at the same time allow each drive to operate independently.

Most RAID systems use the *data striping* method to store data. In this method, the storage space is partitioned into several units into which data is distributed. Each unit is called a *stripe*, and all stripes are interleaved to ensure that the combined space comprises joined stripes from each drive. In essence, the system treats RAID as a single logical storage unit.

Note

> It is not necessary that all RAID systems use the data striping method. In fact, as you will read later in the section, RAID 1 does not use the data striping method.

An electronic device serves as an interface between the computer and the array of disk drives. This device is called a RAID Controller and is shown in Figure 2.9. The RAID controller works in a manner similar to the disk controller currently used by the hard disks on your system. It is a chip or a circuit that translates the data from the computer into a form that can be understood by the disks.

LEVELS PRESENT IN RAID   RAID as a technology has come a long way from its initial configuration. The developments in RAID have led to a number of different configurations, known as "levels," that have been standardized. There are a number of levels in RAID, such as RAID 0, RAID 1, RAID 2, RAID 3, RAID 4, RAID 5, RAID 6, RAID 7, RAID 10, RAID 53, and RAID 0+1. Each of these levels has its own advantages and disadvantages, and the numbers assigned to them are not necessarily indicative of the relative superiority or effectiveness of each level. There are slight but significant variations between these levels. The simplest RAID configuration either stripes or mirrors data across two or more drives. This type of configuration does not offer reliable levels of data protection and performance improvements. More advanced configurations include varying levels of fault tolerance and performance enhancers with three or more drives. The Berkeley scientists of the University of California have contributed five of these levels. The one thing common among all the RAID levels is that at least two or more disks are virtually combined to appear as a single large storage device.

Figure 2.9
The RAID Controller serves as an interface between the computer and RAID.

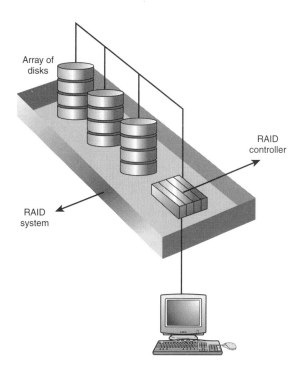

Array of disks

RAID controller

RAID system

RAID 0   RAID 0 is among the simplest of the RAID configurations that uses the data striping method, where data is striped or stored across the disk drives, as shown in Figure 2.10.

Each of the hard disks, D1, D2, and D3, have stripes numbered as 0, 1, 2, and 3. The data is partitioned across blocks, where each block is written to an independent disk drive. Improved input/output (I/O) performance is possible because the I/O load is spread in parallel across many drives. RAID 0 can be implemented with a minimum of two drives.

Do not even consider this level of RAID if you want to store business-critical data, because this level offers no fault tolerance. However, if you want faster access to data alone, then this RAID level is best suited for you.

Figure 2.10
RAID 0 is a striped
disk array.

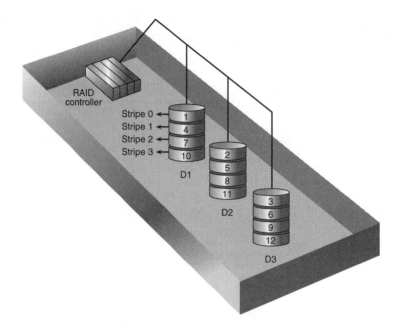

RAID 1   RAID 1 requires the hard disk drives to be split into groups of two, as shown in Figure 2.11. Any one of the disk drives in each pair of drives serves as the primary storage device; the second disk serves as the secondary storage device. RAID 1 uses the disk mirroring method. *Disk mirroring* is the process of duplicating the data stored in one disk or group to another disk or group to provide data redundancy. The data striping method is not applicable here. The RAID 1 implementation requires a minimum of two drives.

RAID 2   RAID 2 is an enhanced version of RAID 1. This technique uses multiple drives that match each other, similar to the disk mirroring method in RAID 1. The improvement over RAID 1 is that the one-to-one mapping of the disks has been eliminated, which makes RAID 2 much more flexible. The theoretical data transfer rate is also exceptionally higher than RAID 1.

RAID 2 employs the hamming code Error Correction Code (ECC) method for ensuring fault tolerance, as shown in Figure 2.12. This method provides built-in error detection. ECC adds the numerical values of data by using a formula to obtain a checksum, which is stored on specific blocks on the disk drives. This level of RAID is practically of no value if you use SCSI disks because SCSI has an in-built error correction system.

This error detection method is used to check whether the data transmitted is received intact at the receiving end. In this method, a numerical value accompanies every transmitted message. This value is obtained using a formula based on the number of bits that the message contains. The receiving end uses the same formula after receiving the message to ensure that the same numerical value accompanies the message.

Figure 2.11
RAID 1 is a disk array
that uses the disk
mirroring method to
store data.

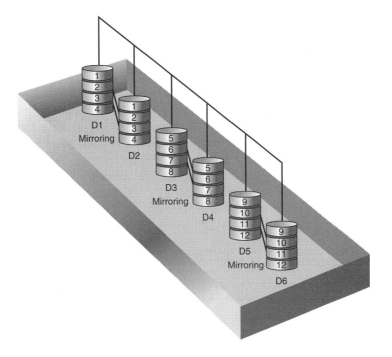

Figure 2.12
RAID 2 uses the Error
Correction Code for
verification of fault
tolerance.

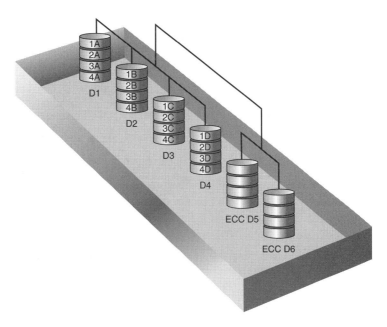

This checksum is then added on to the end of the data block for verification of fault tolerance. As soon as the data is read back from the drive, ECC tabulations are again computed,

and the specific data block checksums are read and compared with the latest tabulations. The data is intact if the numbers match. If there is any inconsistency, the lost data can be retrieved by using the first or earlier checksum as an indicator.

RAID 3   RAID 3 is a simplified version of RAID 2 that also incorporates the feature of data striping. RAID 3 consists of an array of disk drives, one of which is assigned for parity. Parity checking is a simple technique used to validate the accuracy of data transmissions. In this system, an additional parity bit, which is a binary digit, is appended to data being transmitted. If the total number of bits to be transmitted is even, the parity bit is set to one; else, the parity bit is set to zero. At the receiving end, the total number of bits received is checked. If this value is even, then it implies that an error has occurred in the transmission. This is not the best or even a very reliable method of error checking because if you have two bits in error they counterbalance each other. The reason why this method is still used is that it is very unlikely that you could have such a situation in personal computers.

RAID 3 uses the striping method to store replicated data that is striped in the form of bits or bytes across the disk drives. One of the disk drives is assigned to store ECC information. In RAID 3, data recovery is achieved by calculating the exclusive OR (XOR) value of the information stored on the other drives. This XOR calculation helps in parity generation, as shown in Figure 2.13.

Figure 2.13
RAID 3 transfers data with parity generation.

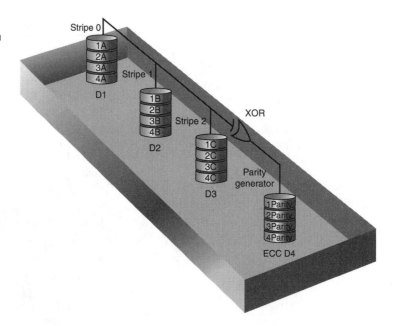

RAID 4   RAID 4 is similar to RAID 3 except that data is distributed in sectors or blocks and not in terms of bits or bytes. Another difference is that RAID 3 needs to access all the disk drives in the array, whereas each disk drive in the RAID 4 array can operate on its own.

The other major advantage with RAID 4 is that all the parity information is stored on a single dedicated drive. This makes the total capacity required for the redundant information less. RAID 4 works on the principle of parity generation, as shown in Figure 2.14.

Figure 2.14
RAID 4 consists of several data disks with a common parity disk.

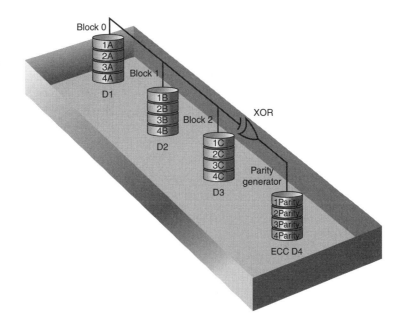

Implementation of RAID 4 requires a minimum of three drives. The cost per megabyte is quite low because only one drive is dedicated to storing redundant data. This RAID level is fast when performing read operations. However, in the case of write operations, the need to update parity data makes the write process considerably slower. This does not have a large impact when you are working with large amounts of data and sequential writes, as opposed to small random writes.

RAID 5   RAID 5 is similar to RAID 4 and works on the principle of parity generation. The minor difference is that parity is distributed across the drives and is not dedicated to a single drive, as shown in Figure 2.15.

The RAID 5 implementation also requires at least three drives. The cost per megabyte is the same as that of RAID 4. The point to note in a RAID 5 implementation is that because the parity data is distributed across the drives, the reads are slower than RAID 4 arrays. However, in the case of small and random reads, RAID 5 has a slightly better performance compared to RAID 4. There is not much to choose between RAID 4 and RAID 5 in terms of the write speeds because both the levels do not support simultaneous data writes.

RAID 6   RAID 6 adopts the same parity generation principle as RAID 5, but with two parity stripes, as shown in Figure 2.16.

Figure 2.15
RAID 5 has several data disks with parity data distributed among disks.

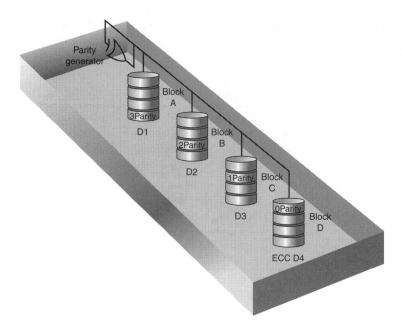

Figure 2.16
In RAID 6 there are two separate parity schemes.

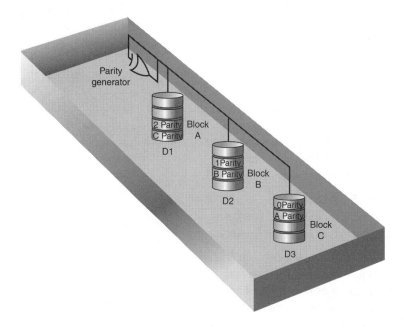

Data is striped on a block level across the set of drives with a second set of parity calculated and written across all the drives. The main advantage in RAID 6 is that this level would be able to recover from the failure of two drives. However, in RAID 5 you can normally recover all the data only in the case of a single drive crash. This is possible because of the use of the double parity generated.

RAID 7   RAID 7 is a registered architecture created by Storage Computer Corporation. The working of RAID 7 is similar to RAID 3. However, in RAID 7, data is striped across the array and a separate disk is dedicated to parity, as shown in Figure 2.17. Moreover, RAID 7 has an embedded OS that optimizes the read and write operations of individual drive elements. The most notable feature of RAID 7 is that it provides an asynchronous data transfer system. Each drive has an independent data path and its usage in RAID 7 is asynchronous. This enables RAID 7 to access each drive independently of the other drives; that is, it enables simultaneous access. The use of the real-time embedded OS allows RAID 7 to control the transfer of data to and from the central cache. Each device or interface also has a cache, which is connected to the central cache through a high-speed bus.

Figure 2.17
RAID 7 performs an asynchronous data transfer.

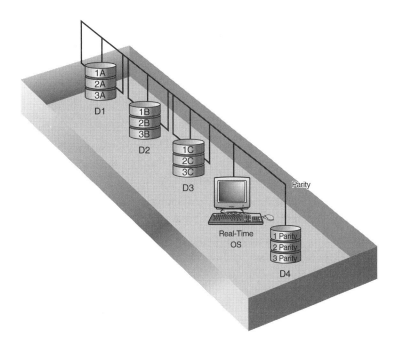

The use of the embedded OS and the asynchronous control of the data bus and the data paths between the central cache, local drive cache, and parity drives makes the performance of RAID 7 read and writes much faster compared to RAID 3 or RAID 5. RAID 7 provides faster read and write access to both large chunks of data and small random access of data.

RAID 10   RAID 10 works on the mirroring method. Each stripe in RAID 10 is a RAID 1 array of drives, as shown in Figure 2.18. RAID 10 is a combination of both RAID 0 and RAID 1. The data is first striped across drives and then mirrored. This level provides high performances for both read and write operations. However, the drawback with this level is that the cost is also high.

Figure 2.18
RAID 10 uses mirroring as well as striping to ensure security of data.

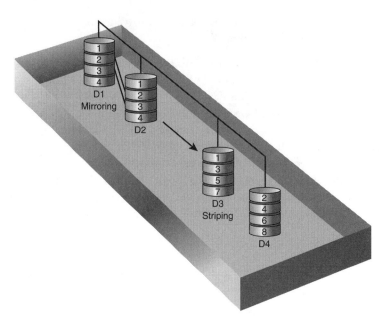

RAID 10 does not follow the technique of parity generation. The fault tolerance of RAID 10 is the same as that of RAID 1. The RAID 10 implementation requires a minimum of four drives.

RAID 53   The configuration of RAID 53 is very similar to that of RAID 3, in that it uses RAID 3 arrays. The data is striped across multiple RAID 3 arrays and works on the principle of parity generation, as shown in Figure 2.19.

RAID 53 should actually be identified as RAID 03 because each stripe in RAID 53 is a striped (RAID level 0) RAID 3 array of drives. The fault tolerance value is similar to that of RAID 3.The RAID 53 implementation requires a minimum of five drives.

The problem with RAID 53 is that it is very costly to implement. This RAID level also requires that all the drive spindles are synchronized. This could restrict your choice of drives to only those drives that are compatible and perform at the same speed. Because byte striping (RAID level 0 striping) is used, the maximum available formatted space is significantly decreased.

Each RAID level has its own advantages and disadvantages. When you select a RAID level, you must check whether it meets the requirements of the applications it is going to support. For example, RAID 5 is typically used for database servers because of its random access speeds. The RAID level that is best suited for a given type of application is determined by the performance requirements and the advantages and disadvantages of each RAID level, as shown in Table 2.1.

Figure 2.19
RAID 53 is another
form of RAID 3.

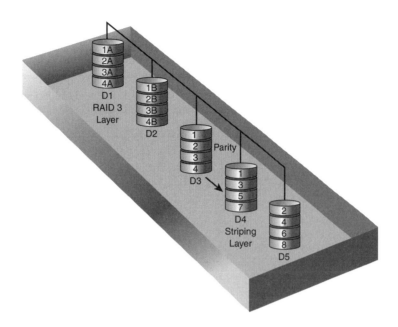

TABLE 2.1   WHEN TO USE EACH RAID LEVEL

RAID Level	When to Use
RAID 0	Use this configuration if you want RAID, can't spend too much, and can survive on backups. Your most critical need is speedy access.
RAID 1	Use this RAID level if reliability is a primary need and cost is not a concern. This level is typically used only in small systems where not more than three drives are available.
RAID 2	This level is too costly and hardly a practical solution. In most cases, you might not even be able to find a vendor to support this level.
RAID 3	This level is suited for large I/O operations and provides redundancy through parity.
RAID 5	Typically used in database servers, this level provides high performance for small and random access.
RAID 6	Typically used for medium-sized databases where data accessibility and security are a premium. However, not all vendors provide this RAID level.
RAID 7	This level is best suited for applications that require a RAID 5 kind of setup and need to have fast access for both random and large read and writes.
RAID 10	This level is best suited for applications that require fast access and redundancy. This level is suited for mission-critical applications but costs a lot more than some of the other RAID levels.

JUST A BUNCH OF DISKS

JBOD stands for Just a Bunch of Disks. JBOD refers to hard disk drives that are connected to the computer/server through multiple slots. Both RAID and JBOD follow the same concept of a set of disk drives. However, the former has some advantages over the latter. In the case of JBOD, the partitioning of disk drives is not present as in the case of RAID. In JBOD, a number of drives are grouped together to form a single large logical volume.

JBOD, unlike RAID, does not provide any fault tolerance; it is just an aggregation of the storage capacity. JBOD also hinders performance, because it is difficult for a user to access the individual drives in the whole unit. The entire capacity in a JBOD is consolidated into a single logical unit. Therefore, it is not possible to optimize data storage. For example, you cannot select a faster drive to store more frequently accessed data. It is also difficult to provide independent drives for different users to access, because the storage capacity is not partitioned.

JBOD is a cheaper alternative to storage needs in places where RAID costs are prohibitive. In spite of the fact that JBODs offer no fault tolerance and redundancy advantages, it is still considered a cost-effective solution. Because JBODs need a controller card, there is a tendency to compare JBODs with RAID 0. The comparison stems from the fact that any system that can be configured as a JBOD can also be configured as a RAID 0 system. In spite of the disadvantages that JBOD has when compared to RAID, JBOD has the following merits:

Drive capacity waste is prevented. JBOD allows the user to make optimum utilization of the capacity of drives because it combines the storage capacity of multiple drives. Consider a case where you have three separate disks of 10, 20, and 30GB, respectively. If you create a JBOD configuration, you will be able to get a total storage capacity of 60GB. On the other hand, if you configure it as a RAID 0 system, the total storage capacity will be restricted to 30-40GB. This advantage is particularly applicable in the case of a system that is expanded to accommodate more disk drives.

Simpler disaster recovery is ensured. If a drive present in the JBOD system fails, it is easier to recover data from the remaining drives. In comparison, if any drive in RAID 0 fails, the data on every disk in the array is lost, because all the files containing the data are striped together and there is no redundancy provided.

PROTOCOLS

For every storage device to be connected to a new SAN setup smoothly, it has to fulfill certain conditions. The conditions vary with the type of storage device. In case of non-SAN devices, gateways can be used to connect them to SAN.

With storage area networks, data access takes place with ease. Unlike the traditional storage setup, in SANs the server gives the client direct access to the storage devices and the client handles the read or write actions by means of block-level SAN protocols.

PROPOSALS TO EXTEND SAN PROTOCOLS

The heterogeneous storage environment is made possible because of the SAN open model protocols. There are proposals to extend the SAN protocols so that it is adaptable with other file sharing protocols, such as Microsoft's CIFS, which is used for Windows NT or Windows 2000 servers, and UNIX's NFS protocol.

Some of the file sharing protocol extensions are Soft Lock, SAN server buffer disabling capability, and Extent List Capability. The Soft Lock is a new form of file and record locking scheme. Its function is to automatically withdraw a lock when there is a contention. Based on the type of operation being performed, the Soft Lock is either shared or exclusive.

The SAN server buffer disabling capability is an important feature to prevent the loss of modifications to files. When the client requests a direct disk write permission, the SAN server transfers all buffered information about the file to the disk and then permits the client to update the file. This ensures that there is no conflict between the buffer and the disk data.

The Extent List Capability feature has the function of reporting to the client that certain disk blocks are allocated to a file. This enables the client to directly transport data to and from the disk.

The proposed SAN protocols are from SNIA File System Working Group White Paper Excerpt authored by Tim Williams of CrosStore and with enhancements by the SNIA File System Working Group.

Integration of various platforms and sharing of data can now be done with ease. The implementation of minor enhancements on the NAS protocols discussed earlier enable network clients to directly access and transfer data to the SAN storage devices. The change in the working of the NAS protocols has enabled SAN to function seamlessly and ensure externalization of storage.

SAN SOFTWARE

The basic purpose of the SAN software is to provide a simplified storage management system that will help you synchronize the working of the other components of a storage area network. SAN software enables the synchronized functioning of the storage area network. It manages all the other entities, such as the infrastructure, servers, and storage systems. This entity can be made up of single consolidated SAN management software or a collection of management software for the different devices in the storage area network. It controls the various SAN devices and the functionalities associated with them.

There are number of SAN management software available in the market. Some of these are complete management software solutions for the entire storage area network, and others are specific software for managing individual devices. The individual device management software is exclusive to each vendor.

This section discusses Hierarchical Storage Management (HSM) solutions, which is a product of UniTree Software Inc. HSM is primarily concerned with storage space management. HSM, when used along with RAID systems, provides an ideal method for managing the storage capacity to get the most out of the available storage resources. This SAN software provides a storage management solution that is suitable for both small and mainframe computing environments.

In HSM, the secondary storage capacity is made to appear larger than its original size by integrating it with the tertiary storage, such as tape and optical devices. For example, if you have a 30GB RAID 5 system, a 20GB JBOD, and a 20GB RAID 3 system, HSM will virtually combine the storage space and treat the entire storage capacity (70GB) as a single unit. HSM will enable you to store up to 70GB (in this example) and internally manage the individual storage space on each device to give the best performance.

HSM is not a means to take backup, although it can also be used to perform backup operations. It protects the data continuously to keep the data intact. The conventional backup solutions create a snapshot of the source device's data to avoid any data loss.

HSM is unlike the archive solutions. In the case of an archive solution, you must specify the data that is to be archived to initiate the process of archiving. After the data is archived, it is deleted from the current location. When you need to read or modify the data, you must open the archive. On the other hand, HSM moves the data automatically from the hard disk to the tape, depending on the frequency of data access. This capability gives the users a seamless view of the data.

HSM fundamentally balances disk space and the speed at which the data is retrieved from the storage devices. Each storage device has a varying cost factor associated with it. Therefore, you can set the hierarchy of the various devices such that HSM can ensure optimum utilization of storage space.

HSM follows a three-pronged approach to ensure speedy access to data:

- Move rarely accessed data to cheaper media.
- Move frequently accessed data to faster media.
- Manage the movement of data transparently.

Any new data that enters the system is stored on media such as disk array systems or JBODs, which provide fast data retrieval. HSM monitors data access and transfers the data that is not frequently accessed to cheaper media. If you start accessing data that is stored in cheaper media quite often, the data is transferred into faster media.

Regardless of the type of media, the user who is accessing the data does not know the source from which the data is retrieved. HSM hides the background shifting of the data. The data appears to remain the same to the user and the applications that use it.

HSM is just one of the various SAN software products available. It is possible to achieve multiple management models by using single SAN software, such as HSM, or by combining a number of specific SAN software. The SAN architecture enables you to design a heterogeneous storage environment that can be managed with ease.

TRANSFERRING DATA IN A STORAGE AREA NETWORK

The business needs of today are such that data needs to be accessed and retrieved quickly. It must be stored such that it can be retrieved at a fast pace for later use and sufficiently well protected through backups. Therefore, all data cannot be present in the same place for long. You need to be able to transfer data to provide a place for the current data. There are three modes of transferring data:

- Server-to-storage transfers
- Storage-to-storage transfers
- Server-to-server transfers

Assume that the software development center of the fictitious company, Westside Inc. employs these three modes of transferring data based on its requirements. The nature and need of the transfers are discussed in the following sections.

PART

I

CH

2

SERVER-TO-STORAGE TRANSFERS

The basis for storage area networks having come into existence is server-to-storage transfers. The growing demands posed by this type of data transfer over existing LAN setups was one of the driving factors that led to storage externalization through SANs. When the volume of data to be transferred is huge, it is cumbersome to copy the data to the storage device. This is unlike the case of the traditional system, where the server transfers the data over the LAN to the storage device or to another server with the dedicated set of SCSI-based drives directly attached to the servers. Figure 2.20 shows the server-to-storage transfers.

In the case of a NAS-based network setup, the server will request the NAS devices for the required data over the LAN connection. This data will be picked by the server and sent to the client system over the LAN again. In a SAN setup, the server-to-storage transfer happens behind the LAN. The data is transferred between the server and the storage devices over the storage area network instead of the LAN. This kind of setup externalizes the storage from the LAN.

Assume that currently the software development center at the fictitious Westside Inc. works on an Ethernet setup. In the current setup, the need for a server-to-storage transfer or the reverse transfer is almost a continuous process and occurs when LAN clients want to access information on NAS devices. The data transfer in the Ethernet setup happens over the Ethernet. In server-to-storage transfers on a SAN setup, the server transfers the data directly to the storage devices over the Fibre Channel connection. The other problem that could be avoided by Westside Inc. by implementing a SAN is that the need for server-to server communication to access shared data is decreased. In a SAN setup, each server can access the shared data independently without depending on another server to serve the data. This access model does not use a LAN for data transfer. Figure 2.21 shows the server-to-storage type of data transfer.

Figure 2.20
The difference between the ordinary copy function and server-to-storage transfers is that the transfers are a faster way to copy data.

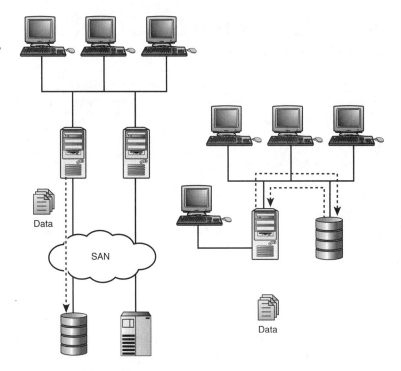

Figure 2.21
The server transfers data to the storage devices over the Fibre Channel connection.

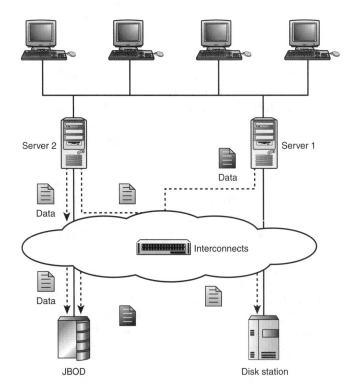

STORAGE-TO-STORAGE TRANSFERS

When the entire content of a storage device needs to be transferred to another storage device, storage-to-storage transfer helps. In this type of data transfer, the data is directly transferred from one storage device to another without having to pass through a client. In the traditional method, the applications had to invoke the read and write functions to transfer the data. The drawback of this method was that the load on the client was increased.

There are a number of advantages involved in storage-to-storage transfers. The servers do not have to perform the function of data protection and can therefore be used for dedicated use. Disaster recovery can be accomplished also. The SAN servers make the data sharing across platforms possible. Therefore, multiple copies of the same data need not be maintained.

→ For more information on data sharing across platforms, **see** "Network Attached Storage," **p. 18**

The process of backing up data is made simpler and is made more secure. The probability of data passing through an overloaded server and the potential risk of losing data is minimized. Storage-to-storage transfers enable centralized data management.

The storage-to-storage transfer system can be implemented in several different ways. This type of transfer is implemented depending on certain conditions that the source and destination storage systems must satisfy, such as the storage capacity, compatibility of protocols, and connection topology.

→ For more information on designing the transfer model, **see** "Design Considerations for Storage Area Networks," **p. 160**

The strategies that are commonly used in implementing the storage-to-storage transfer system are Push, Pull, transfers within clients, and transfers at some intermediate location.

In case of the Push strategy, the file that needs to be transferred is pushed from the source storage device to the destination storage device. In this type of transfer, both the storage devices need to have the same protocol.

In case of the Pull strategy, the file that needs to be transferred is pulled from the source device to the destination device, which initiates this process. This strategy also requires both the storage devices to have the same protocol.

The strategies of transfers within clients and transfers at some intermediate location need the SC-API functions and are used in cases where the Push and Pull strategies cannot be used. These two strategies are slower than the Push and Pull strategies.

Note

The push and pull strategies function only if they are supported at both ends.

The storage area network ensures the security of data, as it automatically monitors the data transfers that occur. Every time a data transfer takes place, the *metadata*, which is the information about data, is transferred to the backup server, as shown in Figure 2.22. In a storage-to-storage transfer, the data is transferred from one storage device to another on the SAN network. The server does not have to monitor the transfer of data. However, the metadata is transferred to the controlling SAN server so that the server will be able to look up for the data.

Figure 2.22
Data is moved directly from the disk station to the tape library and the metadata is sent to the server.

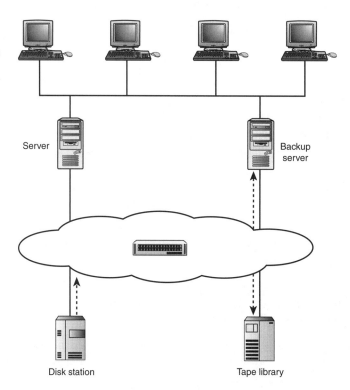

→ For more information on designing the transfer model, **see** "Design Considerations for Storage Area Networks," **p.160**

SERVER-TO-SERVER TRANSFER

This type of transfer system is similar to the transfer systems discussed earlier. The merit of this system is that it does not consume LAN bandwidth. Moreover, the servers appear to be directly connected to each other. The connection between the servers can either be through a fail over link or through the storage area network. To the users on the LAN it appears as if the servers are directly connected because they can interact without using the LAN bandwidth.

Assume that there is a requirement in the software development center of Westside Inc. in New York that the data in Server A be transferred to Server B. The FTP application performs the data transfer. If a storage area network was implemented in Westside Inc., the data transfers from Server A to Server B would be faster than the earlier setup. The implementation of SAN provides this advantage because the data transfers take place over the Fibre channel connection of the SAN.

As demonstrated by the example of Westside Inc., the implementation of a SAN helps in all three types of data transfers. The implementation of a SAN on your network would not only move the storage off the LAN, but also make the data transfers faster and more efficient. The SAN also indirectly increases the speed of the existing LAN setup, because it removes the load of these data transfer operations from the LAN backbone.

PART

I

CH

2

SUMMARY

There has been an increase in the requirements with the emergence of the Internet, mission-critical applications, and the data-centric model of working, for the volume and security of data to be stored. This led to the growth of storage system capacities and newer ways to store and manage data storage. SAN came as a solution for the requirements mentioned earlier. To enable data access across platforms with ease, the platforms needed to be integrated. SAN integrates the different formats in which information is stored through its architecture.

The SAN architecture consists of four layers: infrastructure, servers and hosts, storage systems, and software. The SAN architecture is composed of interfaces, interconnects, and fabrics.

SAN predominantly works on Fibre Channel connections. However, it also works on other connection interfaces, such as SCSI, ESCON, and so on. The extensions to the NAS protocols made it possible for SAN to provide for a truly heterogeneous storage environment. The SAN software, which is the controller, enables you to put the various components of SAN in place and manage them.

There are three basic methods to transfer data: storage-to-storage, storage-to-server, and server-to-server. Under each system of data transfer, SAN is more effective that other networks.

PRODUCTS ARENA

In this column, we shall see the use of a product called Seascape, which is one of the latest products from IBM. Seascape has an enterprise architecture that promises to change the way storage management will function in the future. Seascape addresses the complicated problem of network storage through storage servers.

Earlier storage systems had hardware controllers with microprocessors to perform core operations. Seascape has a set of portable software that will perform the functions of the hardware controllers. The Seascape range of products come as independent products that can be snapped together to create a virtual pool of storage. The independent blocks concept enables easy upgrade and additions or extensions to the products.

STORAGE AREA NETWORKS AND THEIR COMPONENTS

CHAPTER 3

Storage Area Network Interfaces

In this chapter

PARALLEL STORAGE AREA NETWORK INTERFACES

An *interface* is a point of communication between processes, entities, or devices. In terms of networking, the interface serves to establish a means of communication between the devices it connects. There are two categories of interfaces: parallel and serial.

A *parallel interface* is an interface that can transmit more than one bit of data at the same time. A *serial interface* transmits data in the form of packets. Serial interfaces are discussed later in this chapter.

INTEGRATED DRIVE ELECTRONICS/ADVANCED TECHNOLOGY ATTACHMENT TECHNOLOGIES

Integrated Drive Electronics (IDE) is a type of parallel interface that is used in hard disks. IDE is synonymous with many other names, such as ATA, EIDE, Ultra ATA, and fast ATA. Actually, the IDE interface that is currently available in hard disks uses the Advanced Technologies Attachment (ATA) to provide a truly integrated interface. The original IDE interface, developed by Quantum, was composed of (and referred to as) *hardcards*, which were mounted to expansion slots. This was not a very efficient system. The size and weight of the hard disks, and the heat the hard disks generated, made them unsuitable for use with hardcards.

AT Attachment technology connects the current hard disks to a regular bay drive through a system bus. To avoid misinterpretation of the IDE with other interfaces, it is commonly referred to as IDE/ATA. The IDE/ATA hard disk is most popular for modern PCs because it provides high performance and reliability and is inexpensive.

IDE, as the name implies, has a controller built onto the hard disk. One of the benefits of having a built-in controller is that the number of cables and other parts required for the setup is low and these drives are easy to install. The signal pathways adopted are shorter in length; therefore, these pathways enhance the reliability of the disk drive.

There is a set of standards that aims at describing the IDE/ATA interface. A number of organizations, such as American National Standards Institute (ANSI), Information Technology Industry Council (ITIC), National Committee for Information Technology (NCITS), and T13 Technical Committee (T13) have contributed to setting up the ATA standards and developing them. The first AT Attachment Packet Interface (ATAPI) standards were defined by the Small Form Factor committee, which primarily takes care of defining standards for material issues, such as PC cables. T13 is the committee that now holds specific responsibility for the IDE/ATA interface. Some of the different standards that are currently recognized by standards committees are ATA-1 (ATA), ATA-2, ATA-3, ATA Packet Interface, ATA-4, ATA-5, and ATA-6.

ATA-1

A certain set of transfer modes and features describe the original IDE/ATA standards. It has two hard disks with a single channel that is shared by the *master and slave*.

The master and slave concept can be explained on the basis that each IDE/ATA channel is capable of supporting either one or two devices. With each IDE/ATA device having its own integrated controllers, it is required that some order be maintained on the channel, to enable some demarcation between the two devices. Therefore, the solution is to provide each device with a designation as either master or slave. The controller can address data and commands to the drives. If a command is addressed, the target drive responds to the command and the other drive ignores the command. The terms "master" and "slave" are assigned only as names and have no significant effect upon the working of the device. The only difference is that the master is recognized first during the boot process, and then the slave is identified.

Another feature of ATA is that it provides support for Programmed Input Output (PIO) modes 0, 1, and 2. The *programmed I/O* method is the conventional technique of data transfer over the IDE/ATA interface. This method enables the CPU of the system and the hardware to have the capability to control the data transfer that takes place between the hard disk and the system. The PIO modes refer to the classification of the different speeds of the programmed I/O. The three modes, 0, 1, and 2, have the data transfer rate of 3.3MBps, 5.2MBps, and 8.3MBps, respectively. The cycle time of the three modes is 600, 383, and 240 nanoseconds, respectively. It is important to remember that the PIO modes are mainly defined with respect to the cycle time.

PART

II

CH

3

> **Note**
>
> *Cycle time* is the time taken for each transfer of data to take place. The *maximum transfer rate* is the inverse of the cycle time multiplied by two. The reason is that the IDE/ATA interface is two bytes wide.

An important feature of ATA is that it provides support for single-word *Direct Memory Access* (DMA) modes 0, 1, and 2 and multiword DMA mode 0. The programmed I/O method has the drawback of high overhead apart from taking care of the system CPU involved. The idea of eliminating the CPU's involvement and allowing the hard disk to communicate directly with the system memory seems more feasible. Direct Memory Access is the name given to a transfer protocol that enables a peripheral device to be capable of transferring information directly to the memory or receiving data from it, without the need for the system processor to carry out the process. The traditional DMA makes use of regular DMA channels. There are two types of DMA modes that are defined: single-word and multiword. In the *single-word mode*, the transfer of data is carried out one word at a time. The other type of classification is *multiword*, where the data is transferred at the rate of more than one word at a time.

> **Note**
>
> A *word*, in this context, refers to two bytes of data.

ATA-2

The ATA-1 standards are not capable of meeting the demands of the new hard disks in terms of higher performance, increased size, and higher data transfer rates. Therefore, ATA-2 replaced ATA-1 with a number of improved features. ATA-2, in addition to the PIO modes that ATA-1 offered, provides support for PIO modes 3 and 4. ATA-2 also adds the faster multiword DMA modes 1 and 2 to those supported by ATA-1. ATA-2 further improves performance by adding commands to enable block transfers of data.

Block mode permits the grouping of multiple read or write commands over the IDE/ATA interface to enable the commands to be handled on a single interrupt.

> **Note**
>
> An *interrupt* literally interrupts the other jobs being performed by the processor when it issues a signal that data can be transferred from the hard disk.

ATA-2 also has an improved Identify-Drive command. When the software issues queries, this command permits the hard disks to answer by providing accurate information in terms of their characteristics.

ATAPI-5

AT Attachment with Packet Interface – 5 (ATAPI-5) provides support to Ultra DMA modes 3 and 4 with data transfer rates of 44.4 and 66.7MBps, respectively. *Ultra DMA* is a protocol that is used to transfer data to and from hard disks. Ultra DMA is built on the Direct Memory Access technique that is used to transfer data from memory to a device without passing through the CPU. DMA channels are very useful in speeding up data transfer rates and accordingly are useful in real-time applications. All these standards and versions are backward compatible. ATA-3 standard made minor modifications to the previous standard, ATA-2. The ATA-3 interface provides greater reliability during high-speed transfers as compared to ATA-2. ATA-4, the standard next in line, provides nearly twice the speed of ATA-3 by reducing the timing window in the protocol. ATAPI-5 is the generation that is currently adopted. This standard was published in the year 2000 by ANSI with minor changes to ATA-4 that nonetheless significantly increased the throughput time to almost double the existing speed of ATA-4. ATAPI-6, the next generation of ATAPI, is expected to secure its position in the near future. This standard, at the time of this writing, is still to be completed. The changes proposed to this standard aim at increasing the speed of access of UltraDMA.

> **Note**
>
> Apart from the existing ATA standards, there are a number of standards and versions of ATA are being introduced in the market on a regular basis based on user requirements. Each version and standard is trying to beat its predecessors in terms of speed, consistency, or other features. ATA is a fast growing standard that currently enjoys quite an amount of acceptance in the market.

SMALL COMPUTER SYSTEM INTERFACE

The *Small Computer System Interface* is an interface popularly recognized as SCSI, which is pronounced as "scuzzy." SCSI is a parallel interface that originated as a multipurpose I/O bus for use in PCs. SCSI permits the connection of devices to a PC or other systems with data being transmitted across multiple data lines. In the conventional PC hardware setup, each device made use of a separate controller. This resulted in a number of controller cards of different types, such as one card for the tape drive and one for the hard disk. In these technologies, one or more dumb peripherals are attached to a controller. These dumb peripherals serve the purpose of controlling the I/O operations. SCSI then gained recognition as it brought about a specification that required intelligent peripherals and controllers where one controller card can manage a set of seven devices. SCSI offers benefits such as high bandwidth, multitasking, low overhead, and also high-velocity cable.

SCSI STANDARDS

The first SCSI standard evolved as SCSI-1. It defined the transfer modes and fundamental SCSI features, such as signaling characteristics and cable length.

PART

II

CH

3

> **Note**
>
> *Cable length* is the maximum length of a SCSI cable. Cable length is affected by the signaling speed and signaling type of the interface. For example, if the signaling speed is high, the SCSI cable could be longer.

One of the features of SCSI cables is that it is flexible. The cable can be bent easily without affecting its performance. It is a necessity that each SCSI cable match the specific electrical requirements associated with the methods and signaling speeds supported.

SCSI-1 devices offer an asynchronous data transfer rate of 1.5MBps and a synchronous transfer rate of 5MBps. An advantage of SCSI-1 is that it can process many overlapped commands at the same time. SCSI-1 drives can overlap I/O functions with the remaining SCSI drives that are a part of the setup and perform the processing of data in a parallel manner. The main drawback with SCSI-1 is its incompatibility with other devices.

→ To learn more about data transfer methods, **see** "Modems," **p. 88**

The SCSI-2 standard arrived as a solution to the incompatibility problems of SCSI-1. SCSI-2 aimed at making the SCSI hardware offered by different SCSI vendors interoperable. SCSI-2 provided a higher synchronous data transfer rate of 10MBps. The specification comprised a 16-bit wide data path that offers a doubled throughput of 20MBps. SCSI-2 can support 15 devices with the additional feature of parity checking. The higher rate of data transfer SCSI-2 to improve the cabling length. SCSI-2 also introduced the feature of *command queueing*. Command queueing enables parallel and multiple requests to be sent to the devices on the SCSI bus. SCSI-2 included new command sets to provide support to the use of more devices, such as CD-ROMs and scanners, in addition to hard disks. Another highlight of SCSI-2 is that it is backward compatible with SCSI-1.

A new standard, SCSI-3, emerged as a combination of multiple standards. The new standard also introduced new command sets for processing certain primary and block commands. SCSI-3 adopts the dual features of an 8-bit data path with a data transfer rate of 20MBps, as in Ultra SCSI, and a 16-bit data path with a data transfer rate of 40MBps, as in Ultra Wide SCSI). Both Ultra SCSI and Ultra Wide SCSI are backward compatible with SCSI-2.

One factor that you need to keep in mind is that a few SCSI vendors and manufacturers are studying the market requirements with respect to interfaces. After this study, they improve or update their SCSI product and introduce it as a new standard. The outcome is that there are a number of SCSI versions available in the market today and there is a possibility of more versions being developed.

However, the different versions do not actually cause a threat for one simple reason that each new version is compatible with the earlier versions. The SCSI standard recognizes virtually every peripheral device. Currently, only SCSI-1 and SCSI-2 cannot be upgraded to the latest versions, such as Ultra160 SCSI or another LVD-based SCSI. The primary reason for this incompatibility is that the original versions were based on 8-bit data bus, unlike the latest versions, which need a 16-bit data bus.

ULTRA2 SMALL COMPUTER SYSTEM INTERFACE

Ultra2 SCSI is another SCSI standard, which uses the *Low Voltage Differential* (LVD) technique. Ultra2 SCSI is designed as a computer disk interface that is compatible with older SCSI devices. This interface is available in the market as 68- and 80-pin configurations. Ultra2 SCSI is an advancement over earlier SCSI technologies because it offers improved speed and reliability.

Note

The LVD signaling concept makes use of two wires and creates complementary signal pairs by using differential voltage between the two wires. The use of LVD reduces power costs significantly.

Ultra2 SCSI offers the benefits of backward compatibility, enhanced flexibility in configuration, faster data transfer, and increased bus bandwidth. These benefits are most suitably implemented in cases such as RAID systems, servers, workstations, digital broadcasting, multimedia, and Internet technologies where the data transfer rate is required to be very high. Ultra2 SCSI reduces overall power consumption because of an increase in the bus transfer rate to 80MBps.

The design flexibility is higher in the Ultra2 SCSI devices in comparison to the other SCSI interfaces because the cable lengths are increased to nearly 12 meters. You can connect more devices to a system by using Ultra2 SCSI. Systems that make use of the Internet and other server-oriented applications require high transfer rates and large storage capacity. Ultra2 SCSI can provide connectivity to up to 15 devices without giving any chance for bottlenecks to occur. The distinction between SCSI-2 and Ultra2 SCSI (both can connect to 15 devices) is the capability of Ultra2 SCSI to span devices across a wider area. The length of SCSI cable and the speed of transmission are better in Ultra2 SCSI than SCSI-2. There is also the advantage of being able to connect more devices.

Consider a situation where you are using the Ultra2 SCSI controller card and the immediate requirement is to upgrade it to Ultra160 SCSI. The backward compatibility feature of Ultra2 SCSI allows this upgrade.

Caution

If you remove the Ultra2 SCSI controller, the Ultra2 SCSI interface might begin to act like a SCSI-1 device, in which case you could not take advantage of the performance enhancements Ultra2 SCSI offers.

PART
II

CH
3

ULTRA160 SMALL COMPUTER SYSTEM INTERFACE

The SCSI standard has been continuously improving and the developers of SCSI have gone one step further in providing another SCSI technology, Ultra160 SCSI, which offers improved performance and higher reliability as an interface. Ultra160 SCSI offers the following benefits:

- Easier manageability
- Higher speed of transfer
- Improved data integrity
- Improved operating efficiency on the whole

The SCSI generations moved from SCSI to LVD or Ultra2 SCSI. Ultra2 SCSI offered quicker data transfer, increased bus bandwidth, and also enhanced flexibility in terms of configuration. Then, Ultra160 SCSI came in as a product based on the feature set of Ultra3 SCSI that further improved performance. Ultra160 SCSI provides a data transfer rate as high as 160MBps because of characteristics such as domain validation, double transition clocking, and CRC, which it adopts from Ultra3 SCSI. The following are the base characteristics of Ultra3 SCSI products:

- Double transition clocking
- Domain validation
- Cyclic redundancy check (CRC)
- Packetization
- Quick arbitration select (QAS)

Before the advent of Ultra160 SCSI, the single transition clocking mechanism was used to transfer data over the SCSI bus. *Single transition clocking* restricts the data transfer rate to half the value of the clock speed. Ultra160 SCSI achieves a greater transfer rate with double transition clocking. In this mechanism, the increase in data transmission rate is accomplished without increasing the clock speed. The data transfer rate for Ultra160 SCSI is 160MBps, compared to 80MBps for Ultra2 SCSI, because the data is transferred over the SCSI bus by a double transition clock, which increases the speed of the data transfer across the lines. In environments where many devices are on a bus, this method yields improved performance.

The domain validation feature ensures that the determined transfer rate is compared with the actual rate adopted. In the previous versions of SCSI, the host controller was responsible for deciding the data transfer rate for each connected device, but with no assurance that the connection would adopt the determined transfer rate. In Ultra160 SCSI, in the case that errors are detected, the rate is reduced until no errors remain. Domain validation thus provides support in reducing the cost of ownership by ensuring drive availability and reducing device installation issues, such as invisible legacy components (extenders and so on) and improper terminations.

In the pre-Ultra160 SCSI era, if devices that did not support negotiated transfer rates were there, they would remain inaccessible. However, with domain validation, the host controller would keep trying different permutations to access the device. This process is similar to the dial-up connection process. The host controller would keep trying alternatives until a successful connection was established. This helps to ensure that installation problems are reduced.

Note

In the process of establishing a connection, the host controller could reduce the data transfer rates or abandon double transition clocking.

The earlier versions of SCSI were able to detect the transmission errors by using the parity check method. CRC offers an error-detection feature that ensures high-speed data transfer. CRC checks not just a byte but validates the entire data transmission as one unit, which results in enhanced data reliability.

CRC has existed for years as a part of products of FDDI, Ethernet, and so on. When data is transmitted, the transmitter divides the data by a specially selected prime number. The remainder obtained as a result of the division is the CRC value, which is appended to the data and transmitted. At the receiving end the receiver divides the appended data and the CRC value using the same process. If this results in a remainder that is equal to a constant, it implies that the data has been transmitted correctly. If the remainder is not a constant, it implies that an error has occurred in the data transmission.

CRC has been incorporated into Ultra160 SCSI to ensure that error rates can be minimized during hot-swaps. It also assumes importance because the data transmission rates are considerably higher than in Ultra2 SCSI.

Tip

Although Ultra160 SCSI supports both parity checks and CRC, only one of the two systems can be used on a single data transmission.

Note

Parity checks check whether a transmission has any problems. The sender calculates a parity bit for a transmission and attaches it to the transmission. The receiver calculates the parity bit for the transmission received and checks to validate whether the parity bit matches with the one sent by the sender. Errors in transmission are corrected through re-transmission.

Packetization is a feature that was added in Ultra160+ SCSI (later version to Ultra160 SCSI). This feature aims at improving the operating efficiency of SCSI by reducing protocol overheads and increasing data transfer rates. Packetization enables Ultra160+ SCSI to transmit multiple threads of data per connection cycle. It achieves all this by using a packet structure similar to Fibre Channel.

→ To learn more about Fibre Channel, **see** "Fibre Channel Architecture," **p. 113**

Ultra160 SCSI has a leading edge in comparison with the other interfaces. Its data transfer rate of 160MBps is greater than that of other interfaces. Ultra160 SCSI improves system performance significantly by supporting multitasking. Finally, Ultra160 SCSI is inexpensive, because the markets offer a wide variety of SCSI products. Ultra160 SCSI promises to offer improved reliability, flexibility, and speed, and in high-performance environments these factors give Ultra160 SCSI the lead over Ultra2 SCSI.

Another characteristic of Ultra160 SCSI is that it is compatible with the Ultra2 SCSI devices. Both Ultra160 SCSI and Ultra2 SCSI make use of the same cables, terminators, and connectors. The Ultra160 and Ultra2 SCSI devices can also be mixed on the same bus, because the Ultra160 host controllers are able to support the Ultra2 SCSI devices. The benefit of mixing these two devices is that each device can operate at its maximum speed over the shared resources and in effect increase the speed of total processing.

The additional manageability and performance of Ultra160 SCSI is very appropriate in digital video environments, which require intensive data throughput capabilities and multinode server clusters. In situations where RAID configurations are employed, certain devices can fail and will need replacement, which increases the workload. The high bandwidth feature of Ultra160 SCSI would prove useful in absorbing the additional workload.

The ability of Ultra160 SCSI to negotiate transfer rates provides you with the ability to ensure a connection in cases of hot-pluggable drive replacements. Hence, this feature makes this SCSI widely applicable for corporate intranets, data warehousing, and data mining operations.

Because Ultra160 SCSI devices provide a significant data transfer rate, they prove useful in servers, workstations, Internet, CAD/CAM, multimedia, video, and digital broadcasting applications that have such a data transfer requirement.

INTEGRATED DRIVE ELECTRONICS IN COMPARISON WITH SMALL COMPUTER SYSTEMS INTERFACE

SCSI scores many points over IDE as an interface and is usually the preferred interface in higher-end machines. The drawback of SCSI, in comparison with IDE/ATA, is that it is expensive and thus does not prove beneficial for home users.

The SCSI and IDE/ATA manufacturers are regularly redefining the standards based on the market requirements. Therefore, SCSI and IDE/ATA share a similarity in terms of having a number of standards that could be confusing. However, the SCSI standards can be easily distinguished because each SCSI protocol has a name to specify its capabilities. Therefore, there is little dependency on using the name of the standard to identify its transfer rates or any other characteristic information.

SCSI is a high-level protocol in comparison with IDE. IDE is an interface, whereas SCSI is actually a system-level bus that has intelligent controllers on each SCSI device. These controllers work together to control the flow of information on the channel. SCSI is not limited to providing support for hard disks only, which is the case for IDE/ATA, but supports different types of devices, such as tapes and CD-ROM drives. SCSI provides higher performance and compatibility than other PC interfaces due to the fact that it is designed to work like an additional bus for peripherals.

The following sections compare SCSI and IDE/ATA in terms such as cost, configuration, ease of use, and performance.

COST

On the cost scale, the IDE/ATA interface has the upper hand due to many reasons. SCSI makes use of additional hardware, such as a host adapter, terminators, and cables. Fewer SCSI products are manufactured, which makes them more expensive in the market. SCSI products offer high performance, so customers who need a high-performance interface buy SCSI products even at a high price. SCSI is mostly applicable in high-end systems, whereas IDE/ATA, due to its cost-effectiveness, is more commonly used in low-end systems.

PERFORMANCE

Although SCSI is supposed to offer higher performance than IDE/ATA, the actual performance level could vary based on the system setup. For example, a performance-related factor is the data transfer rate of the device. The data transfer rate of a product differs based on the number of devices that are employed. Both IDE/ATA and SCSI provide maximum data transfer rates, so the transfer rate does not ordinarily influence the choice between the two. The transfer rate is a deciding factor only when a large number of hard disks are used, as is the case for RAID; in these cases SCSI is preferred because it improves the aggregate performance.

In the case of single devices, IDE/ATA takes the lead over SCSI with respect to speed, because the overhead of managing the channel and sending commands is high for SCSI interfaces. Consider a situation where the data transfer needs to be performed between multiple devices.

In such an environment, SCSI has the capability to execute multitasking and command queuing, which enables the devices to execute multiple operations simultaneously. In such a case, if IDE/ATA is carrying out one set of transactions, then the device tends to block the channel temporarily so that other devices cannot be accessed. If two devices are put on two different channels, then it is possible to have simultaneous access through the IDE/ATA interface. However, this also results in the problem of limiting the expandability of IDE/ATA. Having different devices on different channels can lead to a slack in the performance because of the cross-channel communications, which can create a number of complications in the actual implementation.

If different devices, such as CD-ROMs and hard disks, are mixed on an IDE/ATA interface, a performance degradation results. This degradation is due to the fact that two different protocols are operating on the same channel in IDE. This does not happen in the case of SCSI.

With regular advancements in technology, SCSI and IDE/ATA are both being constantly upgraded to the latest requirements to offer performance higher than before. In this case, IDE/ATA beats SCSI, because the expenses incurred by upgrades, such as installing additional hardware, are lower than that for SCSI. The price of SCSI is reasonable only in the respect that it is better suited for handling multitask operations. The IDE/ATA interface is the sensible choice for simple applications.

SIMPLIFIED USE

If the setup involves few devices, then it is easier to use IDE/ATA. There are no buses that need to be terminated, no different cables types to use, fewer software driver problems, and only one type of signaling is required. SCSI has all the issues that are not encountered with IDE/ATA. The complex SCSI interface on hard disks makes use of low voltage differential (LVD) signaling, which makes it difficult to set up SCSI.

The complications with the IDE/ATA configuration arise when a large number of devices need to be placed on the channel. If the number of devices is increased, there is a performance setback in IDE/ATA. In such a case, SCSI is a more feasible solution, because it is possible to place seven devices on the SCSI bus without hindering the performance; only the termination factor requires attention. SCSI also possesses a significant advantage over IDE/ATA in terms of the method it uses for hard disk addressing. When multiple hard disks are used, IDE/ATA (unlike SCSI) is susceptible to conflicts between the different settings and BIOS routines.

Note

Termination factor refers to the fact that every bus connection needs to be properly terminated at both ends to ensure proper functioning. (This is very similar to a bus and tag network system.)

SCALABLILITY

In terms of scalability, SCSI has a clear lead over IDE/ATA. Whereas IDE/ATA is restricted in the number of devices it can connect, SCSI can connect 7 or 15 devices, based on whether the data path is 8-bit or 16-bit. This advantage makes SCSI worth its high price when scalability is a concern. IDE/ATA provides support to four devices that can be increased to eight only with a lot of difficulty.

MULTI-DEVICE SUPPORT

The SCSI interface, unlike IDE/ATA, has the benefit of supporting different types of devices. SCSI entered the market as an interface promising high performance; therefore different types of hardware came into the market to be supported by SCSI. For a long period, IDE/ATA gained recognition only as a hard disk interface. With technologies growing, IDE/ATA systems in the market have been on the rise and manufacturers are bringing out more hardware devices that are compatible with IDE/ATA. The SCSI interface still supports more types of devices in comparison with IDE/ATA. The main demarcation in terms of device support is that SCSI can support certain external devices, whereas IDE/ATA is completely restricted to the PCs. If you require support for devices outside the personal computer world, you need to turn to SCSI. SCSI is more widely used by different manufacturers, such as Apple (which seems to be adopting IDE/ATA also), UNIX, and minicomputers. SCSI also enables you to connect devices on different systems over one bus, provided you have taken care of other issues, such as file systems, software, and so on. This is currently not possible with IDE/ATA.

AVAILABILITY

SCSI wins over IDE/ATA with respect to the number of different kinds of devices, such as hard disks, tape drives, and CD-ROMs, but loses out with respect to the number of different models that are available for each device type. The IDE/ATA interface is more widespread in the market because the devices that are available for IDE/ATA are more than that for SCSI.

This factor is significant in terms of hard disks. The choice for hard disks for the IDE/ATA interface varies from small-end models to high-performance systems. SCSI is restricted in its choices especially for the small-end machines. It is an arduous task to find reasonably priced disk drives for a SCSI setup.

SOFTWARE COMPATIBILITY

During its formative years, SCSI faced a number of compatibility and support problems. The primary reason for this was the fact that the SCSI interface was not a native interface of PCs. On the other hand, IDE/ATA served as the most common (that is, native) interface for PCs, so software compatibility problems never occurred. SCSI required the use of extra drivers and additional software to enable older operating systems, such as DOS and Windows 3.x, to function with SCSI devices. Today, SCSI devices are compatible with most of operating systems, which provide support for a number of SCSI adapters and devices.

USAGE OF SYSTEM RESOURCES

SCSI and IDE/ATA utilize system resources on the same scale when a single channel is used. However, when IDE/ATA employs two channels it makes use of more system resources than SCSI. SCSI is the better choice for avoiding problems related to system resources. By default, most PCs have dual channels (unless you have disabled one) and this results in the IDE/ATA interface consuming more resources. The usage of system resources by the interface results in other processes and applications being left with fewer resources. The effect of additional system resource usage is that the net speed of the PC slows down.

SUPPORT FOR NON-PC PLATFORMS

In terms of support for external devices, SCSI takes the initiative. The external SCSI devices can be suitably employed for applications that need to share data or devices between machines. These devices provide the advantage of sharing or moving information between different platforms. IDE/ATA does not support more than one system, whereas you can connect more than one system on the SCSI bus.

A SUMMARY OF HOW SCSI AND IDE/ATA COMPARE

The comparison between SCSI and IDE/ATA interfaces can be summed up in the following statements. In terms of price, IDE/ATA is cheaper than SCSI. For IDE/ATA, the performance factor is high for single devices and varies from moderate to low for multiple devices, whereas SCSI provides a high performance value in most of the cases where multiple devices are used. SCSI is more scalable than IDE/ATA. SCSI is highly software-compatible while the compatibility for the IDE/ATA interface varies from moderate to high.

SERIAL STORAGE AREA NETWORK INTERFACES

Serial interfaces send data as packets in a series over a wire, which reduces overhead and simplifies the data transmission process. You can use different types of serial interfaces in storage area networks, such as high-performance parallel interface (HIPPI) and Serial Storage Architecture (SSA).

HIGH-PERFORMANCE PARALLEL INTERFACE

High-performance parallel interface (HIPPI) is a point-to-point protocol that enables the transmission of a huge amount of data over a short distance at high speeds, as in the case of LANs. HIPPI serves as a parallel interface to connect devices such as multiple computers and storage resources to work as if it were a single device on a LAN.

HIPPI-PH relates to the physical layer and a small section of the data-link layer of the OSI-reference model.

HIPPI-PH is the standard that implements the physical layer of a HIPPI link. According to the standard, HIPPI implements a point-to-point connection over a maximum distance of 25 meters by using copper cables. The standard specifies that HIPPI can be implemented by using either one or two twisted-pair copper cables that adopt a parallel 8-bit data path. The 800 Mbps HIPPI makes use of a 32-bit data bus. The 1600 Mbps HIPPI makes use of a 64-bit data bus.

HIPPI-PH is a *simplex channel*, in other words, it has the ability to transfer data only in one direction (half-duplex). To implement a full-duplex channel, two HIPPI channels can be used. As HIPPI is a point-to-point protocol, the electrical and the protocol characteristics are very simple to implement. HIPPI does not support multi-drop. The limitations posed by the point-to-point connection system considerably simplify the electrical and protocol aspects of the HIPPI. Crossbar switches and other networking methods are being considered to achieve the functional equivalent of the multi-drop feature. An addressing mechanism is also included to support these networking concepts.

Note

Multi-drop is a connection system in which non-simultaneous data transmission occurs between two or more devices (which means there could be multiple receivers). This is used in half-duplex channels. In a point-to-point channel, the data transmission is between two devices only.

Note

A cross-bar switch channels data between any two devices connected to it without affecting the rest of the network (unlike in a bus topology).

→ To learn more about the half-duplex and full-duplex modes, **see** "Ethernet Local Area Networks," **p. 135**

HIPPI can be efficiently used for transferring data packets of varying sizes and has the advantage of low latency. The signal sequences of HIPPI provide look-ahead flow control that enables the average data rate to approach the peak data rate, regardless of the distance (even over tens of kilometers). The transfer of data and flow control is carried out in bursts.

Note

A *burst* is a group of words sent during contiguous CLOCK signals. A burst can contain from 1 to 256 words. A burst that contains fewer than 256 words is called a *short burst*.

HIPPI offers support for error detection. HIPPI uses byte parity on the data bus to detect any errors in transmission. However, it does not provide any error correction. The HIPPI vendors foresee that error recovery might be implemented at the higher-layer protocol.

In the byte parity check, each data burst is succeeded by a Length/Longitudinal Redundancy Checkword (LLRC). This LLRC is used along with the byte parity to check the transmission for any errors in a data burst.

Note

LLRC is a single word that is sent on the data bus from the source to the destination after every burst. LLRC is used to inform the destination of the length and duration of a burst and to match against the actual length of the transmission received.

To transmit data over HIPPI, it is necessary to first establish a connection. Data is then transferred from the source to the target in the form of single or multiple data packets over the connection. Each data packet can consist of zero or any number of bursts. Each burst can comprise up to 256 words. Bursts with less than 256 words are transmitted either as the first or the last bursts. The process of dividing data into sub-components is known as *data framing*. In HIPPI, data transfer follows a structure of data framing, as shown in Figure 3.1.

Figure 3.1
In the data framing model in HIPPI, each transmission is broken down into words and LLRC.

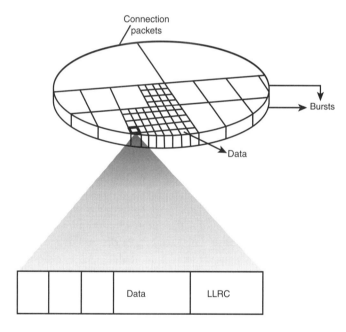

The amount of wait time between bursts and packets can differ. The maximum wait times depend on the data flow to or from the upper-layer protocols and the data flow to or from the opposite end of the channel.

The interface signals during the data flow is displayed, as in Figure 3.2.

The source sends the Interconnect S-D signal to the target. The target responds by sending the Interconnect SD-S signal. These Interconnect signals make use of single-ended emitter-coupled logic (ECL) drivers and receivers while the remaining signals use differential ECL drivers and receivers. *ECL drivers* are high-speed logic drivers that are used to reduce the noise levels in transmissions. The numbers with the 'data bus' and 'parity bus' signals represent the number of signal lines that are used.

Figure 3.2
This sequence of interface signals between the source and the target transmits a set of data bursts.

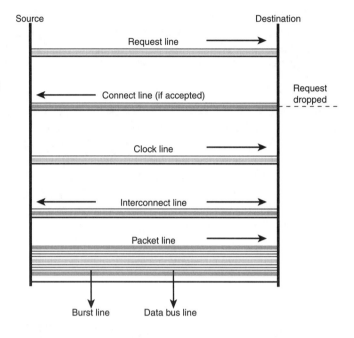

Note

The control and data signals are all timed with respect to the constant 25MHz CLOCK signal with a period of 40 nanoseconds.

Consider a scenario where a connection is set up between the source and the target. Next, one packet containing four bursts of data is sent, where the first burst is the shortest. This packet is then followed by another burst packet. At the end of the entire transmission, the connection is terminated. The waveforms generated in such a scenario would be as displayed in Figure 3.3.

Figure 3.3
The timing sequence transmits a packet with four data bursts, which generates these HIPPI waveforms.

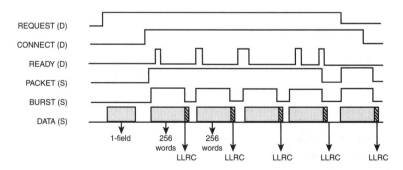

The source provides the I-field on the 'data bus' and then transmits the REQUEST signal. The REQUEST signal is transmitted to the target, which decides whether it wants to respond to the connection. If the target wants to respond to the connection, it then sends back a CONNECT signal. The I-field handles the control and addressing issues. The contents of the I-field are not mentioned in the HIPPI-PH standard but are determined by the standards of the upper-layer protocols.

Note

I-field is a 32-bit information field transmitted as a part of the sequence of operations to set up the connection between the source and the destination.

In case the target decides not to respond to the REQUEST signal, it can either not react in any way and maintain the signal to be *deasserted* (a logical convention to represent an inactive connection), or it can send a connection reject cycle. In the case of sending a connection reject cycle, the CONNECT signal is asserted for 4 to 16 clock cycles so that a signal is sent to the source indicating that the destination does not want to establish the connection. After the source receives this message, it releases the channel.

If the connection is established, it is possible to transfer single or multiple packets to the destination. The packets that compose one or more bursts are delimited by the PACKET signal. The bursts are delimited by the BURST signal.

The LLRC checkword implements a longitudinal parity of all datawords in the burst and the lengthcount of the burst. The LLRC checkword is sent from the source to the destination on the data bus during the first clock period after the burst.

If there are 4-bit and 8-bit errors within a burst, these errors cannot be detected by the error detection mechanism LLRC offers. The byte parity proves to be insufficient in this case.

When the destination is ready to receive a burst from the source, it issues a READY signal for each burst it is prepared to receive. In this manner, the destination can control the flow of data. The source might receive the READY pulse even before the source is actually ready to transmit the next burst; this ensures that there is no time lag between the bursts. When the cable length time is less than the time required to send the multiple bursts, the flow control is not dependent on the distance. This situation requires a burst buffer for every Km.

Note

Burst buffer refers to the buffering of each burst before it is forwarded to the next location.

The INTERCONNECT signals perform the task of indicating to both the source and destination that the cable(s) are connected and that the other end is ready. These signals also indicate whether the 800Mbps or 1,600Mbps HIPPI option is being used.

For packets you need to transfer over a HIPPI connection, the HIPPI-FP standard is defined. This standard enables the packets to be split into three areas: Header_Area, D1_Area, and D2_Area, where each area begins and ends on a 64-bit boundary. Header_Area defines the size and offsets of D1_Area and D2_Area. The purpose of D1_Area is to contain control information, whereas D2_Area contains data that relates to the control information.

The Serial HIPPI specification denotes an extender to enable the serial transmission of data between the HIPPI-PH nodes. Unlike HIPPI-FP, which is a standard, Serial HIPPI is a specification that is agreed upon by the manufacturers (and is also stated to be unlikely to be a ANSI or ISO standard).

SERIAL STORAGE ARCHITECTURE

The Serial Storage Architecture (SSA) is designed by IBM, keeping in mind the features that it needs to offer, such as usage of longer cables, high performance, fault tolerance, with more devices per bus. IBM introduced SSA to replace the older versions of SCSI.

A key feature of SSA is that it makes use of the spatial reuse concept. *Spatial reuse* enables an increase in the aggregate bandwidth because it allows simultaneous traffic to move on a bus. The SSA systems are configured in the form of loops with daisy chained connections maintained between the devices, in contrast to the parallel SCSI storage systems built on a chain or a bus. Each SSA device can support two loops by using the two links (in and out). The spatial reuse concept makes use of both loops for simultaneous transmission of data, hence increasing the bandwidth, but the maximum bandwidth of a link is only 20MBps.

It is possible to access parallel SCSI devices from an SSA system or vice versa by using an SSA-to-parallel SCSI bridges product. If a bridge device is used, the spatial reuse concept is not applicable to the parallel SCSI devices.

Although the basic transfer rate of a single SSA port is only 20MBps, because of the dual ports and full-duplex transmission, the aggregate transfer rate can reach up to 80MBps. SSA aims at increasing the total bus bandwidth from 80MBps to 160MBps with the help of the spatial reuse feature. SSA is also intended to double the basic speed per link from 20MBps to 40MBps. However, to actually reach the speeds stated, a lot more changes need to be done, both at the adapter and bus levels.

In multihost or clustered systems where aggregate bandwidth and connectivity are key factors, SSA can be suitably employed, but SSA is not very appropriate for single-stream, bandwidth-intensive applications because the spatial reuse concept cannot be applied to extend the use of bandwidth in a connection that has only a single stream.

SSA works on the addressing mechanism where information about the path to the device, which the packets need to pass, is required. In situations where a device is added or removed from the path, the old address is not applicable and needs to be restructured. The addressing scheme used in SSA specifies the exact routing to the device. If any intermediary devices are removed, then the address is no longer valid. In such cases, the address is restructured; that is, the entire path to the device is remapped.

ENTERPRISE SYSTEMS CONNECTION

With growing enterprises needing to increase the speed of data transfer, the data centers of today need to be designed to meet the following requirements:

- Transfer data over longer distances to enable systems such as processors and control units to be remotely located and still be interconnected.
- Share the available resources as the network grows in size and manage them dynamically.
- Serve as an interconnect to LANs and WANs.

Enterprise Systems Connection (ESCON), as a new data center, is a name for a group of IBM products consisting of interrelated hardware and software products and technologies designed to meet the previously stated requirements. ESCON serves to interconnect S/390 mainframes with other mainframes, clients, attached storage devices, and other devices by using optical fiber technology and switches known as ESCON Directors. The fiber optic cabling in ESCON enables the network to be spread over a distance of 60 Kms by using chained directors. Connecting the ESCON directors in a chained connection (linking one to the other) can expand the distance.

→ To learn more about directors, **see** "Directors," **p. 106**

The ESCON technologies are very beneficial to an enterprise. Data center resources can be shared between hosts and application users with the help of this technology.

ESCON offers a very high data transfer rate and is one of the technologies that are widely implemented as a part of SANs. ESCON actually replaced the bus and tag cables that performed the task of interconnecting mainframes and attached devices.

PART

II

CH

3

> **Note**
>
> Bus and tag is a complete communications channel specification, defined by the Federal Information Processing Standard (FIPS-60). It makes use of two copper cables to connect between devices. One of the cables is for the data (bus) with the other cable for the control signals (tag). The data transfer rate ranges from 1.5MBps to 4.5MBps.

FIBRE CHANNEL

Fibre Channel is a high-speed serial storage interface designed to be an improvement over SCSI. The word "Fibre" in Fibre Channel is spelled as is written here and not as the American spelling of "fiber" for a reason. "Fiber" refers to the fiber optic cable where copper wires are not used. "Fibre," however, can be implemented by using fiber optic cables as well as copper cables.

The purpose of the Fibre Channel interconnect is to provide bi-directional and point-to-point communications between servers, workstations, storage systems, hubs, and switches. Fibre Channel offers a number of advantages, such as increased efficiency, high performance, scalability, ease of use and installation, and support for popular high-level protocols.

Fibre Channel Arbitrated Loop (FC-AL) is a significant enhancement of Fibre Channel designed specifically to meet the needs of storage interconnects.

Fibre Channel overcomes the distance limitation of SCSI (which is only 25 meters) because it can support up to 10Kms. Due to this feature, Fibre Channel enables faster transfer of data even between distantly connected devices. It can support bandwidths up to 4GBps with a data transfer rate of 100MBps when data is transferred only in one direction (half-duplex mode) and a rate of 200MBps in both directions (200MBps). Chapter 5, "Fibre Channel," covers Fibre Channels in greater detail.

Fibre Channel can support different types of protocols, such as TCP/IP, SCSI, and ATM on the same physical medium, such as copper or optical fiber cables.

Fibre Channel can connect a number of systems and storage devices efficiently in a storage area network. It makes use of switches and hubs to create a well-bounded cluster. These clusters offer high performance in areas such as general computations, file services, and data management.

→ To learn more about hubs and switches, **see** "Hubs," **p. 101**

Fibre Channel, as an interface, enables a number of devices to be added or removed from the loop without affecting the process of data transfer. This interface also provides error-detection by attaching error-detecting codes to each packet of data that is to be transferred to the destination. When these packets are received at the destination, the codes are checked; if an error is detected, the destination sends back a request to repeat the transfer.

STORAGE AREA NETWORK INTERFACES: A COMPARATIVE STUDY

You have seen the different types of interfaces supported by storage area networks. Each of these interfaces has a number of advantages and features that make them worthwhile. However, if you need to select an interface to implement in your storage area network, you will need to be able to compare the different interfaces. This section details the basic differences between the different SAN interfaces.

COMPARING SERIAL STORAGE ARCHITECTURE AND SMALL COMPUTER SYSTEM INTERFACE

Both SSA and SCSI are storage interfaces but SSA has the following advantages over SCSI:

- In SCSI, the cables are bulky, which makes routing difficult. The SSA cables are a tenth the size of the SCSI cables and hence routing is simpler.

- SSA devices have on-board terminators, whereas the SCSI devices require external terminators.

- In SCSI, a maximum of 16 devices can be supported by an Ultra SCSI bus. SSA can connect up to 128 devices on a loop.

- The bus length for SCSI is limited to six meters, whereas the devices in SSA can be at a distance of 20 meters from one another.

- In a conventional SCSI, 50- or 68-pin connectors and cables are used, whereas SSA makes use of a four-pin connector with a four-conductor copper wire cable. The benefit is that the connector as well as the installation and configuration expenses are reduced.

COMPARING SERIAL STORAGE ARCHITECTURE AND FIBRE CHANNEL

Fibre Channel and SSA are two types of serial interfaces that have the following common features:

- Both Fibre Channel and SSA employ the technique of transmitting data in the form of a stream of bits over the data path.

- Both architectures can transmit high-speed serial bit streams by making use of fiber optics.

- Both interfaces can provide a higher bandwidth in competition with parallel SCSI.

- Both technologies can support more devices over greater distances in comparison to SCSI.

The parallel SCSI-1 version does not offer many benefits for the latest technologies, but Ultra-SCSI promises greater backward compatibility and bandwidth at less cost to make up for SCSI-1.

Consider a case where two SSA drives malfunction. This malfunctioning causes a drastic loss in the means to access data. If an SSA drive is removed, this results in the host adapters restructuring the addressing as well as reanalyzing the I/O operations that are being carried out to ensure that there are no errors. The addresses of devices in the SSA architecture need to be recalculated when a device is removed from or added to the SSA loop. These recalculations eventually result in the delay of the I/O operations, because the host adapters or controllers take time to settle on which of the devices are still a part of the network. Any new operations that have not begun might need to be reinitialized.

When disk drives are removed, you need to install devices known as *canisters* unless you replace the disk drives replaced simultaneously. The canisters perform the task of maintaining a loop if a device is removed from the loop. These canisters serve as a bypass circuit for the canister or the device and also maintain the signal integrity of the group in SSA. Even if one of the canisters is removed, the host adapters need to reconfigure the SSA loop to restudy the devices that are still a part of the loop.

SSA vendors point out that SSA has an advantage over SCSI due to its Spatial Reuse feature. SSA also can sustain simultaneous transmission, because it enables more than one transmission to be carried out on the unused links at the same time. Theoretically, the amount of data that can be transferred is more when there are multiple well-balanced CPUs on the network.

PART

II

CH

3

Practically analyzing the situation, any read or write data transfer cannot be more than 20MBps that is the same for Parallel SCSI and less than the speed of Ultra SCSI. SSA has a greater capability to increase performance in the case of multiple devices. It offers the same performance for single devices as Parallel SCSI.

It might happen that when more nodes are added to FC-AL, the latency or response time is increased. When frames are viewed by a device and then passed on to the other device in line, this results in latency or *wormholing*. Both Fibre Channel and SSA have a share in this wormholing, but SSA requires more time than Fibre Channel due to its overheads.

With the spatial reuse feature, SSA promises a higher aggregate bandwidth where multiple devices are used, whereas Fibre Channel ensures a greater bandwidth for an individual device.

COMPARING FIBRE CHANNEL AND SMALL COMPUTER SYSTEM INTERFACE

The Fibre Channel-Arbitrated Loop-based storage systems can have a data transfer rate as high as 200MBps with an expected advancement of up to 400MBps in the near future, whereas SCSI (Ultra160 SCSI) can offer only up to 160MBps. A single-host adapter can support up to 127 FC-AL devices, which results in a significant reduction in implementation and maintenance expenses. This addressability of nodes in FC-AL is better than in SCSI. SCSI works on parallel data paths with the requirement of complex and expensive cabling. In contrast, Fibre Channel is a simple serial protocol that does not require an expensive cabling structure.

SUMMARY

SAN design makes use of interfaces to connect servers, workstations, storage devices, and other systems. Interfaces are categorized into two types: parallel and serial. The parallel interface enables the transfer of more than one bit simultaneously to establish communication between two devices. There are many types of parallel interfaces: IDE/ATA, SCSI, and HIPPI. The serial interface enables the transfer of data in the form of packets. There are different serial interfaces available: ESCON and SSA. Multiple standards are evolving in these interfaces based on industry requirements. Each product or standard aims at offering improvements in terms of data transfer rate with a higher bandwidth and increased scalability in the SAN environment.

PRODUCTS ARENA

Tekram Technology has developed a SCSI product known as DC-390U2 Series controller. DC-390U2 Series comprises an Ultra2 Low Voltage Differential (LVD) SCSI controller kit along with internal LVD cables and terminators. This product provides a data transfer rate of 80MBps by using the Wide LVD SCSI devices. It can support up to 15 devices. The controllers used in this product follow the LVD SCSI standard to offer improved performance with longer cable lengths and a reduction in bus noise. Model DC-390U2W is capable of supporting SCSI-2, Ultra-Wide, and Ultra2 SCSI devices. With the aid of Symbios 53C141 Isolation Integrated Circuit (IC), all the devices can work at their maximum speed without causing any kind of performance degradation to the Ultra2 bus. If Ultra2 and Ultra-Wide SCSI devices are mixed on DC-390U2B, the performance of the SCSI bus is degraded to 40MBps. The asynchronous SCSI bus transfer rate is 5MBps. The synchronous bus transfer rate is 80MBps with the LVD devices.

PART

II

CH

3

CHAPTER 4

STORAGE AREA NETWORK INTERCONNECTS

In this chapter

INTRODUCING INTERCONNECTS

A computer network is a set of computers or nodes interconnected by a communication system. With the ever-expanding span of LANs, interconnecting devices are needed to connect systems on different platforms. Some of these interconnecting devices are modems, hubs, repeaters, bridges, and switches. Which specific interconnecting device you use depends on the specific requirements you have. The following sections describe the different kinds of interconnects and help you understand how they work in a SAN environment.

MODEMS

When a standard telephone line is used to transmit data, it transmits analog signals. However, computers store and transmit data in a digital form.

Note

An *analog* signal is an electric signal that is continuous in nature. A *digital* signal is a discrete, discontinuous signal represented in terms of the binary states, zero and one.

A *modem* is a device that converts the digital signal from the transmitting system to an analog signal, transmits the converted signal over a telephone line, and then restores the transmitted analog signals back to digital format for the recipient system. The process of converting one type of signal to another type is called *modulation*. The process of restoring the converted signal is called *demodulation*; hence the device gets the acronym, modem.

Modems connect computer devices or entire networks located at distant regions. Modems can operate in two modes, through a dedicated connection or through a dial up connection. In a *dedicated connection*, the modem is constantly connected to the telephone line and is active all the time. A typical example of a dedicated connection would be an integrated services digital network (ISDN) line.

Note

Before digital telephone lines were available, the only way to link the distant devices of a network was through modems. An Ethernet that is connected through modems is a good example of a dedicated connection.

The more commonly used mode of connection when using a modem is the *dial-up access* method. In the case of a public switched telephone network (PSTN), a connection is established only when the need to connect to the network arises. A typical example of such a connection would be the way users would connect to the Internet through their home PCs.

The function of the modem is to enable networks to perform a limited transfer of data. The problem that affects this process is that the connectivity available is limited due to the restricted bandwidth offered by modems. Modems are like network cards, which offer an access point for the transmission medium. In the case of modems, telephone lines serve as the access point to transmit analog signals to another device, which might in turn be a modem on the network.

The question that arises here is that if a modem can connect two systems that are on different networks, isn't it similar to connecting the two networks? The point to note here is that the systems are connected through a telephone line. The difference in connecting to systems through a direct cable connection, coupled through modems, and through a telephone line is that the telephone line is connected to a switchboard (through which the connection is established). You cannot connect two systems directly through a modem. However, you can connect the two systems through a SAN interconnect.

Until recently, modem manufacturers judged the performance of modems by using a parameter called the baud rate. *Baud rate* refers to the oscillation speed of the sound wave transmitted or received by a modem. The improvements in this field of technology have made baud rates a less significant unit of measure. The data transfer rate in bits per second is an improved measurement standard over the baud rate. The data transfer rate of modems currently varies from 14.4kbps to 56kbps.

Note

Bits per second is considered to be a better performance rating factor for the simple reason that it measures the actual data transferred. The baud rate measures only the oscillation of sound waves, which does not tell you how much data is actually transferred, and therefore how much of it remains to be transferred.

Modems are categorized based on the transmission method they adopt to send and receive data. The two types of modems thus identified are

- Asynchronous modems, which follow an asynchronous transmission mode
- Synchronous modems, which follow a synchronous transmission mode

ASYNCHRONOUS TRANSMISSION

Asynchronous transmission is a simple and affordable technology that is ideally suited for transmission of character data and for environments where characters are transmitted at inconsistent intervals, as is the case where users enter character data. The frame that is adopted to transfer data is as shown in Figure 4.1.

The term *asynchronous* means not on par with time. Asynchronous transmission does not follow a clocking mechanism to ensure that the transmitting and receiving devices are synchronized. However, this does not mean the transmission happens in a chaotic environment. Asynchronous transmission uses *bit synchronization* to synchronize the devices used for each frame of transmitted data.

In the bit synchronization method, each frame initializes on a start bit. This bit enables the receiving device to adjust to the timing of the transmitted signal. The messages that are transmitted are kept short to check that the transmitting and receiving devices remain synchronized until the entire message is transferred.

Figure 4.1
The frame has a start bit, parity bits, and data bits to transmit character data.

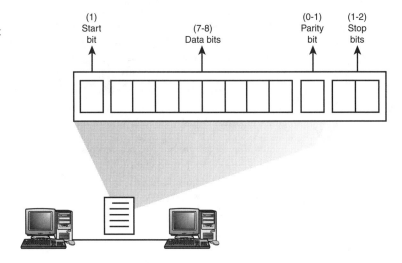

Figure 4.1 displays a frame in asynchronous transmission that is partitioned into four components. The components are

- The start bit
- Data bits
- The parity bit
- The stop bit(s)

The *start bit* indicates to the receiving device that a frame is starting and also enables the receiving device to synchronize itself according to the message.

The *data bit* follows the start bit and consists of seven to eight bits, when the data getting transmitted is character-based. In cases when the data is not character-based, such as an image file, each byte of the image is sent one at a time. Each byte consists of eight bits, and therefore you cannot use parity when transmitting image files.

Tip

If you have to transmit non-character based files with parity, you need to use UUencoders and decoders to convert the data from 8-bit to 7-bit.

The parity bit is a component that detects transmission errors. However, not all asynchronous transmission methods use this bit because it is optional and not always reliable.

The *stop bit* indicates the end of the data frame.

The working of a parity bit: When a set of data bits is transmitted, a binary digit is added on to it. If the count of the data bits being transmitted is even, the parity bit is set to one so that the total number of bits being sent is odd. On the other hand, if the count of the data bits is already odd, the parity bit is then set to zero. When the data bits are received, the total is verified. If the value is not odd, then an error is reported.

The advantage of asynchronous transmission is that the hardware required for it is less expensive in comparison to its alternative, synchronous transmission. Modems use the asynchronous transmission method. Asynchronous transmission is often used for terminal-to-host and PC-to-PC communication.

The limitation of asynchronous transmission arises from the necessity of adding the start, stop, and parity bits to each character that gets transmitted, which makes the process slow. The bit overhead of asynchronous transmission is high and results in a waste of bandwidth. The signals that asynchronous transmission generates are not appropriate for transmitting large amounts of data.

SYNCHRONOUS TRANSMISSION

Synchronous transmission synchronizes the clocks that are on the transmitting and receiving devices. With this synchronization, the requirement for the start and stop bits is overridden. This type of synchronization is achieved by two means. One method is to transmit the synchronization signal along with the data. The other method is to use a separate communication channel to carry the clock signals.

The network adapter cards make use of the synchronous transmission method.

Figure 4.2 displays the two structures in which a message could be transmitted in synchronous transmission.

Both methods of synchronous transmission start with a series or a pair of synch signals. These synch signals perform the same function as the start bit in asynchronous transmission. They indicate the beginning of the frame and notify the receiving device of the same. Synch signals employ a bit pattern that is distinct and cannot be repeated anywhere in the frame. This distinctive feature of the synch signals ensures that the receiving device can easily identify the presence of a new signal.

Figure 4.2 illustrates the different types of data that can be transmitted by the synchronous transmission methods. In synchronous transmission, unlike in asynchronous transmission, multiple characters can be transmitted in a single data frame.

One of the advantages of synchronous transmission is that the overhead bits, such as the synch, CRC, and end bits, cover an insignificant region of the data frame. This means that the available bandwidth can be utilized more efficiently. Additionally, synchronization enables the devices to work at an improved speed. Finally, the CRC method promises better error detection.

Figure 4.2
The different structures of a message are transmitted using the synchronous transmission technique.

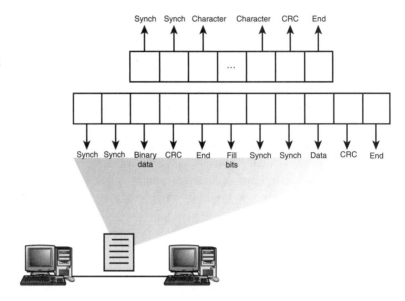

The drawback with this type of transmission is that the transmitter and receiver need to be constantly synchronized during the transmission of a frame. When the frames are long, the time taken for transmission may be quite high. Another obvious drawback is that the expense involved in employing complex circuitry for this transmission method is high.

When the data frames are long, the parity method of error detection is not appropriate. The reason is that when an error occurs, the series of bits might get affected and the parity method might not be able to point out the error. In this scenario, the *cyclic redundancy check* (CRC) technique is the most suitable method for error detection.

In the CRC method of error detection, the transmitting device uses an algorithm to calculate the CRC value. This CRC value summarizes the total value of the bits in the frame; this is added to the frame. The receiving device uses the same algorithm to recalculate the CRC value of the frame. After the CRC value is calculated, it is matched with the attached CRC value. If these values do not match, an error has occurred during transmission. If they do match, this means that the data is preserved.

REPEATERS

Consider a scenario where the analog or digital signals are distorted during the transmission process. The option of having a device that could regenerate the transmitted signal would seem to be a logical solution. A repeater does just that. A *repeater* is a network device that replicates a signal. There are separate repeaters for both analog and digital signals. The analog repeater can only amplify the signal, whereas the digital repeater can actually rebuild the distorted signal to a significant extent.

Networks need repeaters due to the limitations in the different types of transmission media used to connect the devices in a network.

→ To read more on the types of transmission media, **see** "Types of Primary Cables," **p. 22**

Each transmission medium can transfer data reliably only to a certain limit beyond which the data suffers from attenuation. Repeaters overcome this problem by stretching the range to which data can be transmitted or received efficiently.

A repeater can repeat a signal from one port (an interface on the computer) to another to which it is linked or connected, as shown in Figure 4.3.

Figure 4.3
A weak signal is regenerated at the repeater.

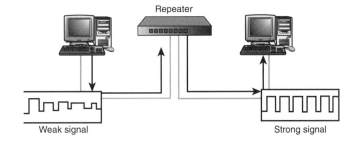

Repeater

Weak signal   Strong signal

The repeater is functional at the Physical layer of the OSI model.

Although repeaters function as regenerators of signals, they do not perform the following tasks:

- Filter or modify the signal.
- Use the data address, because a repeater's sole property is to regenerate the signal.
- Perform any error check on the data bits or signal while regenerating. This is regardless of the fact that the bits of data might be corrupt.

A suitable application of the repeater is shown in Figure 4.4.

The repeater in Figure 4.4 connects two Ethernet cable segments. The repeater doubles the potential distance covered by the network.

The benefits of repeaters are their reasonable price and simple circuitry. Repeaters can only be used to connect networks with similar data frames. However, in case you have two networks, such as token ring network and a switched Ethernet that have different data frames, repeaters cannot be used to connect the networks. Most current day repeaters can connect segments that have similar frame types with different types of cabling.

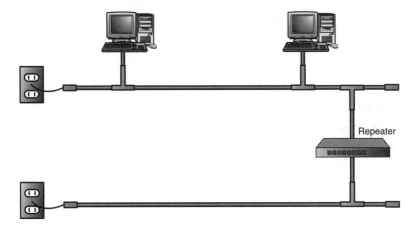

Figure 4.4
The repeater doubles the length of the network in an Ethernet LAN.

Some repeaters, such as analog repeaters, can only amplify signals, thereby increasing the strength of the signal. The fallout of this amplification is that when the strength of the signal is improved or increased, the noise on the network is also increased. Another problem is that this type of a repeater cannot improve an already distorted signal.

Another point to be remember about repeaters is that, beyond a certain limit, even repeaters cannot extend a network, as they might be hindered by the network design, which limits the size of a network. An aspect you should consider when you design networks is the maximum time a signal can possibly be in a channel. This factor is called *propagation delay*. It is the maximum time taken by a signal to arrive at the most distant point on the network. In cases where the propagation delay is crossed with no signals propagated, a network error is believed to have occurred. If the highest propagation delay of a signal is estimated, the maximum cable length for the network can be calculated. The repeaters adopt a 5-4-3 rule to depict that five segments can be connected with four repeaters and only three of the five segments can be occupied.

BRIDGES

Bridges are devices that connect two segments of a LAN or two LANs themselves. A bridge can connect two LANs that are similar or different. A bridge can increase the maximum size of a network, as shown in Figure 4.5.

Whereas a repeater transmits all the signals that it receives, a bridge transmits only those signals that need to reach the destination computer on the other side of the bridge, as shown in Figure 4.5. Each device on the network has its own specific physical address with which it is recognized. A bridge actually reads the physical address of a packet and retains the information in the form of an internal learning table. The procedure involved in transferring a packet to its destination will be clearer after you study Figure 4.5.

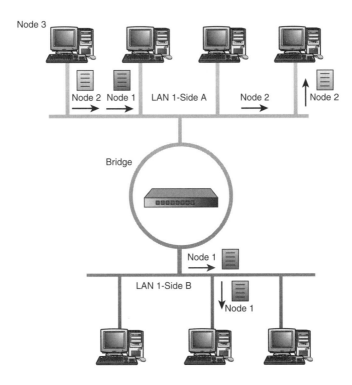

Figure 4.5
A bridge separates the signals on a LAN type of segment.

These are the steps for transferring packets in a network connected through a bridge:

1. The bridge, which is centrally located, receives all the packets from both sides of LAN 1.

2. The bridge refers to the internal table for the physical addresses.

3. The packets on Side A of LAN 1 that address the devices on that side are not transferred to the other side by the connecting bridge. It is the same for packets on Side B of LAN 1 that address the devices on that side. The reason for this is that these packets can be delivered without the aid of the bridge.

4. The remaining packets on Side A of LAN 1 that are addressed to the devices on Side B of LAN 1 are retransmitted with the aid of the bridge. Similarly, the relevant packets of Side B of LAN 1 are retransmitted to Side A of LAN 1.

Bridges are classified into two types, transparent bridges and source routing bridges. The *transparent bridge*, also known as a learning bridge, is transparent to the device that transmits the packets. The bridge learns about the devices present on either side of it. This type of bridge learns about the devices with the aid of the data-link information that it reads on the packets traversing the network. Based on the information that the bridge reads, the internal address table is created. This address table is automatically updated when a device is added to or removed from the network. Ethernet networks regularly use transparent bridges.

A *source routing bridge* is a type of bridge that reads the information attached to the packet by the transmitting device. This information provides the route to the destination network segment. To decide whether this stream of data needs to be transmitted, the source routing bridge studies this information. The source routing bridge is commonly employed on a token-ring network.

A bridge is most applicable in simple networks. Its drawbacks prevent its usage in complex networks. The problem with bridges is that the packets that need to be sent to all users on a particular subnet are actually transmitted to all the devices that form that part of the network.

Consider a scenario where two bridges are connected between two nodes, as depicted in Figure 4.6.

Figure 4.6
This is how bridges work in a complex network.

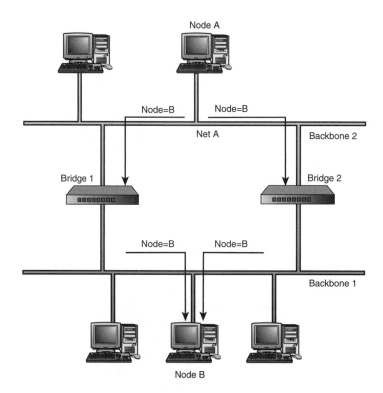

Net A, with two bridges, Bridge 1 and Bridge 2, is the point from which data is transmitted. Both the bridges have the means to pick up and forward a packet from Net A. Consider the case where both the bridges pick up the packet and transmit it to node B, which results in node B getting the same packet twice. If your bridges are configured properly, a Spanning Tree Algorithm would prevent duplication of packets.

PART

II

CH

4

Note

Simply put, the Spanning Tree Algorithm "blocks" one of the ports of the bridge, which drops the packet, on receipt. In case there is a failure in transmission, the bridge is "unblocked." This implies that at any given time only one of the two bridges will be active.

Another problem that could also arise is if the bridges begin to pass the packets in unending loops, causing a large number of packets to flood the network. The second problem would result in the packets never reaching their destination device. This problem can be avoided by configuring the bridge to use a conservative approach in activating new nodes. The activation of new nodes often results in the creation of loops on the network.

You can use bridges in complex networks by means of an algorithm known as the *Spanning Tree Algorithm*. The algorithm helps the bridges build a logical network without the hassle of redundant paths. Even if one of the paths stops working, the logical network is reconfigured to skip the inactive path.

Bridges can partition busy networks into a large number of segments. When a network is so designed that a great number of packets can be delivered without using the bridge, the traffic overload on the network segments is considerably reduced. Bridges, as stated earlier, can extend the physical size of a network. Bridges can also be used to link a LAN segment with another LAN segment through a synchronous modem connection.

Bridges are, however, limited in joining LANs that make use of heterogeneous network addresses. In other words, if you have networks that use different classes of IP addresses, then you cannot use a bridge to connect the networks. The primary reason for this constraint is that bridges work on the Data Link layer of the OSI model, which uses physical address of the devices for recognizing them.

Note

Interconnects, such as gateways or switches, help you connect networks that use different address classes, because these interconnects work on the Network layer of the OSI model. This layer uses logical network addresses to map the different devices.

ROUTERS

Routers are widely applicable in connecting a LAN with one or more WANs, because routers can easily determine the most efficient route to follow. Routers, in comparison to bridges, are also used to translate packets between different cabling systems. A router permits the control and grouping of multiple devices connected together on the same network segment by partitioning a LAN segment into different network segments.

Routers have the ability to divide a large network (LAN or WAN) into smaller network segments. The significance of routers is that they, unlike bridges, can connect different types of networks, such as an Ethernet network segment and a token-ring segment.

Routers are generally of two different types, static and dynamic routers. *Static routers* rely on the configuration of the internal table of locations (addresses) to specify a suitable route. *Dynamic routers* are able to determine the most suitable routes with the aid of the header information present in the packets as well as from other routers.

Routers also create internal tables of network addresses. In addition, they make use of algorithms to decide the most suitable route to pass a packet to any network. If the router is not attached to the destination network segment, the router can still pass on a packet to the network through the most appropriate route.

Consider a scenario where router A is aware that a packet needs to be sent to router C and not router B, as shown in Figure 4.7.

Figure 4.7
This series of networks is interconnected by routers A, B, C, D, and E, which enable the packets to be routed through different paths.

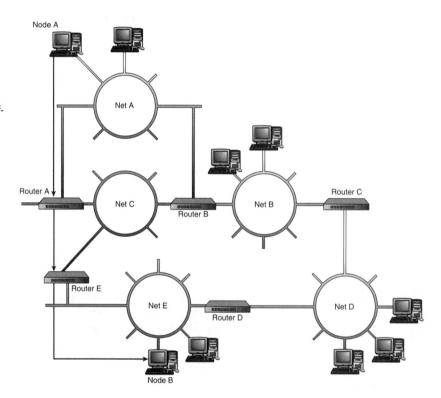

Router B provides an alternate path to that provided by Router A. Routers are capable of handling this type of problem because they exchange the routing information to make sure that no packets are caught in loops. The advantage of redundant paths is that even if Router A fails, Router B can provide an alternate for the packets, as shown in Figure 4.7. Routers are slow in comparison to bridges due to the processing that routers carry out on packets.

Brouters

Brouters are a combination of bridges and routers. Brouters are capable of delivering packets with the aid of protocol information. In cases where the network layer protocol (for routers) is not supported, the brouter serves as a bridge and processes the packets by using device addresses.

SAN Routers

In a SAN environment, routers enable resource sharing. The main idea behind implementing a SAN solution is that the storage resources are shared independently of a LAN. If a number of hosts are provided with direct access to shared storage devices, it is a challenge to data sharing management. Consider a situation where two servers attempt to write to the same storage device. The consequence is that the data or system gets corrupted. A SAN router, such as a Pathlight SAN router product, provides an answer to this problem with channel zoning. *Channel zoning* is a technique that enables the effective sharing of storage resources in a SAN type of environment. This technique controls the access between different channels (or ports). Channel zoning not only manages and protects zoning but also permits the creation of multiple overlapped zones. These zones must share common SAN connectivity channels, as shown in Figure 4.8.

PART

II

CH

4

Figure 4.8
In this example of channel zoning, a SAN router enables the creation of three separate overlapped zones.

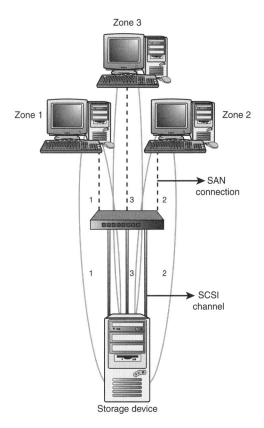

The SAN router can be used to configure SAN zoning. The administrator is provided with the SAN router's management software. Go back to the example of the Pathlight SAN router, which contains management software that provides simple dialog boxes to specify the required connections for each SAN router on the network. To ensure that all the connections are made, the administrator can easily select the check boxes in the Access Settings dialog box whenever a connection is made. if a check box is not selected, Pathlight's channel zoning ensures that the hosts are not aware that the channel or storage device (based on which check box is not selected) is present and that it needs to be connected. The Pathlight product is being used here only to illustrate the use of the interface, which could vary from router to router. However, the concept of router management is going to be the same regardless of which one you use. A SAN router has the capability to handle all complexities that can arise.

GATEWAYS

Gateways are a means of connecting two different networks. Gateways also enable the connection of networks based on different protocols. Gateways are implemented either as hardware, software, or a combination of both. Gateways remove the layered protocol information of the packets that pass through them and replace the layer with the packet information required by the second protocol, as shown in Figure 4.9.

Figure 4.9
A gateway connecting two dissimilar protocols enables different platforms to interact.

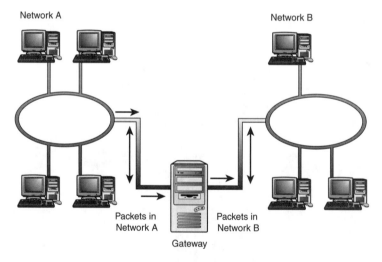

Network A

Network B

Packets in Network A

Packets in Network B

Gateway

Gateways are similar to routers in their working, because they are aware of the destination to which they need to direct the packets.

HUBS

Hubs are common connection points or points of convergence for the devices that form a network. Data from one or more directions arrive at this point of convergence and are then distributed from this point to the required devices, as shown in Figure 4.10.

Figure 4.10
The hub in this example connects a LAN.

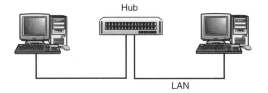

A hub topology is composed of a main circuit to which a number of outgoing lines can be connected. Each line provides one or more connection ports for devices to be attached. This is the general topology adopted by access providers for Internet users who are not connected to a LAN. The bus network and the ring network are other common network topologies. Hubs are also referred to as wiring concentrators.

> **Note**
>
> A *concentrator* is a device that integrates multiple channels into a single transmission medium to ensure that all the individual channels are active at the same time.

A bus topology is a network topology in which the systems are connected using a shared cable, which is often referred to as the *backbone*. A typical bus topology is represented in Figure 4.5, where each segment of the LAN is on a bus topology. This topology uses contention to communicate and must have terminators at the ends to ensure effective functioning.

A ring topology, on the other hand, is a topology in which the systems are connected in a circular manner. The advantage of this topology is that the signals are regenerated at every node, which ensures that the quality of the signals is preserved.

Returning to the hub topology, a hub is generally used to connect the segments that are part of a LAN. A hub contains numerous ports and when a data packet reaches one port, it is copied to the other ports so that all the segments of the LAN are able to observe all packets. Hubs can be classified into three categories:

- Passive
- Active
- Switching

PASSIVE HUBS

Passive hubs serve the sole purpose of combining the signals from various network cable segments. They are not made up of any type of electronic component and do not carry out the processing of the data signal. All the devices connected to a passive hub transmit the data packets that are then transferred through the hub.

Passive hubs, instead of amplifying the signals, actually absorb a portion of the signals. Therefore, the distance between a hub and a computer should be less than half of the acceptable distance between two computers on the network. For example, consider a case where the maximum distance between two computers on a network is approximately 400 meters; in this case, the distance between a hub and a computer should not exceed 200 meters.

Passive hubs are easy to configure and are inexpensive. The main problem with passive hubs is their restricted functionality. Due to their limited functionality, passive hubs are used mostly in small networks where the number of computers on a LAN is few and the distance between the devices is small. Hubs, like repeaters, adopt the 5-4-3 rule, with five network segments being connected to four hubs, where only three of the five segments are populated, as shown in Figure 4.11.

ACTIVE HUBS

Active hubs, in contrast to passive hubs, are composed of electronic components. These electronic components serve the purpose of amplifying signals and strengthen or correct distorted signals. The process of improving or cleaning up a signal is known as *signal regeneration*. The signal regeneration process provides the following advantages:

- The distance between the devices connected can be suitably increased.
- The network is less prone to errors.

These advantages overcome the drawback of the active hub circuitry being more expensive in comparison to the passive hub. Because an active hub partially carries out the function of repeaters, it is also known as a multiport repeater.

INTELLIGENT HUBS

Intelligent hubs are improved active hubs with a few additional functions that add intelligent features to the hubs, such as hub management and switching.

Hubs support network management protocols. These network management protocols permit hubs to send the data packets to a central network console and allow the console to control the working of the hubs. For example, if network errors are generated, the network administrator at a central console has the right to instruct a hub to shut down the connection that is responsible for the network errors.

A *switching* hub is composed of complex circuitry that quickly routes the signals between the ports on the hub. The switching hub is more specific in its operations. A distinction of the switching hub is that it does not repeat or duplicate any packet to the ports connected on the hub. It repeats the packet only to the port that is connected to the destination computer of this packet. In other words, this hub actually reads the destination address of each data packet to forward the packet to the relevant port. A switching hub actually works like a bridge. A switching hub, due to its advanced circuitry, is the most expensive hub when compared to the other types of hubs.

Figure 4.11
The passive hub structure follows the 5-4-3 rule, where five segments are connected to four hubs and three segments are populated.

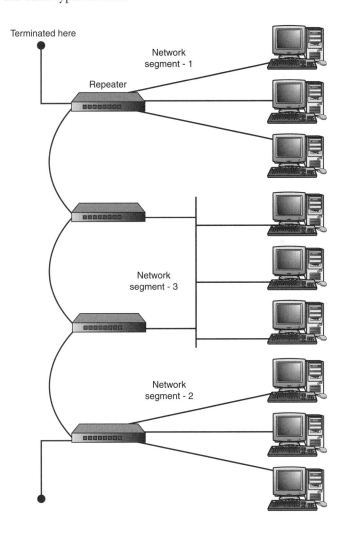

PART

II

CH

4

SWITCHES

Switches are devices that filter and then move the packets between the segments of a LAN. Switches can support any type of packet protocol, because they operate at the Data Link layer of the OSI reference model. Switches are assigned different names based on the network segments that they connect. For example, when the switches are used for Ethernet networks, they are referred to as switched Ethernet LANs.

LOOP SWITCHES

The initial deployment of SANs used SCSI interconnects in a single-server environment with storage hubs. This proved to be the most reasonably priced and effective solution.

→ To learn more about SCSI, **see** "Small Computer System Interface," **p. 67**

With the indication that multiple servers sharing a centralized pool of storage will reduce the cost of ownership significantly, industries began to include switching for more complex applications. Storage devices need to support multiserver applications. Therefore, these servers need to access the shared storage resources constantly. Loop switch helps meet the demand for this continuous and consistent (stable) access.

A loop switch also offers zoning. *Zoning* enables the partitioning of the network and attaches each server to storage resources or particular disks, as shown in Figure 4.12.

Figure 4.12
Zoning between servers and storage devices enables servers on different platforms to share a common storage device.

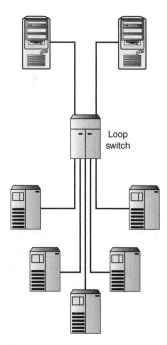

Most of the SAN switches currently used are based on the Fibre Channel supported protocol, Fibre Channel Arbitrated Loop (FC-AL). The switch products used earlier adopted the "fabric" type of protocol, which is not very suitable for consolidation applications. Chapter 7, "Designing Storage Area Networks," covers Fibre Channels in more detail.

Fabric-based switches, referred to as *backbone switches*, are difficult to implement due to the complexity of the protocol. The other factors that contribute to the difficulty in implementation are that backbone switches are nearly four times more expensive than a storage hub and require interoperability testing to determine their reliability. The best alternative to backbone switches is SAN-loop switches. Loop switches are less expensive in comparison to backbone switches. Loop switches also provide the required constant access and offer the zoning feature, because these switches are based on the industry standard FC-AL protocol. Thus, loop switches promise speedy deployment of SANs.

In a multiserver environment for a small network, loop switches replace the hub without altering the network in any manner. These switches enhance storage performance, because they allow constant access between the servers and the storage resources, as shown in Figure 4.13.

Figure 4.13
The loop switch is employed instead of a hub to connect pooled server and storage resources.

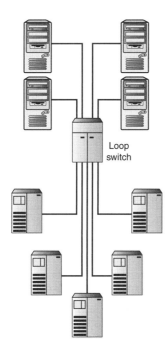

SAN Loop Switches Versus Hubs

Loop switches offer improved performance and increased availability in comparison to hubs. The improved performance feature of loop switches is due to the increased bandwidth. In the case of hubs, only two of the devices can communicate at a time, whereas in the case of switches multiple devices can communicate at the same time, which improves utilization of the available bandwidth.

Switches offer higher performance than hubs because their latency is lower. In the case of hubs, when a message is transmitted, it is passed on to all the devices that are connected, regardless of the sending and receiving devices. Due to this factor, the latency value and the length that a message needs to travel are calculated to be equal to the total length of the distance between the hubs and the devices attached to it. In the case of switches, the message is not transmitted to all the devices. It only travels the distance from the sending device to the receiving device, so the latency is low.

When there is any change in the status of the devices (such as the addition of a new system) connected to the interconnecting device, a loop initialization protocol (LIP) is initiated. A LIP is also generated when a connected device malfunctions. These LIPs need to be kept away from the communicating (busy) devices, because they hinder communications. They should instead be sent to devices that are idle. Switches manage these LIPs efficiently to offer better system availability.

DIRECTORS

SANs can create connections between the storage devices and servers of a large organization across a WAN. SANs ensure storage connectivity for enterprises, because they ensure an improvement in performance. Directors are a type of SAN switch that aids in delivering improved performance, scalability, management, and high availability even in the case of component failures.

The director-class switch is an essential support for SAN. Directors enable SAN to earn nearly 99.9999% uptime, apart from balanced connectivity when a device is added or removed. Directors provide higher availability and bandwidth in comparison to fabric switches. Fabric switches require a number of inter-switch links, resulting in bandwidth bottlenecks in enterprise SANs. These fabric switches add complexity to SANs that result in application failures. Fabric switches, unlike directors, do not ensure high availability.

Directors are designed in such a manner that they promise undeterred operations with minimum performance degradation. Consider a situation where the controller in a SAN breaks down. The director device continues to carry out its operations while the failed component is replaced. Consider the same scenario with a fabric switch being used instead of the director. In this case, when any component fails, the entire operation needs to be temporarily suspended until the fabric switch is replaced, leading to high downtime.

Directors are highly scalable. They allow a number of ports to connect network servers to enterprise storage devices. Directors also enable direct data connectivity from one port to another with the expected latency to be less than two microseconds.

SUMMARY

In a SAN environment, interconnects are the devices that link the storage resources to the servers. The different types of interconnects are modems, repeaters, bridges, routers, gateways, hubs, switches, and directors. Modems are devices that perform the digital-to-analog and analog-to-digital conversion of signals to transmit data. Repeaters are network devices that replicate or regenerate weak signals to prevent any type of data loss. Bridges pass data packets between segments of LANs, whether similar or dissimilar, with the aid of internal addresses. Routers split a large network into smaller logical network segments and assign an address to each segment. Gateways are devices that enable connections between two dissimilar protocols; the most suitable application is the Internet. Hubs serve as points of convergence between a number of ports. Switches, such as backbone and loop switches, filter and transmit packets between network segments.

PRODUCTS ARENA

IBM has introduced a number of products, including switches and hubs. One such hub product is the 8228 Multistation Access Unit, which is a Token Ring Hub. The 8228 Multistation Access Unit ensures connections of up to range of eight devices to a Token-Ring LAN. The cables from devices are easily attached to this unit by using the IBM Cabling Connector. This IBM product also supports interconnection with other hubs. The 8228 Multistation Access Unit configures a ring when it detects signals from all of the eight connections.

The 8270 Nways LAN Switch Family is an IBM Token-Ring switch product. The 8270 Nways LAN Switch is planned for customers who want to eliminate bandwidth congestion at a low cost by using a stand-alone Token-Ring workgroup switch. The Model 800 in this family is a fully configurable switch that can connect up to 30 dedicated or shared segments and can be configured to use redundant power supplies. The Model 800 is provided with slots for eight Universal Feature Cards (UFC).

PART

II

CH

4

CHAPTER 5

FIBRE CHANNEL

In this chapter

INTRODUCING FIBRE CHANNEL

Fibre Channel is a technology standard that enables data transfers between systems at very high speeds. Currently, Fibre Channel can transfer data at a rate of up to 1GBps.

On an average, the processing power of computer chips is said to double every 18 months. That has been the case over the past 20 years or so. However, it is also a known fact that for the real power of the processor to be used, you need 1MBps of I/O for every MIPS of processing power.

Note

> *MIPS* stands for million instructions per second. It is an old measure of a computer's speed and power.

In an environment that has a very low I/O capacity, there is unlikely to be a significant difference between a system that has a high MIPS and one with a low MIPS. This is where Fibre Channel enters the scene. Its high power, high-speed connectivity enables network administrators to bridge the gap between stated MIPS and actual MIPS achieved.

WHAT IS FIBRE CHANNEL?

Fibre Channel is not a cable that connects the system and the storage device. It is an interface like SCSI or ESCON, except that it is about three times as fast as SCSI (more about this is covered later in this chapter). Although the name Fibre Channel gives the impression that it's a channel that works on fiber optic cables, that is not the case. Fibre Channel is more than a channel and also works on cables other than optics.

Note that the word *Fibre* in Fibre Channel is spelled the French way, instead of the American way (Fiber). The primary reason for this is that the interconnections between the nodes (systems and devices) need not necessarily be on fiber optic cables. In fact, the connections could be even through a copper wire. Some people often refer to Fibre Channel as the Fibre version of SCSI.

Fibre Channel is a standard that has been accredited by American National Standards Institute (ANSI). There are many Fibre Channel products available on the market today, such as Fibre Channel switches and Fibre Channel disk drives.

WHY FIBRE CHANNEL?

The uses of Fibre Channel have been widely acclaimed. However, there are a number of skeptics on the use of Fibre Channel. The main argument of the skeptics is that SCSI is great and Ethernet is also good, so why do we need to move to a technology that is not yet proven?

Their argument is that with Ultra SCSI 2 at 80MBps, and plans emerging of Ultra-SCSI-3 reaching an even faster 160MBps, SCSI seems to be quite sufficient for the needs of the users. In the present day scenario, a single microprocessor cannot even max out Ultra-SCSI, so the need for Fibre Channel is far off. The biggest disadvantage with Fibre Channel is that it is not compatible with legacy systems. It cannot connect to the existing SCSI devices and thus entails a huge amount of investment.

The Ethernet advocates argue that Fibre Channel is going to have a tough time establishing itself in the arena of server-to-server connections. The primary reason for this is that Ethernet data transfer rates are on the rise. Many people feel that Gigabit Ethernet will be the rule of the intranets.

Although each of these alternatives has points in its favor, neither discounts the use of Fibre Channel. Ethernet is 30-50 percent less efficient to Fibre Channel in terms of speed and latency. Unlike Ethernet, Fibre Channel also provides for error handling on the chip through the use of features like Cyclic Redundancy Check (CRC).

Channels, such as ESCON and SCSI, are designed for high-performance areas. They work on dedicated, short-distance connections between the systems and storage devices. The traditional network offers more flexibility and enables connections over larger distances. Fibre Channel aims to integrate the benefits of both technologies to provide a fast and reliable connection that could span a large distance.

Figure 5.1 illustrates this concept. In scene A, the systems are directly connected to the storage devices. This enables the processor to access the resources, but the data on the device would be native to it.

In scene B, the systems are connected to the Ethernet, which holds shared storage devices. This enables the systems to access storage devices located at a distance from the system. In scene C, the systems are connected to a device, which in turn is connected to the storage devices. The Fibre Channel connection in scene C enables the devices to be located at a distance from systems and still enables direct communication with the devices using protocols, such as TCP/IP, FICON, FCP.

PART

II

CH

5

Note

The scenario depicted in Figure 5.1 (scene C) is similar to the function of an Ethernet adapter bound to multiple adapters. In an Ethernet setup where IP, NetBIOS, and SNA are all used simultaneously, the protocols are bound to the network adapter card. This enables the network adapter card to receive and broadcast in any one of the bounded protocols. Similarly, Fibre Channel has many protocols that are bound to it, for example, FCP, which is the protocol used in SCSI, as already mentioned in Chapter 3, "Storage Area Network Interfaces."

Fibre Channel technology is a high-speed serial interconnect technology ideally suited for connecting servers to shared storage devices. It is also widely acclaimed as an interface between storage controllers and drives.

Figure 5.1
These three scenes compare the different systems for connecting the storage devices in a network.

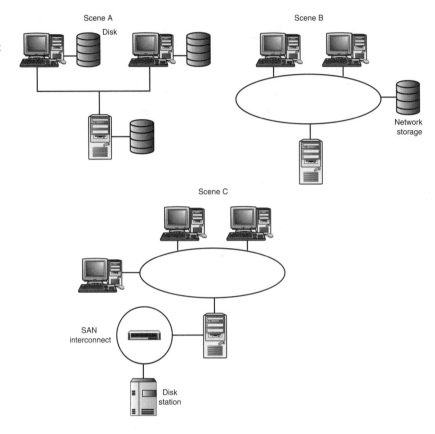

Fibre Channel provides a raw bandwidth of a little over 1Gbps. This in effect would translate to around 800Mbps, the other 20% going towards overhead. On a half-duplex environment, you would get 800Mbps or 100MBps. In a full-duplex environment (that is dual-ported), it works out to 200MBps. This is far more than the speeds offered by any other interface.

→ To learn more about half-duplex and full-duplex environments, **see** "Ethernet Local Area Networks," **p. 135**

→ Comparing Fibre Channel with various other technologies will help you know exactly how to design Fibre Channel connections. To learn more about designing a Fibre Channel connection, **see** "Designing a SAN Topology," **p. 167**

Fibre Channel is still growing; the prediction of Fibre Channel connections being able to span over 10KMs is not yet fully realized. Currently, Fibre Channel connections can span about 2KMs without the use of any additional extenders or repeaters. The 10KM mark is slated to be reached very soon; probably it will be possible by the time this book comes to the market.

FIBRE CHANNEL ARCHITECTURE

In recent years, several advancements in technology have resulted in the need for high-speed data links. High-performance computers have become the need of the hour in the data communications industry. However, merely adding more computing power to the processor is not going to answer this need). If the real power of the system is to be harnessed, the latency in accessing memory and storage has to be cut down. The existing network interfaces have proven inadequate in addressing this issue.

Fibre Channel provides for a practical, inexpensive, and yet expandable method to transmit data between storage devices and the attached systems. The factor that enables Fibre Channel to transmit data faster than other interfaces is based on the fact that its architecture is quiet different from that of the others. The Fibre Channel communication protocol provides for a method to implement a high-availability SAN. But before you get into the intricacies of how Fibre Channel is designed, you should be able to distinguish Fibre Channel from a normal channel.

When *channel* is mentioned, the first thing that comes to one's head is the television channel. That is actually a perfect analogy for explaining the difference between a channel and an interconnect. The television hardware is the same regardless of the channel you watch. You have only one cable connected to your television. The transmission on the cable is aided by technologies that make it possible to simultaneously transmit many frequencies.

When the word channel is mentioned in a networking context (especially storage), the reference is to a type of data transmission that typically occurs between servers. The data communication between servers and storage device is called *network data communication.* Channels are typically more hardware intensive and aim to transport data at very high rates with low overheads. A network, however, consists of a collection of nodes with its own protocols. The network is more software-intensive and consequently slower. Fibre Channel attempts to join both types of data communication. So in effect, Fibre Channel is neither a cable nor network topology. Fibre Channel enables an intelligent interconnection of all the devices.

Although it is called Fibre Channel, the Fibre Channel architecture resembles neither a channel nor a real network. The Fibre Channel architecture is broken up into five layers. As in the ISO-OSI model, the Fibre Channel layers are arranged in a manner that enables layer-wise development. The five layers of Fibre Channel can be mapped to the ISO-OSI model.

The Fibre Channel layers are divided into two parts: Physical and Signaling layer and Upper layers, as shown in Figure 5.2.

PART

II

CH

5

PHYSICAL AND SIGNALING LAYER

The physical layers include the three lower layers of the Fibre Channel architecture: FC-0, FC-1, and FC-2. The physical layer controls the core of the Fibre Channel operations and forms the crux of Fibre Channel.

Figure 5.2
The different components are mapped to the Signaling and Upper layers of the Fibre Channel architecture.

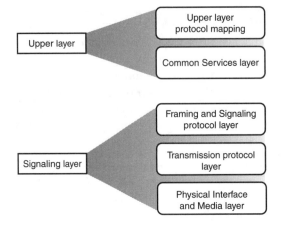

FC-0

FC-0 is the lowest layer in the Fibre Channel architecture. It defines the physical link in the system. It also defines the physical media, such as cabling, connectors, and transmission rates. This level is designed for maximum flexibility and enables the use of a large number of technologies. Typically, an end-to-end communication route consists of different types of link technologies that are integrated to achieve maximum performance at the least possible cost.

The FC-0 layer, which is also known as the Physical interface and media, provides for a safety system for laser data links. The safety system, or Open Fibre Control (OFC) system, was designed because the optical power levels exceed the limits defined by the laser safety standards.

The OFC system acts as a safety lock for point-to-point fibre connections. If the fibre connection in the topology is broken, the ports send a series of pulses (in the wavelength that is within the standards) until the physical rupture is repaired. After the connections are restored, the necessary handshake procedures are followed to re-establish the connection.

Note
A *handshake* is a process of negotiation among ports to arrive at the mechanism to transmit data in a given connection.

FC-1

FC-1 is the second layer in the Fibre Channel architecture. It provides methods for adaptive encoding of the transmission. The encoding enables binding of the maximum length of the code, maintains DC-Balance, and provides word alignment. This layer, also known as the Transmission protocol, is used to synchronize data for transmission.

Note

DC-Balance is an adjustment that is used to ensure that any noise in the transmission due to additional voltage is removed.

The FC-1 transmission protocol includes special serial encoding and decoding rules, special characters, and error control. The information transmitted is in the form of 8 bits at a time in a 10-bit transmission character. The transmission code being generated must be DC-balanced to ensure compatibility with the electrical requirements of the receiving units. The primary goal of having a transmission code is to improve the transmission characteristics of information across a fibre.

The encoded information byte is in a hexadecimal format composed of eight information bits: A, B, C, D, E, F, G, and H. The variable z is used as the control variable. The transmission protocol encodes this information byte into a binary format with the bits, a, b, c, d, e, f, g, h, i, and j. The control variable now contains either a D, which signifies data characters, or a K for special characters. Each transmission character is named in the $Zxx.y$ format where Z is the control variable of the original un-encoded signal. The byte xx contains the decimal equivalent of the binary numbers E, D, C, B, and A. the byte y contains the decimal equivalent of the binary numbers G and H.

This might seem to make little sense. However, all that the previous paragraph is intended to convey is that a normal (un-encoded) Fibre Channel transmission with a hexadecimal value "BC" is equivalent to "K28.5" after it is encoded.

FC-2

The FC-2 layer serves as the transmission mechanism of Fibre Channel. The FC-2 layer, also known as the Framing and Signaling protocol, defines the framing protocol and flow control. The *framing protocol* determines the framing rules for the data to be transmitted. The FC-2 layer is self-configuring and supports different Fibre Channel topologies. The primary function of the layer is to specify data transmission methodologies/mechanisms that are independent of the Upper layer protocols.

The FC-2 layer aids the transportation of data by following a set of rules to frame the data:

- Ordered Set
- Frame
- Sequence
- Exchange
- Protocol

ORDERED SET   An ordered set consists of a four-byte transmission, which contains data and special characters. The primary function of an ordered set is to obtain bit and word synchronization and establish a word boundary. It is easy to recognize an ordered set because each one begins with a special character. Ordered sets are divided into three types:

- Frame delimiters, which include the start and end (SOF and EOF) ordered sets. The frame delimiters either precede or follow the frame and signify the beginning or end of frames. In a fabric or N_Port sequence control, there can be multiple SOFs and EOFs.

- Idle ordered set is a signal sent to notify that the port is currently ready and can accept frame transmissions.

- Receiver Ready ordered set is a signal sent to notify that the interface buffer is available for receiving further frames.

FRAME   Frames are the basic components of a Fibre Channel connection. The frames contain the actual information to be transmitted. They also hold additional information, such as the address of the source and destination ports and link control information. Frames can be broadly classified into Data Frames and Link_control frames. The Data frames can be further classified into Link_Data frames and Device_Data frames. The primary function of the Fabric is to transport the frames. The Fabric receives the frames from the source port and routes them to the destination port. It is the function of FC-2 layer to break the data to be transported into frames (according to the frame size) and reassemble the frames.

As shown in Figure 5.3, each frame begins and ends with a Frame Delimiter. The frame header contains all the control and link information, such as device protocol transfers, source address, and destination address.

Figure 5.3
The frame structure of data on Fibre Channel depicts the different components of a frame and the overall transmission structure.

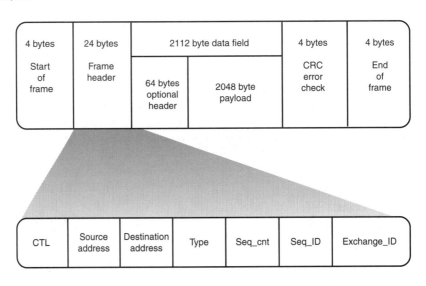

The 64-byte optional header, if used, contains additional link control information. The payload per frame is fixed at a maximum of 2112 bytes. It contains the actual information to be transported between the ports. Each frame also has a four-byte Cyclic Redundancy Check (CRC) error check component that precedes the EOF delimiter.

SEQUENCE A sequence is formed by a set of frames that are transported unidirectionally from one port to another. In a sequence, all the frames are numbered with a sequence count. The task of error recovery is handled by the Upper layer protocols.

EXCHANGE An exchange is determined for a single operation in terms of one or more non-concurrent sequences. An exchange could be unidirectional or bidirectional. An exchange is made up of sequences, and only one sequence in an exchange can be active at any given moment. However, multiple sequences from different exchanges can be active simultaneously.

PROTOCOL The protocols are generally specific to the higher-layer services. Although Fibre Channel provides its own set of protocols to manage its operation environment for data transfer, the following protocols have been specified in the standards:

- Primitive Sequence Protocols, which are specified for link failure.
- Fabric Login protocol, which is used for interchanging service parameters between the port and fabric.
- N_Port Login protocol, which is used for exchanging service parameters between ports prior to data transfer.
- N_Port Logout protocol, which is used to request removal of the service parameter information from the other port. This helps to free up resources at the receiving port end.

The FC-2 control process helps to pace the flow of frames between two ports, and between ports and Fabric. The flow control is dependent on the service classes (about which you learn more later in this chapter).

UPPER LAYER

The Upper layer includes the two top layers of the Fibre Channel architecture: FC-3 and FC-4. The Upper layer enhances the functionality of Fibre Channel and provides a greater scope for interoperability.

FC-3

The FC-3 layer defines all the common services for nodes. FC-3, also known as Common Services, defines the functions that span multiple ports on a single node. In other words, it provides functions that enable advanced features to be used on a node. Some of the functions currently supported by this level are:

- Striping, which is used to multiply bandwidth. Multiple N_Ports are connected in parallel to transmit an unit of information across multiple links.
- Hunt groups, which are an associated set of N_Ports connected to a single node. The advantage of hunt groups is that they enable multiple ports to respond to the same alias address. This decreases the latency in waiting for an N_Port to become available.

■ Multicasting, which is used to deliver a single transmission to multiple ports. Multicasting also enables broadcasts on a Fabric. It results in all the nodes receiving a single transmission.

FC-4

The highest layer in the Fibre Channel architecture, FC-4 defines the application interfaces that can be executed over Fibre Channel. The FC-4 layer specifies the mapping rules for the Upper layer protocols, on the basis of the Fibre Channel levels discussed before.

Fibre Channel is capable of supporting both channel and network traffic. It allows both protocols types to be concurrently transported over the same physical interface. Protocols such as FCP, FICON, and IP can be mapped to the Fibre Channel transport service.

FIBRE CHANNEL CLASSES

The Fibre Channel standard defines multiple service class options. These classes control the flow control (covered under FC-2 layer) and are the key to optimizing the functioning of Fibre Channel systems. Each class represents a mode of operation that would suit a set of applications. There are six kinds of classes that are defined. Of these six classes, Class 1, 2, and 3 are the most widely used. The classes result in flexibility, which forms one of the primary strengths of Fibre Channel.

CLASS 1

Class 1 establishes a dedicated end-to-end connection through the fabric between the devices. Class 1 in effect establishes the equivalent of a dedicated physical connection. After a connection is established between two ports through Class 1, the connection is guaranteed to provide maximum bandwidth. The connection is stable until the communication is complete. If another device requests a connection with the port, that request is not granted.

In an end-to-end connection, the receiving port acknowledges every frame, as shown in Figure 5.4. Class 1 also guarantees that each frame will reach the destination port in the same order as it originated from the source device.

Figure 5.4
A Class 1 connection has been established between Server A and Server B. The request from Server C will not be granted now.

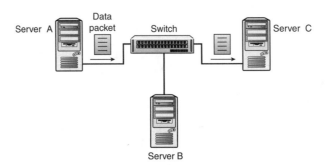

In Figure 5.4, Server A has established a Class 1-based dedicated connection with Server B. For each frame that Server A sends to Server B, the latter responds with an acknowledgement packet. If Server C attempts to establish a connection with Server B, the request is not granted until Server B finishes the current communication with Server A.

The main advantage of a Class 1 connection is that it reserves 100 percent of the bandwidth for the communication. This type of connection is useful in application areas, such as graphic designing and imaging, that require large blocks of data to be transported. All applications that are bandwidth-sensitive and require full use of the available bandwidth are best served by Class 1.

The disadvantage with Class 1 connections is that even if the application is going to use only a part of the available bandwidth, the remaining bandwidth must remain idle. Class 1 connections are therefore also known as "blocking" connections that clog up a busy fabric. If you have multiple systems that require simultaneous access across the fabric, Class 1 is not the best option.

Class 2

Class 1 is often regarded as the best connection option because it guarantees performance and delivery of frames. There is a general misconception that it is necessary to have Class 1 to achieve reliable performance of the Fibre Channel connections.

Contrary to this belief, other classes of service can and actually do offer better performance. Class 2 is a frame-switched connectionless service that enables sharing of bandwidth. It provides a robust link between ports (similar to Class1), but enables multiplexing frames from different devices to be shared over one or many channels. It uses a switched connection to create simultaneous exchanges.

The frames in a Class 2 system are routed through the fabric and each frame can take a separate route. Class 2 does not guarantee delivery of the frames in any particular order. However, as in Class 1, every frame's receipt is acknowledged by the destination port, as shown in Figure 5.5. If for whatever reason a frame is not delivered, a 'Busy frame' is sent to the source device so that it can resend the message.

PART

II

CH

5

Figure 5.5
A Class 2 connection enables multiple systems to interact simultaneously.

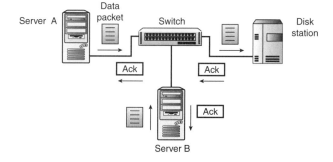

In Figure 5.5, Server A establishes a communication with Server B using the Class 2 option. Now, if Server C attempts to contact Server B, the request is accepted when the switch port is not busy. The Receiver Ready ordered set comes into play here. The switch sends a receiver-ready signal and then accepts requests for transmission for the devices. This enables multiple devices to establish simultaneous connections and make maximum use of the available bandwidth.

Class 2 is suitable for mass-storage applications, server cluttering, and other mission critical applications because it acknowledges the delivery of frames. However, it is not very practical to use SCSI protocols over Fibre Channel. SCSI requires that the frames be delivered sequentially. Several hardware vendors, such as McDATA, have noted this and enable their Fibre Channel switches to ensure that the frames are delivered in sequence.

CLASS 3

Class 3 is similar to Class 2 except that the delivery of frames is not acknowledged. It works in a manner similar to datagrams. The flow control in a Class 3 connection is a buffer-to-buffer flow control. This system prevents loss of frames in transit between two devices, except that an acknowledgement signal would not be received from the destination device.

One criticism of Class 3 connections is that although there is buffer-to-buffer flow control, after the data is transferred to the buffer of the destination devices it can be overwritten. However, to circumvent the problem, the upper-layer protocols must be designed to take over the error recovery process and, if need be, request a resend of the dropped frames from the source device.

Class 3 provides an option that enables Fibre Channel devices to broadcast messages to all the members of a multicast group. This feature enables a device to simultaneously transmit a message to multiple recipients, as shown in Figure 5.6.

Figure 5.6
A Class 3 connection enables multiple systems to interact simultaneously without any acknowledgement packets being returned to the senders.

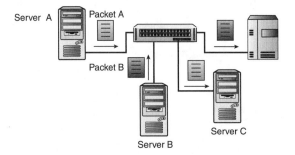

MOVING FROM SCSI TO FIBRE CHANNEL-ARBITRATED LOOP

The last decade has witnessed almost a ten-thousand fold increase in computer performance. At the same time, requirements are increasing for more robust, highly available, and disaster-tolerant computing resources. This is putting a lot of stress on the use of existing computing resources. The performance problems can often be traced to I/O subsystems that are struggling to keep pace.

There are a number of different interfaces (proprietary and otherwise) competing to meet the performance and reliability requirements of modern storage systems. The three major technologies in this race are the Small Computer Systems Interface, Serial Storage Architecture, and Fibre Channel.

SCSI is an intelligent, parallel I/O bus on which various peripheral devices and controllers can exchange information. Because of its longevity in the marketplace, the parallel SCSI interface enjoys a greater foothold on the market which exceeds that of any other I/O interface. The large volume of the market has made SCSI one of the most affordable peripheral interconnect technologies currently available.

→ To learn more about SCSI, **see** "Small Computer System Interface," **p. 67**

One of the main limitations of SCSI has always been maximum length of the bus. Originally, it was limited to six meters, however with the newer standards, with their faster transfer rates and higher device populations, there is an even more stringent limitation on bus length.

Note

There are a number of SCSI extenders available in the market that can be used to extend the maximum length of the SCSI bus to 25 meters. However, even this is not enough in some cases.

PART

II

CH

5

Fibre Channel, with its different topologies and well-modeled architecture, is the best storage interconnect choice today. Migration from SCSI to Fibre Channel is not a major hassle because the standard operating system tools used on SCSI devices can also be used on Fibre Channel devices.

The migration does not have to be a one-time activity. Both systems can exist on the network simultaneously. The migration can therefore be a gradual change. If you implement Fibre Channel, you will find areas where both technologies would have to exist simultaneously. Before migrating to a Fibre Channel environment, you must consider the following issues:

■ Compatibility with existing systems

■ Operating system support and hardware compatibility

■ Fibre Channel management systems

■ Host system incompatibilities between Fibre Channel and SCSI

→ To learn more about migration issues, **see** "Implementing a High Availability Plan," **p. 215**

FIBRE CHANNEL TOPOLOGY

In Fibre Channel terms, the switched network connecting the devices is called a *Fabric*. The *link* is the two unidirectional fibres transmitting to opposite directions with their associated transmitter and receiver. Each fibre is attached to a transmitter of a port at one end and a receiver of another port at the other end. When a Fabric is present in the configuration, the fibre can attach to a node port (N_Port) and to a port of the Fabric (F_Port).

Because Fibre Channel relies on ports logging in with each other and the Fabric, it is irrelevant whether the Fabric is a circuit switch, an active hub, or a loop. The topology can be selected depending on system performance requirements or packaging options.

Fibre Channel architecture offers three topologies for network design: point-to-point, arbitrated-loop, and switched-fabric. All are based on gigabit speeds, with effective 100 megabyte per second throughput (200 megabyte full duplex). All allow for both copper and fiber optic cable plant, with maximum distances appropriate to the media (30m for copper, 500m for short-wave laser over multimode fiber, 10k for long-wave laser over single-mode fiber).

FIBRE CHANNEL COMPONENTS

Before you learn any more about the Fibre Channel topologies, you should know the different components that go into making the Fibre Channel network. A few of the major components that are a part of the Fibre Channel network are:

- Copper cables
- Disk enclosures
- Multimode cables
- Gigabit interface converters
- Host bus adapters

COPPER CABLES

Four kinds of copper cables are defined in the Fibre Channel standard: Broadband, twisted pair, twin-ax, and Baseband cables. The most popular implementations are twin-ax cables (see Figure 5.7).

Figure 5.7
An example of a simple copper cables with connectors.

Copper cables

DISK ENCLOSURES

Fibre Channel disk enclosures permit hot swapping of disks. If a disk is not present, the circuit automatically closes the loop. When a disk is inserted, the loop is opened to accommodate the disk. The disk enclosures utilize a backplane, which has a built-in Fibre Channel loop. At each disk location in the backplane loop is a port bypass that enables hot swapping (see Figure 5.8).

Figure 5.8
Disk enclosures that enables hot-swapping of disks.

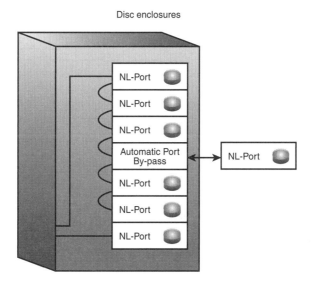

Disc enclosures

MULTIMODE CABLE

Multimode cable is a cable that is dominant for short distances of 2Km or less. It allows light to enter the cable in multiple modes, including straight and at different angles. The many light beams tend to lose shape as they move down the cable. This loss of shape is called dispersion and limits the distance for multimode cable. Multimode connectors, shown in Figure 5.9, can extend this distance.

Figure 5.9
Multimode connectors connect multimode cables.

Multimode connectors

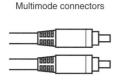

GIGABIT INTERFACE CONVERTERS

Distances in a data center are supported with twin-ax copper circuits and, therefore, hubs, disks, and many host bus adapters come standard with a copper interface. Gigabit Interface

Converters (GBIC) and media interface converters plug into the copper interface and convert it to an optical interface (see Figure 5.10). The benefit is a low-cost copper link and optics for longer distance when required.

Figure 5.10
The GBIC enables the use of cheaper copper connections for short distances and optics for longer distances.

Gigabit interface converter

HOST BUS ADAPTERS

Fibre Channel Host Bus Adapters (HBAs) are similar to the SCSI HBAs and NICs. Typically, HBA uses the PCI bus and has an integrated component that handles all the Fibre Channel protocol processing (see Figure 5.11).

Figure 5.11
This is a simple host bus adapter.

Host bus adapter

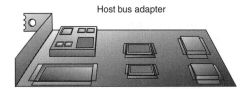

The other components that are used in Fibre Channel include the common network interconnects and interfaces, such as hubs, routers, SAN bridges, SAN gateways, and switches. See Chapter 4, "Storage Area Network Interconnects," for a detailed discussion of the different kinds of interconnects.

Fibre Channel systems are built without restrictions. Virtually any topology that an IT organization requires is possible, as shown in Figure 5.12. The basic building blocks are point-to-point dedicated bandwidth, loop-shared bandwidth, and switched-scaled bandwidth.

POINT-TO-POINT TOPOLOGY

Point-to-point is a simple dedicated connection between two devices, as shown in Figure 5.13.

Figure 5.12
Different networks and storage topologies can be configured using Fibre Channel.

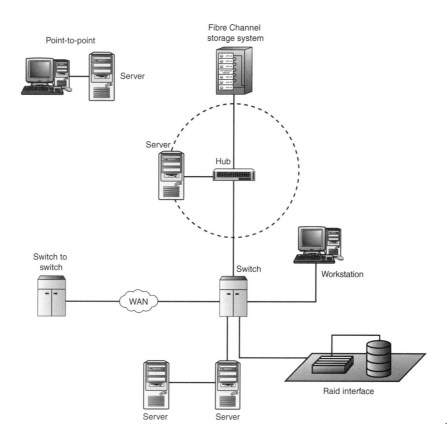

Fibre Channel Network and Storage

Point-to-point

Server

Fibre Channel storage system

Server

Hub

Switch to switch

WAN

Switch

Workstation

Raid interface

Server

Server

PART
II

CH

5

Figure 5.13
This is a simple point-to-point topology connection between the server and the storage device.

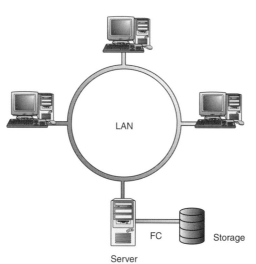

LAN

FC

Storage

Server

The point-to-point topology is used for minimal server/storage configurations. Point-to-point cabling typically runs directly from one device to another without an intervening hub using a subset of Fibre Channel protocol between the two devices. If additional storage devices are to be added, the cabling can be extended. However, this requires the use of the Arbitrated Loop protocol to control the access to the nodes.

ARBITRATED LOOP TOPOLOGY

Before introducing the Fibre Channel Arbitrated Loop topology, it is important that you know the different types of ports supported by Fibre Channel. Fibre Channel ports include N_PORT, F_PORT, NL_PORT, and FL_PORT, which are used to establish links for point-to-point, Arbitrated Loop, and fabric (network) topologies. N_PORT refers to a node or device port that connects to an F_PORT that is part of the fabric, or perhaps to another N_PORT in a point-to-point topology. The "N" indicates a node or device, whereas the "F" indicates the port is part of the fabric. Arbitrated Loop ports are referred to as FL_PORT and NL_PORT with the letter "L" indicating that it supports the Arbitrated Loop protocol. Fibre Channel in simple configurations can be implemented without switches or hubs.

Fibre Channel Arbitrated Loop contains a series of serial interfaces that create logical point-to-point connections between a number of ports, as shown in Figure 5.14. Fibre Channel Arbitrated Loop uses a minimum number of *transceivers* to connect the different ports without using a central switching function.

Figure 5.14
A simple Fibre Channel Arbitrated Loop topology that uses a non-switching interconnect.

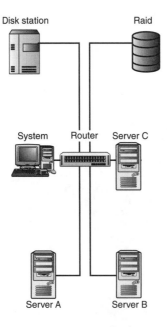

Disk station   Raid

System   Router   Server C

Server A   Server B

Fibre Channel-Arbitrated Loop is a shared gigabit media topology that can support up to 127 nodes. Arbitrated Loop is analogous to Token Ring topology (commonly used in LANs), in that two communicating nodes possess the shared media only for the duration of a transaction, and then yield control to other nodes. As in Figure 5.14, Server A communicates with the disk station, whereas the other ports act as repeaters. In a traditional Fibre Channel Arbitrated Loop topology, only a single pair of ports can communicate at a time.

Arbitrated Loop uses an additional subset of Fibre Channel commands to handle negotiating access to the loop, and specific sequences for assigning loop addresses (Arbitrated Loop Port Address, or AL_PA) to the nodes.

Arbitrated Loop hubs facilitate loop implementation by aggregating loop ports via a physical star configuration. The loop hubs can typically support 7 to 12 ports. However, the hubs can be cascaded to build bigger networks. As with hubs in Ethernet and Token Ring LAN environments, Arbitrated Loop hubs provide greater control and reliability. Arbitrated Loop hubs employ bypass circuitry at each port to keep dysfunctional nodes (nodes that are not working) from disrupting loop traffic.

Fibre Channel Arbitrated Loop-based networks can support data transfer rates of up to 200MB per second. FC-AL is also useful to build networks. Cascading and combining with switches can provide you with innumerable combinations. It can be used to create a highly complex arrangement of storage devices and systems. *Cascading* refers to the process of interconnecting switches to ensure that the network can be expanded. You can create a highly complex network setup by cascading a number of switches, with each switch capable of also supporting a network. The topology would still remain highly scalable and available.

➜ To learn more about cascading switches and other topologies, **see** "Fibre Channel Arbitrated Loop Topologies," **p. 170**

SWITCHED TOPOLOGY

The switched topology is an extension of the point-to-point topology. It enables connection of multiple systems and devices through a switched environment. The switched topology is also referred to as Fabric. In a switched topology, the nodes (systems and devices) are connected to a central switch, as shown in Figure 5.15.

The switch takes care of the process of delivering transmissions from the source devices to the destination devices. The switch sets up point-to-point connections between the nodes and the switch. The nodes that connect to the switch can be workstations, servers, Fibre Channel hubs, or other switches.

➜ To learn more about switches, **see** "Switches," **p. 103**

In a switched topology, up to 2^{24} devices can be connected through a fabric. (For those who want to know, 2^{24} is 16777216). A Fibre Channel switch port can be configured to support a single node or a shared segment of multiple nodes (for example, a loop). However, a switch requires more processing power and memory at each port to properly route frames, and therefore the switch per-port costs are usually more than six times Arbitrated Loop hub per-port costs.

Figure 5.15
This simple switched topology contains a RAID-based storage subsystem and a Disk station.

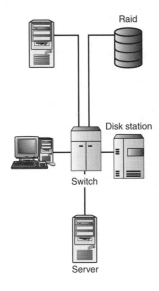

SWITCHING HUBS

A Fibre Channel switching hub is a hybrid technology that offers the advantages of both Arbitrated Loop and fabric switching. A switching hub manages the address space of two or more Arbitrated Loop segments to create a larger, logical loop, as shown in Figure 5.16.

Figure 5.16
Switching hubs provide a switched path between multiple (separate) Arbitrated Loops.

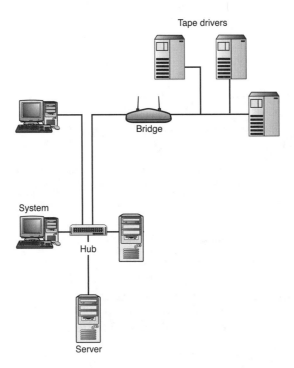

The loops provide a switched path between multiple physically separate Arbitrated Loops. The loops share a common address space, which enables the nodes to address each other as if in a single logical loop. However, each loop enjoys its own 100MBps transport between its own nodes and 100MBps bandwidth to the other loops.

This allows nodes on physically separate loops to transparently communicate with one another while maintaining higher available bandwidth on each physical loop. Switching hub products optimize extended Arbitrated Loop performance. They also give some of the benefits of fabric switching at a favorable price point. Switching hubs can now provide 100MBps of concurrent access between multiple Arbitrated Loops.

FIBRE CHANNEL OVER IP

The purpose of SANs is to externalize storage and provide a faster and safer method to access data across platforms. Fibre Channel combines the flexibility of a data communications network with the special characteristics of channel technologies. Fibre Channel provides for a scalable and reliable network.

The major disadvantage with Fibre Channel is that it must translate the protocols to suit the Fibre Channel setup and then transport them. In some cases, if the recipient device is not able to understand FC protocols, Fibre Channel has to retranslate the transmission. This process brings an element of latency to the high-speed network. Traditionally, Ethernet works on IP-based protocols. Given this fact, the best way to alleviate the drawback is to provide support for transporting IP packets over the Fibre Channel.

In the beginning, SAN was adopted and implemented by large organizations. Geographic diversity and the need for heterogeneous connectivity are business requirements that pushed these corporations to implement SAN. However, the Fibre Channel SANs are a top-tier solution for these campus or data center deployments. Very few solutions were available for connectivity outside the data center. The solutions that did exist were expensive, software-based, and relatively slow. The Layer 1 Physical transport mechanism does not provide the necessary performance, configuration, and statistical data required to manage these remote data services.

With the available bandwidth of IP based networks being installed, SAN extensions are an increasingly attractive option. They allow an end user to connect data centers at opposite ends of a city, as shown in Figure 5.17. However, the challenge is to do so at full wire speed and with the same reliability and availability as the storage traffic within each of the data centers.

Network latency, packet jitters, and guaranteed delivery are the critical issues for the storage data transfers over MAN and WAN infrastructures. These issues are very tightly controlled by the Time Division Multiplexing (TDM) nature of the network. IP networks do not deliver the same Quality of Service (QoS), however by using mechanisms such as VLAN Tagging and UDP port prioritization, traffic can be prioritized for transport across the IP network.

PART

II

CH

5

Figure 5.17
Fibre Channel-based
SAN implemented
over an IP network.

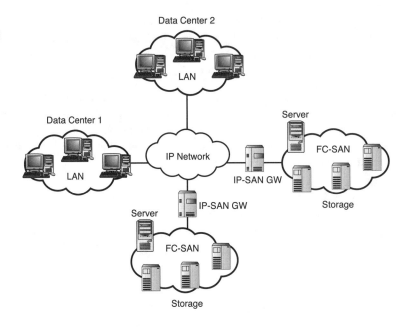

Packet jitters refer to the disruption in transmission, which lead to a disruption in the synchronization.

In order to interconnect these remote storage islands over the IP infrastructure, an IP-SAN Gateway is required to be able to transport Fibre Channel across a gigabit Ethernet network. This gateway technology is responsible for enabling the efficient transfer of Fibre Channel traffic over the IP network. The gateway manages the flow control and jitters and and provides additional robustness for end-to-end packet latency. Encapsulating Fibre Channel traffic into the gigabit Ethernet frames and ordered packet delivery ensures that the network remains fully utilized.

Traffic from one SAN to another can now have the performance, reliability, and scalability of inter-SAN traffic. This extends the benefits of SAN across data center boundaries.

Before linking different data storage sites over IP networks, a careful analysis of the network requirements and service availability should be performed. Under most circumstances, the solution that uses the existing infrastructure is more attractive, because managing new network interconnects requires an additional investment of time and effort. However, if the current setup is too old and incompatible with SAN or you want to establish a separate SAN, you can opt for SAN-compatible devices over FC connections. You might also want to look at getting a new infrastructure if the existing infrastructure slows down SAN performance below acceptable levels.

SUMMARY

Fibre Channel is designed to meet the high data-transfer speed requirements of storage environments. Fibre Channel combines the best advantages of the existing systems and provides: data channel characteristics and networkingcapabilities. With Fibre Channel data can now be transported over longer distances. The Fibre Channel architecture is divided into five layers. Each layer controls an aspect of data transfer. Fibre Channel also provides a set of options or classes of service, which enables different types of connections.

To make all this possible and to provide for a system that is scalable and flexible, Fibre Channel provides three base topologies: point-to-point, Arbitrated Loop, and switched. These topologies can be mixed and matched to provide the ideal setup for your organization. Fibre Channel also enables transmission over IP networks. This allows you to connect distant data centers over existing technologies through Fibre Channel. Fibre Channel has made it possible for data storage to be externalized and has enabled the connection of data centers to provide a truly heterogeneous, high performance, and reliable storage network.

→ To learn more about designing different topologies, **see** "Designing a SAN Topology," **p. 167**

PRODUCTS ARENA

Atto Technology has introduced a range of Fibre Channel-based products. One of them is the FibreBridge 2200R/D. The FibreBridgeTM 2200R/D is a Fibre Channel-to-SCSI bridge that was created to meet the demands of data-intensive environments. The FibreBridge 2200R/D promises to provide certain high-end features that were not available for small-scale operations and offers them at a reasonable price. 2200R/D serves as a bridge between the mid-range and advanced storage technologies in the market. It enables the attachment of SCSI devices to Fibre Channel systems, which results in a faster return on investment (ROI). This product provides the benefit of Fibre Channel-based connectivity to a number of companies.

PART

II

CH

5

The multi-platform 2200R/D is configured within an enclosure. This enclosure allows the product to function as a desktop bridge as well a rack-mounted or drop-in device. FibreBridge 2200R/D product delivers a sustained throughput of up to 98 Mbps and is well-suited for mid-range storage area networking applications. FibreBridgeTM 2200R/D can support SNMP, SCSI enclosure services, and FTP. This product also offers a serverless backup option.

CHAPTER 6

STORAGE AREA NETWORK FABRICS

In this chapter

INTRODUCING FABRICS

Fibre Channel is an interface that connects the different components of SAN. Switched Fibre Channel networks are called *fabrics*. In other words, a fabric is the connection network between two switches. Fabrics yield the highest performance by leveraging the benefits of cross-point switching, which is a low-latency switching system.

> **Note**
>
> Cross-point switching is a type of switching where the switch does not wait till it receives the entire message. It starts forwarding the packets as it reaches the switch, thereby reducing the latency.

The functioning of fabrics can be compared to the traditional telephone system. Each originating port "calls" the fabric by entering the address of the destination port in a frame header. The fabric ensures that the connection between the source and destination ports is configured and that the data is transferred safely. Fabrics can be configured over different kinds of networks to suit different requirements.

Because fabrics can handle more than 16 million addresses, Fibre Channel can accommodate very large networks. It is possible to start with a small network and then increase the number of ports. As the number of ports increases, Fibre Channel's nonblocking characteristic means that the network increases in capacity. This happens because the aggregate bandwidth scales linearly with the number of ports.

SWITCHES

Switches are devices that transfer information from one port to another. Switches sustain the data that comes from each port. They reduce the chances of bottlenecks and ensure that no obstacles are encountered during data flow. Smaller switches, with 16 or fewer ports, are usually serial implementations. Larger switches use parallel switching fabrics.

Switches work around a high-speed bus, and each port has its own controller. This controller places the data packets on the bus based on when the turn of that port arrives. Until then, each port controller listens to signals from the bus for information about when the packets should leave its port. The bus must run at a speed that is sufficient to provide the required bandwidth for all the ports.

A common approach is to use a fabric comprised of small switching elements, resulting in a *matrix*. When a matrix is used, the packets that are transmitted from each port enter one side of the matrix. The switching elements then move the packets to a suitable neighbor, based on some timing functions, such as pulse code modulation. Because each switching element might be connected to a number of neighbors, a packet might need to be switched a number of times before it actually reaches the required output port. However, the use of a matrix ensures that there is no considerable delay in the switching process.

A switching matrix is scalable and can sustain approximately 64 ports. Problems can occur when multiple ports try to send information to a single output port.

Switches are similar to bridges, but the performance of switches is better than that of bridges. Switches are simpler in their functioning, with a lower latency value and a higher bandwidth than that of routers and bridges. Switches can connect two types of Ethernet network segments, such as shared segments (multiple clients) and dedicated segments (single client).

→ To learn more about switches, **see** "Switches," **p. 103**

ETHERNET LOCAL AREA NETWORKS

An Ethernet is a LAN technology that makes use of the star topology. Ethernet LANs generally use coaxial cables and can provide a data transfer rate of 10Mbps.

Note

Ethernet LANs can also be connected over other types of cables, such as copper cables (typically CAT 3 and above), fiber optic, and even wireless connections. The coaxial cables are generally used in an Ethernet setup because of relative advantages of the cable.

→ To learn more about coaxial cables, **see** "Types of Primary Cables," **p. 22**

LANs started as small networks with a limited number of attached devices. Users can make use of shared LANs to meet their demands. Applications of these types of LANs include Ethernet, token ring, and FDDI.

Switches allow numerous servers and storage devices to be shared across one large SAN with their ability to cascade. Switched Ethernet LANs are the means of improving network performance. Switched Ethernet is a type of Ethernet LAN that makes use of switches to connect individual hosts or segments. When individual hosts are considered, the switch replaces the repeater and provides 10Mbps bandwidth to the rest of the network. This type of network is sometimes called a desktop-switched Ethernet.

Currently, Ethernet as well as token ring LANs can provide dedicated support to *full duplex* links, which further provide additional bandwidth to the switched networks.

Note

Duplex or *full duplex* means that data is transmitted in both directions simultaneously. *Half duplex* means that data gets transmitted in only one direction. These concepts are further explained later in this chapter.

Shared, switched, and half-duplex LANs are types of LANs that are distinct in performance and network topology.

PART

II

CH

6

A LAN began as a network where new users could be included whenever the need arose. For example, in an Ethernet network, LANs began with coaxial cables, where each station was linked to the cable, resulting in difficulties during fault isolation. This situation then gave rise to a different type of LAN known as *10Base-T*. 10Base-T adopts a structured concept in comparison to Ethernet that ensures improved fault isolation. 10Base-T, an Ethernet standard, is otherwise identified as Twisted-Pair Ethernet operating at 10Mbps. It makes use of a twisted-pair cable (the T refers to twisted-pair), which is thinner and more flexible when compared to a coaxial cable.

→ To learn more about twisted-pair cable, **see** "Types of Primary Cables," **p. 22**

By using a 10Base-T, all the attaching devices are linked to the repeater. Using 10Base-T is the answer to the problem of fault isolation, and it also offers a methodology for the expansion of LANs. This kind of topology is referred to as shared LANs because all the users of the network share the bandwidth of the network.

SHARED ETHERNET LOCAL AREA NETWORKS

Consider a case in which a 10Base-T Ethernet configuration is used, as shown in Figure 6.1.

Figure 6.1
The 10Base-T network based on the half-duplex concept and using a server with a single network interface card (NIC) results in sharing the bandwidth across all the clients.

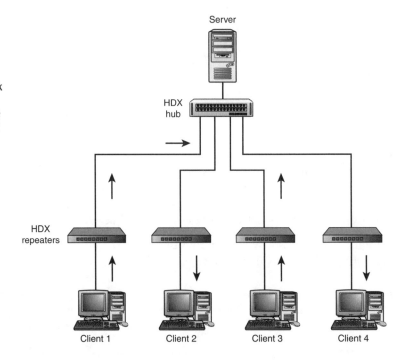

In this configuration, a number of clients are interconnected by means of repeaters. The problem in this type of configuration is that the bandwidth is shared by all the computers, which leads to congestion. If the number of clients is increased, the bandwidth that is available for each client is reduced.

Ethernet's mode of operation in this configuration is referred to as half duplex (HDX). The term *half duplex* indicates that transmission is possible in only one direction. In the case of this network, adapters are used to either transmit or receive data.

In the case of shared LANs, there are multiple adapters, but only one adapter can transmit data at a time. The clients and the servers compete for bandwidth at the same time, but only one of them can use the required bandwidth. When more than one client needs to transmit a packet, the medium access control (MAC) protocol decides which client gets priority and permits it to transmit data first. When a number of clients try to contend at the same time, bandwidth limitations can affect performance.

A feasible solution to this problem of bandwidth limitation is to segment a network and then add server attachments and additional hubs, as shown in Figure 6.2.

Figure 6.2
The 10Base-T network based on the half-duplex concept and using a server with two NICs.

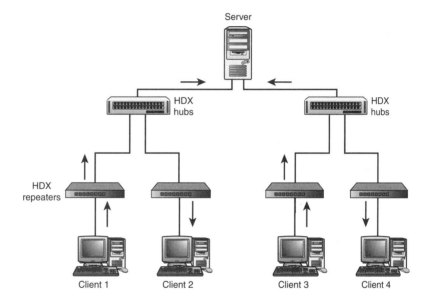

Consider the clients split into two segments, with 1 and 2 in one segment and 3 and 4 in the other segment, as shown in Figure 6.2. Each segment is provided with an independent connection to the server. The separate links let the clients send packets to or receive packets from the server at the same time. In this manner, each client is offered more bandwidth to access the server. This type of arrangement has drawbacks, though. When one client from each segment (client 2 and client 4) tries to access the server, the other two clients (1 and 3) cannot communicate with each other. The reason for this problem is that the clients need to share the bandwidth in their segments. Because there are two 10Mbps paths to the server, the total network bandwidth available is 20Mbps. Within the segments, clients 1 and 2 contend for the 10Mbps bandwidth, and clients 3 and 4 contend for the remaining 10Mbps bandwidth. Another factor to consider is that two clients cannot communicate across segments without using a new router externally or through the server, which acts as

PART

II

CH

6

the router. The only way to overcome the bandwidth problem is to make use of Fast Ethernet. The problem of two clients communicating across segments still remains unresolved. When you run Fast Ethernet, the cost of replacing hubs and adapters is high. To solve this issue, switched Ethernet LANs are the best choice.

SWITCHED ETHERNET LOCAL AREA NETWORKS

LAN segments are generally interconnected with routers or bridges.

→ To learn more about interconnects such as bridges and routers, **see** "Storage Area Networks Interconnects," **p. 87**

When traffic between the segments is high, these interconnects become bottlenecks. Then some new interconnects came into the market that worked with adapters to improve the bandwidth of the existing LANs. These interconnects are called LAN switches and are suitable for Ethernet, token ring, and FDDI. A switch, in general, provides the means to increase LAN bandwidth, because it allows the simultaneous transfer of packets between ports.

SWITCHED ETHERNET SEGMENTS OF THE SHARED TYPE

Network costs need to be controlled without changing the infrastructure in any way. Moreover, the installed equipment should not be drastically changed to be compatible with new technologies. The benefit of using switches is that they increase bandwidth without altering the existing equipment drastically.

Shared switched Ethernet segments are directly attached to the switch ports, as shown in Figure 6.3. Thus, they increase bandwidth and lower latency.

Figure 6.3
Shared, switched Ethernet segments with each port attached to the multiple-station segments enable reduction in the latency.

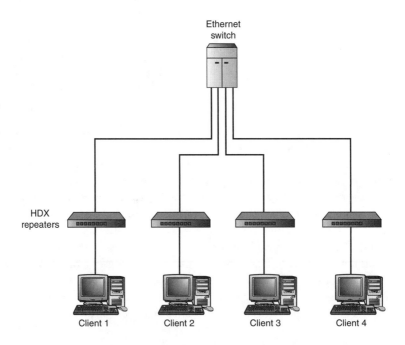

Each switch port is attached to a segment that supports multiple clients, and the switches establish communication between segments.

SWITCHED ETHERNET SEGMENTS OF THE DEDICATED TYPE

Currently, with the number of users on the network increasing, the demand for improved and increased bandwidth is also on the rise. A number of applications with demands for storage networks, such as those employing video imaging and multimedia, are coming into the market. Multimedia (a networked application) needs to ensure that minimum time is used in the process of streaming. This need cannot be met with LANs. This type of requirement can be met by dedicating an Ethernet segment between the switch port and the network segment, as shown in Figure 6.4.

Figure 6.4
A switched Ethernet segment with a dedicated segment between the port and the client is typically used for high-bandwidth applications.

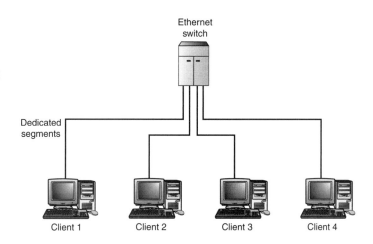

This type of dedicated, switched Ethernet segment is useful for high-bandwidth applications and servers.

THE TRANSITION FROM HALF-DUPLEX TO FULL-DUPLEX MODE

In half-duplex mode, packets cannot be transmitted and received simultaneously. If, between two ports, one port is to transfer data and at the same time receive data from another port, a collision occurs, as shown in Figure 6.5.

Full-duplex (FDX) mode or transmission is a type of transmission in which data can be transmitted and received simultaneously by the same port, as shown in Figure 6.6.

When FDX is used in the 10Base-T network, it does not require any change in the wiring, because it uses the same two-pair wiring scheme as 10Base-T, with one pair for transmission and the other pair for simultaneous reception.

Figure 6.5
In a half-duplex transmission, when two packets are simultaneously transmitted it results in a collision.

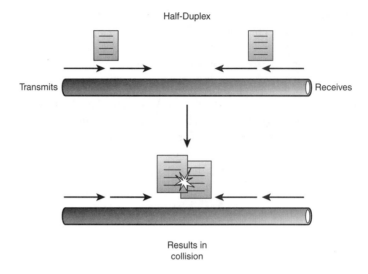

Figure 6.6
The full-duplex concept uses the same port to avoid collision by supporting simultaneous reception.

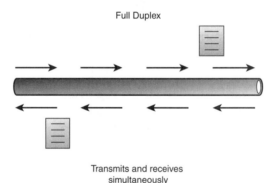

In theory, the FDX operation offers twice the bandwidth that is offered by the HDX operation. The doubling of the bandwidth is possible when the clients that are attached to the end of the links provide a continuous stream of packets for transmission. Also, there is no collision to cause bandwidth loss, as would happen in HDX mode. The advantage is greater in cases where the traffic pattern is symmetric. The FDX links have more of an advantage when they connect switches to each other. The traffic between switches is more symmetrical when the servers are present on both sides of the links between the switches. Another advantage of FDX operation is the elimination of the capture effect, because each station has unrestricted access to the transmission medium.

The *capture effect* occurs when two high-performance Ethernet stations use shared Ethernet in order to communicate. If both the stations need to transmit a set of packets, this results in a collision. The survivor alone has the advantage of getting access to the network with the chance of capturing the bandwidth for a greater period.

SWITCHED FDX LOCAL AREA NETWORKS

In the switched FDX LAN mode of operation, there is a bandwidth gain, and the additional expense for the infrastructure is minimal. In networks, the first bottleneck that is encountered is because of the access requirement to the servers. If this bottleneck is eliminated, performance is improved. One way of eliminating this bottleneck is to replace the LAN hub with a switch that works in FDX mode. Each switch port of the network can support a 10Mbps operation in HDX or FDX mode. For this reason, the shared LAN segments that had multiple networks with more clients now have fewer clients per network. Hence, each port can now be attached to an FDX device after being configured to run in FDX mode.

Consider a situation in which a dedicated FDX connection is provided to the server using an FDX Ethernet adapter, as shown in Figure 6.7.

Figure 6.7
The 10Base-T network based on the full-duplex concept and using one NIC server can be used with switches to exploit the bandwidth.

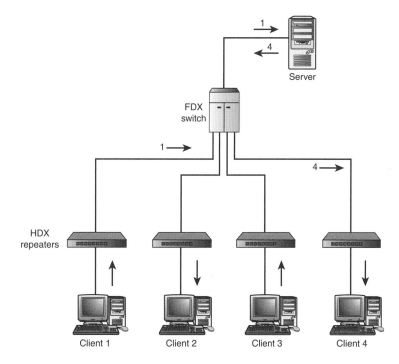

PART

II

CH

6

In this situation, the server has more bandwidth, and it can transmit and receive frames simultaneously. With this configuration, switches can be used to exploit the bandwidth, because multiple segments might need to access the server. This kind of configuration also overcomes the limitations that are encountered when only Ethernet segmentation is used.

The first benefit of switched FDX is that it permits one client to write data to the server while another client simultaneously reads from the server. Even a peer-to-peer connection between the clients is established with the help of the switch, thus eliminating the need for the server to provide routing. Secondly, network and server performances are enhanced, because the switch can be used to switch the packets between any two connected ports. An additional benefit of using switches is that clients can read from as well as write to another server that is connected to a different switch port. The aggregate bandwidth that is now available to each client is increased when compared to two or more servers sharing the same Ethernet bandwidth. Such a configuration is shown in Figure 6.8.

Figure 6.8
The 10Base-T network based on the full-duplex concept and using a server with a single NIC is connected through switches to increase the aggregate bandwidth.

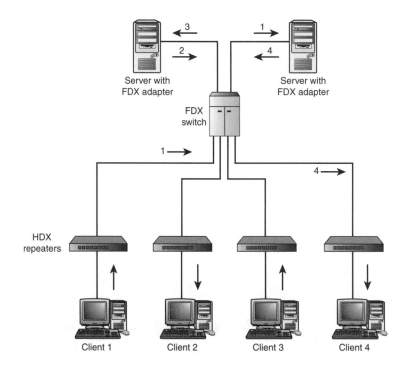

In this type of configuration, the clients on the network segments are connected to the other ports on the switch and can communicate with each other even when the other clients are communicating with the server. In cases where access to the server is still a bottleneck, an additional FDX NIC can be attached to the server and through the server to a free port on the switch. This addition allows two clients to read from the server and two clients to write to the server simultaneously. This technique offers more bandwidth to access the server. Furthermore, even more bandwidth can be provided when accessing the server by adding more FDX network interface cards and then attaching these cards to the free ports on the switch. This addition of FDX NICs is applicable until another component of the server is the cause for a bottleneck. If the other components of the server, such as the disk speed or the processor power, become the cause of a bottleneck, adding FDX NICs does not help improve performance.

This type of configuration allows for bandwidth that is scalable, to and from the server. It also takes care of the cabling, repeaters, hubs, and LAN adapters in the client. It is possible to attach more servers to the unused ports with the help of multiple links, resulting in an increase in aggregate bandwidth. If there are fewer switch ports, multiple switches can be cascaded and used.

In most cases, a few of the slots in the server are not used. If most of the slots are already filled, a second NIC can be added by using a dual Ethernet adapter. This dual Ethernet adapter can provide functionality equivalent to two NICs with the benefit of using only one slot in the server.

SHARED AND FAST ETHERNET LANS

10Mbps switched Ethernet LANs are useful for most applications. An alternative is to use shared Fast Ethernet LANs, running at 100Mbps, to offer more bandwidth to users (for applications that connect high-speed clients and servers). Then all the devices that are attached on the shared LAN share the bandwidth. 100Mbps Ethernet adapters, hubs, and repeaters are required to set up such a network.

SWITCHED AND FAST ETHERNET LANS

If the number of LANs used increases by a large number, even routers, bridges, or 10Mbps switches become bottlenecks to users. To overcome such bottlenecks, 100Mbps or Fast Ethernet switches can replace the existing interconnecting devices.

Attaching a 10Mbps switch to a fast switch requires a high-speed port, which is called an *uplink port*. It is also possible to attach high-speed servers to these high-speed switches to allow the linked users to access the servers.

Consider a network in which a number of 10Mbps shared Ethernet segments are connected using a 10Mbps switch, as shown in Figure 6.9.

The switch uses one of its ports to connect to a workgroup server. As shown in Figure 6.9, the switch is linked to the 100Mbps switch using the uplink port. The 100Mbps shared Ethernet segment is also connected to the clients with the help of the 100Mbps hubs. Two workgroup servers are attached to the hub. You can also see from Figure 6.9 that the hub is connected to the 100Mbps switch, resulting in connectivity between both the workgroups.

Figure 6.9
The switched 10Base-T network based on the full-duplex concept with Fast Ethernet can link two separate work-groups.

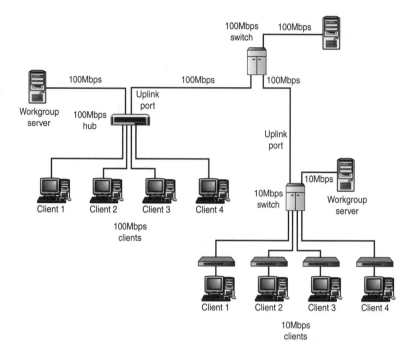

SWITCHED ETHERNET WITH ATM

Now only one issue in terms of building a network needs to be resolved: allowing users to communicate between several sites. Each site might have switched LANs (which can be both 10Mbps and 100Mbps) that are spread throughout the site, as well as ATM LANs. A high-speed wide area network (WAN) is required to interconnect these switches, and ATM is a technology that meets this demand because it is easily configurable.

> **Note**
>
> Asynchronous transfer mode (ATM) is a protocol that transmits data in the form of fixed-size packets or cells. It permits communication between devices even if they are operating at different speeds.

The reason behind using ATM is that it is a scalable technology, in terms of bandwidth, and it also meets the data needs. An Ethernet switch with an ATM uplink port is required to attach a switched Ethernet LAN to an ATM network. FDX and Fast Ethernet LANs can be attached to a backbone, as shown in Figure 6.10.

Figure 6.10
Switched Ethernet is connected through an ATM uplink port to ATM LANs.

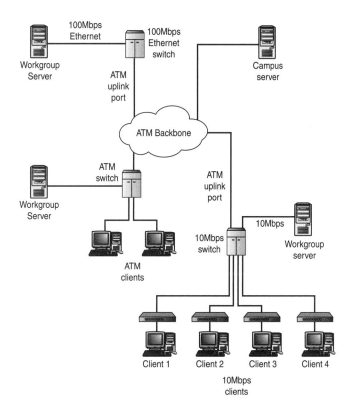

SAN TOPOLOGIES

SAN makes use of three kinds of topologies in its configuration: point-to-point, arbitrated loop, and switched. When these three topologies are interconnected, a fabric is created.

Point-to-point is a simple and easily applied topology for connecting two nodes, and the bandwidth is dedicated to these two nodes. A connection between a storage device and a server uses point-to-point topology. The point-to-point connectivity is also applicable between two CPUs. This type of topology is best used on a small scale.

The *loop* (arbitrated) topology ensures that the bandwidth is shared between all the nodes that are connected to the loop, unlike point-to-point topology. The loop can also be connected node-to-node, but this might cause the loop to stop functioning if even one node malfunctions. The arbitrated loop is cost-effective in terms of the high bandwidth and connectivity it offers. The arbitrated-loop technology can support up to 126 nodes. It is possible to connect a loop to a Fibre Channel switch to further increase a fabric's size.

PART

II

CH

6

The *switched fabric* topology is appropriate for large-scale or enterprise networks in which a number of users are interconnected and need to access or share a common data storage array. A *fabric* is used to connect networks across large distances. The fabric can connect a maximum of 16 million nodes. It offers a maximum bandwidth of 200MBps times the number of nodes. The fabric can comprise one or more electronic switching devices to enable a point-to-point connection between the pairs of nodes.

The fabric is not limited in terms of the number of loops it can connect. To make a comparison, a switched fabric works in a similar fashion to a switched telephone network in that it can provide a dedicated connection between multiple pairs of nodes. In a switched fabric network, the data throughput value is greater than that of point-to-point and loop configurations. The higher data throughput is due to the chances of a number of dedicated paths through the fabric.

→ To learn more about point-to-point and arbitrated loop topologies, **see** "Arbitrated Loop Topology," **p. 126**

FIBRE CHANNEL SWITCHES

Fibre Channel switches work in a style similar to conventional switches and offer increased bandwidth and performance. Fibre Channel switches differ in terms of the number of ports they can support. It is possible to connect a number of switches to form a switch fabric. If multiple switches are connected, it is important to copy (cascade) each switch's configuration into the remaining switches that are connected.

NON-CASCADED SWITCHED FABRIC

A non-cascaded switched fabric can support configurations that are required by large enterprises. This type of configuration can be set up in such a way that it allows every system to have the required access to each switch. In this manner, if a switch fails, it is possible for the system to use any controller and ensure continuous operation. The Fibre Channel switched topology for non-cascading switches is shown in Figure 6.11.

CASCADED SWITCHED FABRIC

A cascaded switched fabric offers interconnections between switches. The main benefit of a switched fabric is that it serves as a logical switch with a single connection working to provide access to all the other ports that are present on the set of switches. The Fibre Channel switched topology for switches with cascading is shown in Figure 6.12.

Fibre Channel protocols allow dynamic as well as permanent data paths between the nodes that are on the switched fabric. A permanent data path ensures a guaranteed bandwidth between two nodes. A dynamic path provides the freedom for any node that is connected to the fabric to communicate with another node as long as a third node is also not trying to communicate with the target simultaneously.

In the current market, where data storage is a necessity, storage area network products are in great demand. These products need to offer high bandwidth, resource sharing, and flexible deployment of devices. Devices such as storage controllers and Fibre Channel bridges can offer nodes with fast connections to the network. The most common types of fabrics are Switched-SCSI, Fibre Channel Switched, and Switched-SSA.

Figure 6.11
The Fibre Channel switched topology consisting of non-cascaded switches is costly but supports fail over.

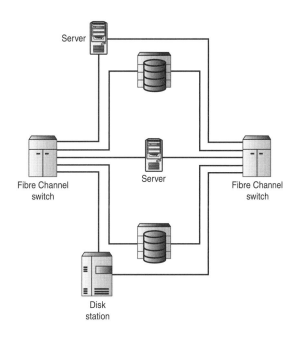

Figure 6.12
The Fibre Channel switched topology consisting of cascaded switches enables automatic fail over and resource sharing.

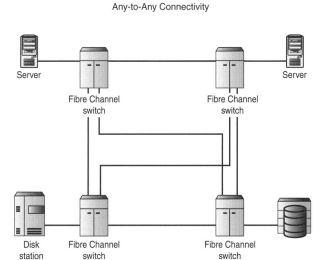

In 1992, IBM, Sun Microsystems, and Hewlett Packard formed the Fibre Channel Systems Initiative (FCSI). They wanted to create an input/output (I/O) technology that would offer enhanced performance as well as permit improved configuration flexibility. The main intent of FCSI was to develop an I/O technology that could support a number of protocols simultaneously over one medium. This gave rise to multiple protocols for Fibre Channel standard supports, such as SCSI, ATM, HIPPI, and TCP/IP. The significant feature of Fibre Channel is that it is possible for data and the network protocol to be present on the same media.

→ To learn more about SCSI and HIPPI, **see** "High-Performance Parallel Interface," **p. 75**

Two choices are available for Fibre Channel SAN fabrics. Fibre Channel directors offer more fault tolerance with no single point of failure. Multiple and interconnected Fibre Channel switches are the second choice. Here, the number of interswitch links is equivalent to the number of port devices required for a complete nonblocking fabric.

The Fibre Channel director is similar to RAID in fault tolerance. The Fibre Channel switch can be compared to JBOD. To state this differently, it is a set of fault-tolerant ports against just a bunch of ports. One feature is that, like JBOD, Fibre Channel switch fabrics can be configured in a high-availability environment. The suitable solution for an organization is decided by factors such as downtime cost, SAN scalability, and the organization's bandwidth requirements.

A COMPARISON BETWEEN FIBRE CHANNEL DIRECTORS AND SWITCHES

A Fibre Channel director does not have any point of failure in its architecture. All its critical components, including the PCB's can be replaced. Fault isolation is brought down to the component level. In case of upgrades being carried out, when required, the upgrades do not disrupt the functioning of the network.

Fibre Channel switch fabrics can be easily managed from a single management console. The Fibre Channel switches that build the SAN fabric have the required hot-replaceable power. A minimum of two Fibre Channel switches is required in a SAN fabric. The latency value between any two ports is consistent and can be easily calculated.

To get a clearer idea of Fibre Channel directors and Fibre Channel switch fabrics in the market, some of their features are compared in the next section.

SCALABILITY

In general, scalability is the factor that measures the rate of growth of a SAN fabric. Fibre Channel directors, in terms of scalability, start with 64 ports in eight-port increments and move on to 128-port, then 256-port, and so on. The scalability of Fibre Channel directors promises to increase with the growth and increased complexity of SAN.

Fibre Channel switches are currently available in both eight-port and 16-port configurations. These numbers might increase in the near future. Switches have single field-replaceable units (FRUs). In other words, if ports need to be added to a SAN fabric, it requires a new switch to be installed and managed.

If Fibre Channel switches need to obtain the same number of high-availability nonblocking ports as that of a 64-port director, an important requirement is a minimum of nine interconnected 16-port switches, each using eight Inter-Switch Link (ISL) ports. Hence, full access to the switches is provided, but not full bandwidth.

In conclusion, regarding scalability, both Fibre Channel directors and switches can easily scale up to approximately 32 ports. Beyond 32 ports, Fibre Channel directors are still easily scalable, but Fibre Channel switches become complex with an increasing number of ports. In terms of scalability, Fibre Channel directors score one over Fibre Channel switches.

COMPLEXITY

The complexity factor is a necessary measure of the IT personnel resources that are needed to install, manage, and troubleshoot a SAN fabric.

Fibre Channel directors follow the three stated factors of installing, configuring, and managing as a single system. In the case of multiple units being interconnected in a fabric, only a single image of the fabric is created. The port capacity can be increased through a nondisruptive installation of additional ports.

Fibre Channel switches can also be installed, configured, and managed as a single fabric, but the number of units needed to achieve a similar port count is high. The interconnectivity factor is an important point to be considered while designing a SAN; a 64-port fabric is interconnected differently from a 128-port fabric.

In terms of ease of configuration, capacity upgrade, and simplicity of management, Fibre Channel directors score another point.

LOOP VERSUS FABRIC TOPOLOGIES

One of the most significant technology choices in Fibre Channel SAN is the addressing mechanism. There are two types of addressing schemes: private loop and fabric mode. These two schemes differ technically in terms of the size of the address field that is associated with every node. The private loop makes use of a sparse 8-bit address field and provides a maximum station count of 126 nodes. The reason behind the address field's being sparse is that it uses specific bit pattern combinations to enable quicker recognition by components such as switches. In comparison, fabric mode makes use of a 24-bit address field and hence is able to offer nearly 16 million addresses. This addressing does not necessarily serve any purpose to an end-user apart from providing information on how it affects the technical power of SAN.

In private loop mode, the complexity of the loop configuration is the same as that of the simple hubs configuration. It is appropriate to examine the loops to identify the devices that are connected, however slow the process. This process can be carried out for a small number of nodes, but it is not possible to execute this process for 16 million (2^{24}) nodes. Instead of attempting to examine the fabric, there is an alternative: Switches offer a name service that is structurally similar to the name services (such as DNS) provided for IP networks.

PART

II

CH

6

Note

Domain Name System (DNS) specifies a procedure to name a group of computers and domains. In DNS, a domain name or an IP address is assigned to the computers on the network. This is useful in identifying and locating computers and services. IP addresses of computers can be traced using DNS services information. With the help of domain names or IP addresses, client computers can send queries to a server.

The nodes, adapters, and switches that need to determine the addresses and identities of the devices connected can question (query) the name service.

The most significant aspect of private loop node is that each loop is treated as an individual (standalone) network, with no connections to the other networks. The difference is noticed when a topology more complex than a simple loop topology is configured. Consider a situation in which two parallel private loops are connected to a single system in which the device drivers are unable to realize that the disks are duplicate images of each other, so two devices get created for each physical drive. To eliminate these multiple images, the technique of switch zoning needs to be applied.

Zoning, in the case of a Fibre Channel environment, is the concept of joining or grouping a number of ports to create a virtual storage network. The zoning concept permits the administrator to create multiple zones within a fabric, where each zone can comprise storage devices, servers, and workstations. The ports that belong to a particular zone are allowed to communicate within the zone but not with ports of other zones.

→ To learn more about zoning, **see** "Zoning," **p. 249**

IMPLICATIONS OF A FABRIC

If the name service is present in the fabric, this implies that the host bus adapter (HBA) needs to be instructed to query the name service so that it can state the identity of the attached devices. The name service, whenever queried, needs to inform the HBA of the current state of the fabric and when nodes leave or enter the fabric. It is possible for the nodes to change state for a number of reasons. For example, a change in state happens when a cable is plugged into or removed from its switch port. Changes in fabric zoning might also result in altering the connectivity between an HBA and a device.

When fabric mode is adopted, every attached device must be capable of managing the 24-bit address and must also be aware of the name-service function. This necessity is a problem for large fabric devices, such as switches and HBAs, and it gets even more complex for smaller devices, such as disk drives. When fabric mode is used, an issue to keep in mind is the requirement of new device drivers for the HBAs. These drivers need to know how to make use of the name service. It is important to note that a Fibre Channel network can operate only in either of two modes: private loop mode or fabric mode. It cannot operate in both modes.

A third type of technology, introduced by Ancor Communications, is called translated mode. It requires that the switch translate the fabric address to a private loop address. Each private loop in the fabric is assigned a prefix address to ensure that there is a distinction with the 7-bit private loop addresses. Therefore, the devices can operate in private loop mode and also participate in the full fabric interconnection scheme.

FIVE-SERVER STORAGE CONSOLIDATION

Consider the case of a consolidation topology with five servers, as shown in Figure 6.13. The five servers are connected to a tape library. They share a common data storage array. Each server contains two HBAs, with one linked to each switch. Notice that both the switches are linked to the data storage array. This provides redundant data paths from each server to the storage array through the fabric.

Figure 6.13
The storage consolidation with five servers and a common storage array is connected through non-blocking redundant data paths.

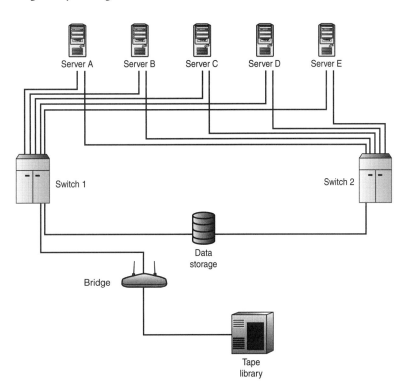

The paths that form a part of this topology can be either fiber-optic or copper cables. This fabric is a nonblocking fabric, because no ISLs are used.

FIVE-SERVER STORAGE CONSOLIDATION USING A REMOTE MIRROR

The five-server storage consolidation topology can be extended by including remote data mirroring. It is possible to locate the mirrored storage up to 10km (kilometers) away from the server by using long-wave fiber-optic cable in the ISLs between the switches. This five-server storage consolidation setup is shown in Figure 6.14.

PART

II

CH

6

Figure 6.14
The five-server storage consolidation with mirrored storage as far as 10km enables creation of a disaster recovery setup.

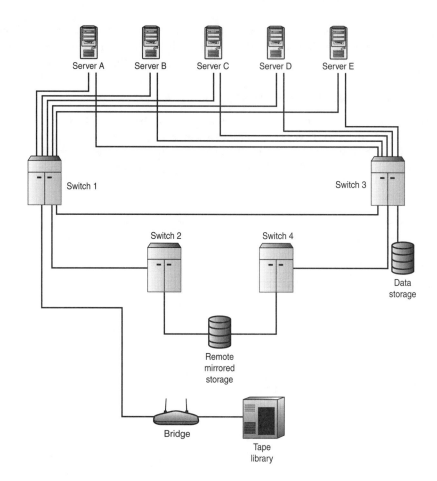

The data transfers that happen between the tape library and the servers need not pass through the ISLs, because the tape library is situated within 1km of the servers. This implies that one ISL between the switches is sufficient to provide fully nonblocked data paths. This type of topology requires the operating system to offer mirroring capability, as in RAID 1, and the data storage arrays offer RAID 0 behind the mirror, thus creating a RAID 10 type of configuration.

→ To learn more about the different RAID levels, **see** "Redundant Array of Inexpensive Disks," **p. 42**

SIX-SERVER STORAGE CONSOLIDATION USING REMOTE STORAGE

Another type of storage consolidation that is possible using fabric switches is the six-server storage consolidation with the aid of remote storage. In this type of configuration, six servers are required to share a common data storage array and a tape library. With the use of long-wave fiber-optic cables between the cascaded switches, it is possible to locate a server 10km away from the storage array. The cascaded switches serve the purpose of getting the

10km distance between the storage devices and the servers. The two ISLs that are located on switches A and B (primary fabric) ensure that a nonblocked bandwidth is provided between the servers, tape library, and storage. However, the path available to the tape library is not redundant.

There is always the risk of a failure of the primary fabric. To be prepared for such a scenario, switches C and D (the secondary fabric) contain two ISLs and the transferred bridge and tape library to provide the required nonblocked bandwidth.

NINE-SERVER STORAGE CONSOLIDATION USING TWO STORAGE ARRAYS

The final topology discussed is the storage consolidation extended to nine servers with another storage array, as shown in Figure 6.15.

Figure 6.15
The nine-server storage consolidation with two storage arrays still has some problems.

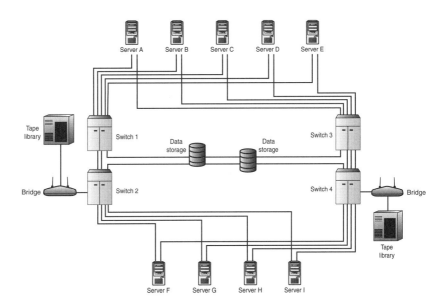

The drawback of this configuration is that blocking can occur in the following situations:

When Server A writes to storage array 2 with Server I reading from array 1 at the same time, data transfer between switches 1 and 2 is blocked. This blocking is present until at least one of the processes is completed.

In the meantime, the remaining seven servers can all access the tape libraries through the ISLs between switches 3 and 4. These servers are prevented or blocked from accessing the storage arrays until one of the servers (A or B) completes its process.

If storage array 1 is assigned exclusively to servers A through E, and storage array 2 is assigned to the remaining servers exclusively, the stated problem can be avoided. The benefits of providing these exclusive rights are that traffic through the ISLs is significantly reduced, and there is no requirement for another ISL. The significance is that the redundant paths between all the devices on SAN are preserved.

SERIAL TRANSMISSION NETWORKS

Storage area networking can also be created around a serial architecture and not just SCSI or Fibre Distributed Data Interface (FDDI), which have their limitations and are expensive. Serial interfaces are the storage device interfaces that are replacing interfaces such as SCSI and IDE.

→ To learn more about SCSI and FDDI, **see** "Small Computer System Interface," **p. 67**

In general, device interfaces are used to connect storage devices to a computer bus. Serial interfaces go one step further to increase the potential of storage architectures to a wide range of networked system configurations. Similar to SCSI, serial interfaced devices can also be arranged in strings, as shown in Figure 6.16.

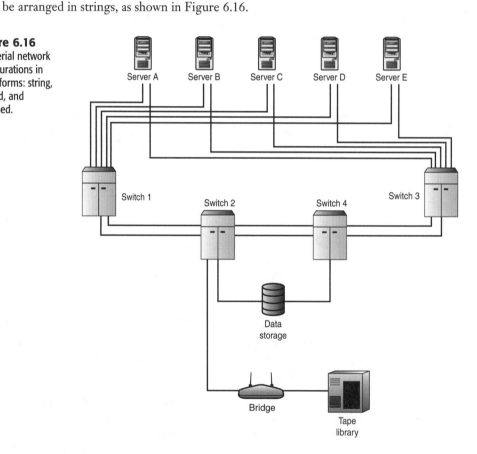

Figure 6.16
The serial network configurations in three forms: string, looped, and switched.

The variation here is that a serial configuration can support up to 128 devices, not seven as with SCSI. Also, multiple host adapters can be plugged into any point on the string, allowing a number of computers to be able to share data. The strings can be closed to form loops that create fault-tolerant networks, because data can now be transmitted in either direction.

The new technology that evolved in LANs relies on a method known as switching. This method creates logical domains, instead of LAN segments, promising higher performance and improved reliability. LAN switching works on the technique of data packets that are transmitted between hubs.

WHY SERIAL STORAGE ARCHITECTURE?

Ethernet uses the collision-based method. The process of collision results in truncation of data packets, which results in retransmission of those packets. Switched Ethernet uses the concept of a "store-and forward" switching hub. It receives the entire packet, verifies the data integrity, and then retransmits it to the next segment, resulting in high latency and more memory usage. Serial transmission is not collision-oriented; it permits the use of fast "cut-through" switches that start the process of retransmitting packets to the next segment immediately. Serial transmission operates in a switched configuration to create a more flexible architecture than traditional topologies, such as Ethernet.

Serial storage architecture (SSA), developed by IBM, is an implementation of the serial technology. The SSA network is comprised of point-to-point links that are attached to SSA-interfaced storage devices by shielded four-wire cable. In their current applications, the servers are connected to the storage devices using SCSI-SSA host bus adapters.

SSA, when connected to switched networks or loops, provides fault tolerance by making use of a dual-port architecture. This dual-port feature allows data packets to be sent in both directions over the loop. If the default path is interrupted, alternative paths to a drive might be found. This dual-port technology improves performance, because the full-duplex support property is enabled. The serial feature adopted by SSA also increases performance, because all the SSA devices in a loop can handle data simultaneously. Multiple transactions are allowed to wait on the SSA loop. This efficient use of bandwidth optimizes performance.

SSA, when compared to SCSI, offers faster, less-expensive performance and a more reliable network. It is simpler to configure an SSA-based storage network than a SCSI network. SSA-based networks are also more flexible and are extremely fault-tolerant. SSA is best suited for mission-critical applications, because they offer increased performance as well as data security. The SAN fabrics are designed in such a way that they provide redundant data paths to all the devices in SAN.

PART

II

CH

6

SUMMARY

Switches are devices that are used to transfer information between a network's ports. The main purpose of using switches is to eliminate bottlenecks in terms of bandwidth usage. Switches can connect different Ethernet network segments.

Switched LANs can work in two modes: full duplex and half duplex. The switched FDX LAN lets you maximize the usage of the available bandwidth. Ethernet LANs can be either shared or switched LANs.

Three types of Fibre Channel topologies are widely adopted in SAN: point-to-point, arbitrated loop, and switched. The switched fabric topology lets you establish a connection between 16 million nodes. Different kinds of switched topologies can be designed, depending on the number of servers and devices used.

Apart from the parallel interfaces, SSA provides you with a serial interface that can be used as a fabric when used in a switched network.

PRODUCTS ARENA

Serial Storage Architecture: The Apollo is a type of high-performance, integrated PCI/SSA I/O processor. With the help of a peripheral component interface (PCI) local bus, it offers a dual-port SSA interface for host systems. Each SSA port interface that is present on the Apollo offers 20Mbps FDX operations. When data frames are input and output on both ports simultaneously, this results in a peak transfer rate of 80Mbps. The Apollo is a device consisting of a single-chip solution with integrated drivers and receivers to allow direct connection with 150-ohm lines. This chip solution also supports loop, switched SSA, and string networks. The Apollo is made up of five major system blocks. The SSA dual-port interface that connects to the SSA networks is a fully integrated interface. The high-performance transfer of SSA frames between the host PCI system and the SSA dual-port block is supported by the 32-bit PCI interface. It makes use of a multichannel DMA engine and supports on-board FLASH ROM programming.

PART III

DESIGNING, MANAGING, AND IMPLEMENTING STORAGE AREA NETWORKS

CHAPTER 7

DESIGNING STORAGE AREA NETWORKS

In this chapter

DESIGN CONSIDERATIONS FOR STORAGE AREA NETWORKS

Storage Area Networks are not theoretical concepts that you study in books. They are technologies that are used in organizations to satisfy their storage needs. SANs, along with Fibre Channel, are a subject of intense study for the simple reason that the options afforded by SANs are plenty. This makes the job of selecting the right design that much more difficult. The next three chapters try to make it easier for you to select a SAN design that will best optimize the existing resources.

Storage area networks are useful in areas that require deployment of large volumes of storage. On a simple scale, you might not be able to appreciate the features of a SAN. However, the implementation of storage area networks in large networks can have a definite qualitative impact on the existing network and its components. A SAN is not just an extension and externalization of storage devices; it's a network in itself. This makes a world of difference to the use of storage devices, given that storage devices were originally built to be attached to a single host computer.

A storage area network could be even a simple two-node connection. Needless to say, this would be quite different from a fully configured network with multiple connections. This chapter covers the different topologies that are possible with SANs and the drawbacks and advantages of each.

It is evident that no two organizations have the same requirements. This section offers basic ideas and guidelines that help you customize your SAN's design to suit your organization's requirements. Designing storage area networks requires a methodical approach. You have to go through the processes of assessment, planning, implementation, and management.

Note
> Some companies, such as IBM and SAN-Architects.com, provide total SAN solutions.

GOALS

Your organization's needs are the key determinant of SAN design. The assessment of the existing network and the requirements for future growth determine the use of a SAN. Remember that a SAN is not just an assembly of components; it is a solution for your storage needs.

Implementing a SAN necessarily implies an additional investment. As in any business, investments cannot be justified if proportionate benefits are not guaranteed to accrue. There is a maxim that states "If it ain't broke, don't fix it." If your current storage setup is sufficient and meets all your needs (current and future), you do not need to set up a SAN.

You need to carefully evaluate all your goals before attempting to implement a SAN in your organization. Your goals can be broadly classified into business goals and technical goals.

BUSINESS GOALS

The benefits of SANs to an organization are plenty. However, the real benefits you will derive depend on your organization's needs and requirements. You need to analyze the existing setup and identify areas that have storage-related problems. Typically, in most organizations that have adopted SANs, trouble areas include lack of connectivity, the inability to share information, the need to expand storage, or bandwidth constraints on LANs.

When storage costs and needs grow and managing resources becomes difficult, SANs can be a solution. If you are moving to a seven-days-a-week 24-hours-a-day schedule, or if you run mission-critical applications where downtimes are unacceptable, SAN can come to your rescue.

Whatever the trouble spots, you need to understand the capability of the existing network setup and match it with your future business requirements and goals. You must accurately estimate future plans and needs before deciding whether to use SANs. For example, if you are in a non-IT business, or you can afford to have some downtime once in a while for reasons of management and upgrades, SANs don't have to be a solution. Of course, this assumes that no other factors will affect the decision.

TECHNICAL GOALS

Technical goals or requirements can be measured in terms of factors such as availability, reliability, performance, manageability, and security. Each of these factors on their own and in unison affect the decision to implement a SAN.

The criticality of applications and hardware is crucial in the estimate of network availability. In an e-business setup, it would be almost impossible to permit downtime. Unavailability of the network could lead to costs of thousands or even millions of dollars. For other businesses, the loss might not be much. You should carefully analyze the cost of downtime and then plan your hardware setup.

When you design a high-availability setup, your costs will be high because of the use of redundant components. Similarly, if you design a setup that has a high level of security, your cost of monitoring will escalate. You must carefully study the trade-offs between features and affordability before arriving at a design that gives you an optimal storage area network.

> **Tip**
>
> Individual cost estimates for each feature can lead to a confusing array of sheets of paper. A total cost of ownership estimate helps you decide on the exact mix of features and required hardware. Cost of ownership is discussed more later in this chapter.

→ To learn more about high availability, **see** "Implementing a High Availability Plan," **p.215**

SAN APPLICATIONS

There are many areas in which SAN can be implemented. SAN in general adds bandwidth for specific applications and eases the bandwidth load on the primary network. SAN is a technology that can find its way into a wide variety of networking environments, as shown in Figure 7.1.

Figure 7.1
There are a variety of SAN applications.

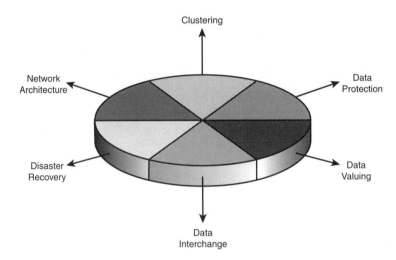

Externalizing storage is one of the main areas in which SANs are implemented. Externalizing storage adds a new network to the existing network. Therefore, the change to the network architecture lets you run a myriad of network-hosted applications. It also lets you integrate storage across platforms.

SANs have found their way into areas such as data warehousing and data outsourcing. The following hypothetical case studies give you a basic idea of the different types of companies in which SANs can be implemented. Later sections of this chapter and later chapters provide you with tips on how to design an ideal SAN setup for each hypothetical case.

CASE STUDY 1

Imagine providing the latest updated online financial information across eight time zones. That would mean transferring huge volumes of data across different Web sites. Added to this is the fact that your Web site traffic is slated to more than triple every year. Now, that's a lot of demand for access to information! That's the situation faced by XYZ.com, a (hypothetical) major online financial consultant.

XYZ.com is an online financial company that lets its members trade stocks and shares online. This company's transactions average about two million dollars a day throughout the year. Since its launch, the company has been experiencing an exponential growth in trading volumes. The company wants to incorporate a robust storage and backup system.

The business directives of the hypothetical XYZ.com are simple: to provide seamless access to all its members across time zones. This is to be achieved while retaining and maximizing the utilization of the existing resources. The current network setup of XYZ.com is shown in Figure 7.2.

Figure 7.2
The high-level net-work design of XYZ.com.

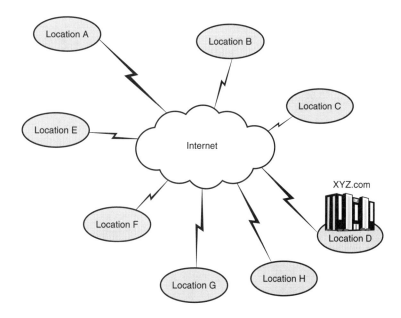

In the current setup, all connections to Location D, where the hypothetical XYZ.com is located, are through a T1-based connection to the Internet. The other locations have a mixture of connection topologies. Location D runs mission-critical Web-based applications that are required to function seven days a week, 24 hours a day. The intranet is shielded from the Internet through firewalls located on the web server.

The existing servers have proven insufficient to handle peak-time activities due to insufficient memory and disk speed. The entire system slows down because of this limitation. Downtime is unacceptably high every time there is a problem. It takes too long to repair the systems when disks fail.

The company's data requirements are in terabytes (TB) and are growing at a rapid rate. XYZ.com moves over to a SAN to ensure that storage is scalable and available.

CASE STUDY 2

HT Industries is a hypothetical company located in Detroit. It deals in heavy engineering precision equipment. The company's operations are highly data-centric. The company's data center is located on the fourth floor of its office. The data center handles all the administrative, billing, and support services for the company.

PART

III

CH

7

The load on the data center over the years has almost outgrown its capacity. The storage space available in the existing building is limited and therefore does not afford much room for adding storage devices.

The storage available for HT Industries is not small. It can store up to 5TB of data in two disk storage subsystems (the 3700 subsystem). Although structurally nothing is wrong with the subsystem, it is a bulky piece that weighs almost two metric tons.

Assume HT Industries wants to expand its storage capacity. However, a number of architects and structural engineers believe the building can house no more equipment of the magnitude that HT Industries needs to install. With the latest set of expansion plans, the data storage requirements are slated to triple in the next two or three years.

This case study has a need that most enterprise planners might find all too familiar: The hypothetical HT Industries wants to transfer all the data held in the old data center to the new one. It also wants to have the whole process completed as quickly as possible. The other condition that sounds familiar is that HT Industries wants the entire process to happen without disrupting the existing operations.

HT Industries is also planning to open another data center that will function as a center for disaster recovery. Cost is not a major constraint for HT Industries; however, it wants to make the best possible use of the existing infrastructure.

Given its requirements, HT Industries acquires a new building to accommodate the storage devices. The company decides to build a SAN setup to manage the new data center. The primary reason for the adoption of a SAN is that the new data center is located far from the old one—about 35 miles away.

CASE STUDY 3

For this example, ABC is a very small company (compared to the first two case studies) that has a network with multiple servers that have directly attached storage devices. ABC has 100 employees working on different projects. The company works on a shift system and therefore requires round-the-clock functionality.

ABC's network setup is based on a centralized networking model that has smart terminals. Currently, four servers manage the network's requirements. Each server has a disk array attached to it through SCSI interfaces, as shown in Figure 7.3. ABC's total storage capacity is about 700GB.

ABC has a contract to develop packages and animation for another company. The only snag perceived by ABC management is that the storage capacity must be doubled to ensure that the animation can be developed and tested.

ABC decides to implement a miniature SAN-based network to meet its storage needs. This seems to be the ideal solution for the simple reason that it does not require additional servers. SANs also let ABC share storage resources across servers and their domains.

Figure 7.3
ABC's network setup.

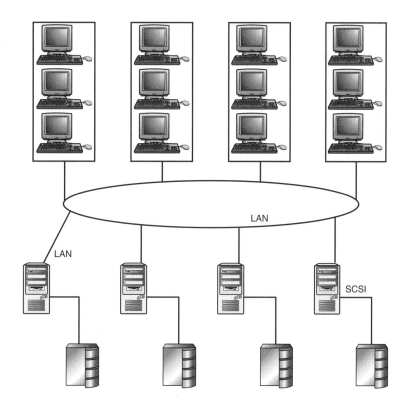

CASE STUDY 4

For our last fictional example, Oil Expo Corporation (OEC) is a worldwide geophysical service provider. The company has a database that contains seismic information on more than 2,000 blocks in a particular region. This is a fair volume of data. This data is used to manipulate and study the region's 3-D seismic images and make exploration decisions based on the study.

The critical seismic data currently occupies close to 1TB of the RAID storage system. Assume OEC wants to double this storage capacity with additional RAID-based storage systems. The speed of data retrieval is important to OEC's operations. To study the seismic information for one square mile, 60,000 to 70,000 records must be extracted and run. An area is represented in terms of seismic traces. About 100 seismic traces put together result in the creation of a graph to depict the seismic activity in the small area.

The data is fed into the system over high-speed networks from a 60-node cluster. The nodes are managed by a set of six servers, as shown in Figure 7.4. OEC requires a system to ensure that the data in the storage devices is secure. In case of system failures, the option of restoring data from backup devices such as tapes would be expensive. Therefore, OEC wants a secure RAID-based system.

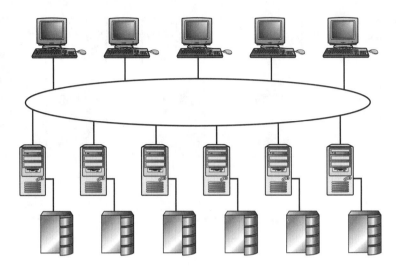

Figure 7.4
The current setup of OEC.

Speed of data retrieval is important to OEC to ensure that the images appear to be real-time studies. OEC decides to move to SANs for two primary reasons: the flexibility in storage space and the ability to retrieve information from the storage devices at rates close to 200MBps.

DESIGN METHODOLOGY

Storage systems are a crucial part of an organization's network infrastructure. With the requirements for storage growing, your storage strategy must be designed to keep pace. You must select the most appropriate technology for the primary storage devices, implement reliable backup strategies, and ensure that a management scheme is in place to monitor the functioning.

In today's environment of reduced resources and time, it has become imperative that quick decisions be made. However, the requirements that have to be met are also getting more complex by the day. To design an effective storage system and implement it successfully, you need more than one person. Implementing a complex SAN setup is a team effort.

As with any network design, to design a SAN setup, you need to go through a certain set of steps to optimize your design. You have to go through the set of steps outlined in Figure 7.5.

SAN assessment is the first step in the SAN design process. The assessment process is basically used to gather necessary information about the current network and requirements. Ideally, this process starts with a site audit. This is an important aspect when planning your SAN design. For example, in Case Study 2, if HT Industries had planned to install all its additional capacity at the existing location, the effect could have been chaotic. Another advantage of doing a site audit is that it gives you a good idea of what kind of setup you are getting into. If the existing setup consists of haphazardly connected systems and a badly configured LAN, you might have to design the SAN in a manner to adapt to the network. Sometimes you might even need to redo some of the existing LAN so that the SAN can function effectively.

Figure 7.5
SAN design method-
ology.

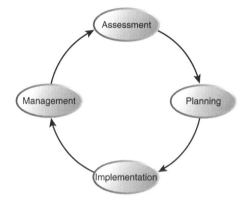

As a part of the assessment activities, you have to take stock of the existing storage and server inventory. You also have to analyze the technical and business issues that might affect the deployment of the SAN on the network. For example, if the network currently has many Macintosh systems, you must plan for the compatibility of the storage devices as well as interoperability issues. The selection of the vendor and devices depends to a great extent on the technical and business issues.

The requirements in terms of the SAN's reliability and availability must be determined. The SAN's topology will be affected by these requirements. As seen earlier, the kind of applications that will be run on the network also determine the SAN's setup. In Case Study 1, XYZ.com's requirement was for a more available and expandable storage system. This means that the SAN setup would use clustering and redundant disks to achieve the objective. However, in Case Study 3, where the emphasis was on a storage system that is faster, the connection channels and storage devices play a major part in the design.

The implementation and management phases cover the stages of installing the devices, planning backup topologies, making the system available, and maintaining and monitoring the system.

→ To learn more about implementing SANs, **see** "Implementing Storage Area Networks," **p. 191**

DESIGNING A SAN TOPOLOGY

The key factor in deciding the correct topology for your SAN setup is based on the requirements. The amount of storage space required and the span of your network are the main considerations when you're deciding on a topology.

The following sections discuss a set of generalized topologies that can be formed in a SAN network. You can either pick a topology mentioned here (which would be great) or adapt the different topologies to suit your requirements. Typically, you might need to mix and match the different topologies to arrive at the right one for your organization.

All topologies mentioned here assume that a Fibre Channel connection will be used. The primary reason is that Fibre Channel connections offer unparalleled speed and reliability. You can design your SAN on any connection technology and still use the topologies explained here.

A SIMPLE TOPOLOGY

In a simple point-to-point connection, the server is directly connected to a single disk array, as shown in Figure 7.6. Although this topology satisfies the requirements to be called a SAN, it really does not offer many options. However, it is a useful server-to-storage connection.

Figure 7.6
A simple point-to-point connection.

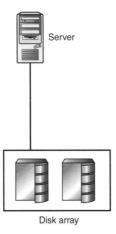

Server

Disk array

This topology provides you with a fast and convenient connection to the disk array. However, if you are looking for a very reliable connection, this is not for you. The reason is that this topology has many single points of failure: server, HBA, cable, and disk array controller.

If you still want to use a point-to-point connection because your requirements are ideally suited for it, consider the following alternative.

Because a simple disk array permits you to have two redundant controllers installed, you can add a second HBA to the server and connect it to the disk array, as shown in Figure 7.7.

Note

Note that high-end disk arrays offer you the scope to have multiple disk array controllers. Select the disk array as per your organization's requirements.

Figure 7.7
A point-to-point connection with two paths.

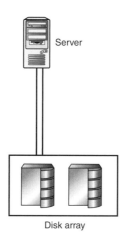

Server

Disk array

In this topology, the server has two HBAs and will therefore work even if one of the HBAs, cables, or disk array controllers fails. The single point of failure in such a connection is the server.

The logical conclusion now would be to add another server. If your disk array has a limited number of controllers, your topology would look like Figure 7.8.

Figure 7.8
Point-to-point connections from two servers.

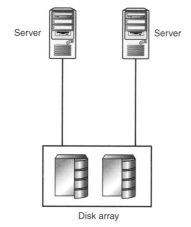

Server   Server

Disk array

In this topology, each server connects to the disk array. However, the single points of failure have actually increased. The single points of failure are servers, HBAs, cables, or disk arrays. That actually makes eight single points of failure. This assumes that the disk array has a limitation of only two controllers. If your disk array lets you have four controllers, you can also cross-connect the two servers. However, if either server fails, the whole chain ceases to function.

PART

III

CH

7

To solve this, you can cluster the servers, as shown in Figure 7.9. You can link both servers to ensure that one server continues to provide you with access to the disk array, even if the other server collapses.

Figure 7.9
A clustered point-to-point connection.

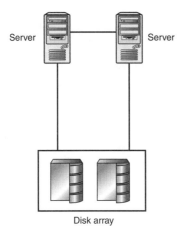

Disk array

The clustered point-to-point connection is the most reliable point-to-point connection, because there are no single points of failure (provided that your disk array permits four controllers). The drawback with this kind of topology is that options for expanding are hardly present. You can pick a point-to-point topology if you need a huge storage space that cannot be directly attached and you are looking for a faster and more reliable method to store and access data from an external storage device without eating up LAN bandwidth.

FIBRE CHANNEL ARBITRATED LOOP TOPOLOGIES

Typically, a SAN is used in an Enterprise network setup. When storage is externalized in such a setup, the storage devices are typically placed farther from the servers. In such a case, the topology that is to be adopted by the SAN must also account for the distance and connections.

When an interconnect is added to a simple point-to-point connection, the topology becomes a Fibre Channel arbitrated loop (AL) topology, as shown in Figure 7.10. This is the simplest implementation of the Fibre Channel arbitrated loop topology.

In Figure 7.10, a hub is used to interconnect the servers and the disk array. Two connections from each server are linked to the hub. Two links from the hub connect to each disk array controller. The single point of failure in this topology is the hub. This topology can be used if there are few servers and you can afford some downtime if the hub fails (not that you would ever encounter such a situation!).

To make this system safe, you can add a second hub and have a topology that has no single points of failure, as shown in Figure 7.11.

Figure 7.10
A simple Fibre
Channel arbitrated
loop topology.

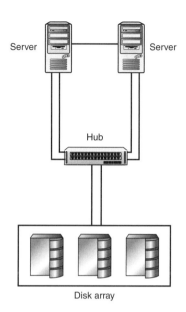

Figure 7.11
A simple failure-proof
FC-AL-based topol-
ogy.

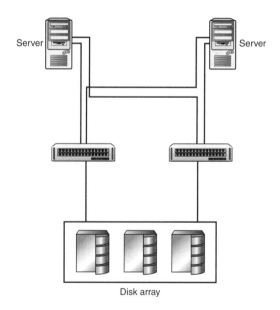

This topology has no single points of failure. This is the simplest topology of a truly reliable
SAN. You can use this kind of topology in an environment that does not immediately
require scalability. In actual work environments, this kind of topology is used to build a separate SAN setup for a very specific requirement. The investment in such a topology is limited. The only additional investment, apart from the required storage space, is for the hub.

This topology lets you expand the setup and span distances with ease. If you want to connect five or six disk arrays to the servers simultaneously, you can just add the devices and connect them to the hubs, as shown in Figure 7.12. As shown in the figure, you can even expand the number of servers that you want to connect to the storage devices.

Figure 7.12
Multiple storage devices and servers connected through a simple FC-AL-based SAN topology.

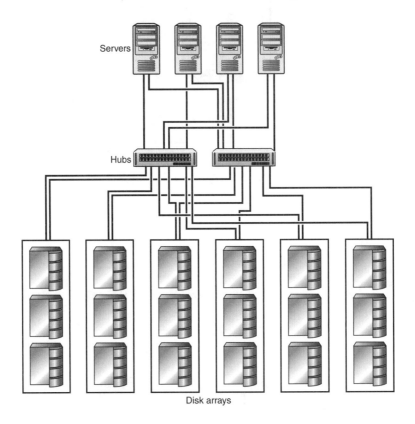

Servers

Hubs

Disk arrays

Consider a graphics company called Grax Enterprises. The company's main function is to develop animations. This process requires developing a large number of graphic images, collating them, and testing them. Grax Enterprises has only three primary servers, a web server, and a mail server. It employs 160 people, but its storage space demands are very high because of the kind of files (graphic) they work with.

Because the company is working on a number of projects, its storage needs are great. Grax Enterprises is also looking for a fast and reliable mechanism to store and retrieve files. The company has decided to implement a SAN. For a company such as Grax Enterprises, the topology illustrated in Figure 7.12 would be useful. The primary reasons for this choice are that the company is small and is located at one place, all development activities are concentrated at one location, and the number of primary servers on the network is small.

Assume that Grax Enterprises wants to use six or eight disk arrays and wants all of them to be connected to the servers. You don't have to rush out and get additional HBAs. The simplest system would be to cascade the hubs, as shown in Figure 7.13.

Figure 7.13
Cascaded hubs being used to expand the storage capacity in an FC-AL-based topology.

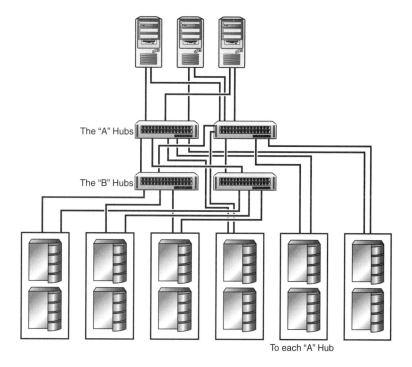

The "A" Hubs

The "B" Hubs

To each "A" Hub

You can connect the servers to a set of two servers. If you are using a 12-port hub, servers would occupy four slots on each hub. Another two ports are needed to connect the hubs to the other set of hubs. This means that you can connect only four devices to the first set of hubs. On the second set of hubs, two ports are taken up to connect to the first set of hubs. The remaining set of 10 ports can be used to connect 10 devices or further cascade the hubs. Actually, you don't necessarily need only two hubs at each stage. You can use three or four hubs at each stage.

Now, suppose that the company has two divisions within a block of each other. What do you do to the topology now? You can use Fibre Channel connections that let you stretch the connections to a distance of a kilometer. The topology might now look like Figure 7.14.

There is just one practical hitch in this topology. It requires you to place the hub in the middle of the connection. The middle of the topology would, in real terms, be somewhere between the locations (and, in most cases, in someone else's office!).

Figure 7.14
A storage area network in an expanded topology.

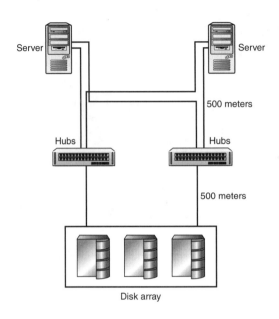

Note

A switched fabric-based topology is more useful when you're connecting devices over long distances. More about such topologies is covered in the next section.

Assume that Grax Enterprises has one office located on White Street, New York and another on 1st Street, New York. The distance between the offices is approximately 2 miles. If you have to connect the offices, you cannot directly use a single hub to connect them. However, this does not imply that you have to keep adding a hub for every 500 meters to make sure that the link is up. If you are looking at a reliable connection, with no single points of failure, that implies adding two hubs for every 500 meters, which is impractical.

A simpler solution is to use a couple of long-wave hubs at each end and connect them over fiber-optic cables, as shown in Figure 7.15. This topology can span up to 10 kilometers.

Although this topology is theoretically possible, it is not a recommended solution for the scenario just discussed. The problem with this topology is that if you are going to use a hub, there is a chance that the transmission could get distorted. The other problem with this topology is that you still need to install fiber-optic cables between the two locations.

FABRIC-BASED TOPOLOGIES

When you need to connect systems over long distances, the ideal interconnect device is a switch. The primary reason to use a switch is that it makes managing the network much easier, because there are fewer devices. The other factor for the use of fabrics over FC-AL-based topologies is that in a loop topology, latency increases in direct proportion to the distance spanned by the network.

Figure 7.15
Connection over long-wave hubs.

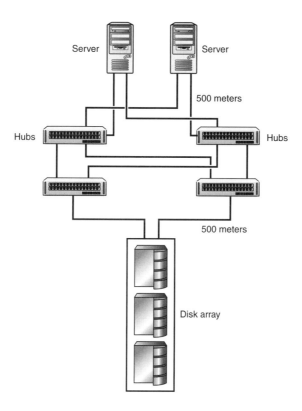

If you have a network that is predominantly concentrated at one location and that has just one server connected to the SAN setup from outside, you might want to use the loop topology. Although this might help you save money, it will cost you performance. The latency caused by the connection to the far-off server affects the performance of the entire loop.

Switched topologies do not look totally different from FC-AL topologies. The difference is that in place of a hub, a switch or a higher interconnect is used, as shown in Figure 7.16.

The investment in a switched network would be higher than for a loop-based topology for the simple reason that a switch costs almost four times as much as a hub. However, most switches come with features such as multiple fans, a dual power supply, and replaceable GBICs. The advantage of using a switch is that it provides isolation between the endpoints.

→ To learn more about switches and fabrics, **see** "Switches," **p. 134**

A switched topology is ideal for medium or large enterprises. It is also useful in environments that require high scalability and availability. However, all this does not negate the use of hubs. Hubs can still be used to cluster storage devices, as shown in Figure 7.17.

The servers can be directly connected to the switches over Fibre Channel connections. The storage devices can be grouped into different clusters, and each cluster can be connected to the switches through a set of hubs.

Figure 7.16
A simple fabric-based topology.

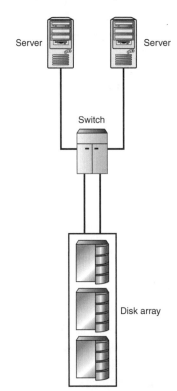

This type of setup might be ideally suited for Oil Expo Corporation (OEC) from Case Study 4. The primary reason to choose this topology is that the number of servers in the setup is few, but the number of storage devices could be many. This kind of setup is also useful in case you want to connect a heterogeneous set of storage devices to the SAN setup.

In the case of HT Industries from Case Study 2, this topology might not provide the highest availability and connectivity to the storage devices. Multiple servers are connected to the network, and you might want to connect them to the SAN. In such a case, you might want to cluster the servers as shown in Figure 7.18.

In the topology illustrated in Figure 7.18, hubs have been used to cluster servers. This is the easiest way to cluster servers. However, if you want to design a really scalable topology, you might want to use switches. Actually, in most LAN setups in organizations, even the 10Base-T LANs are designed over switches instead of hubs. In such cases, connectivity between switches is far better than if routed through hubs.

You might not have as many storage devices as depicted because of the sheer size of the latest set of storage devices. You can currently get storage devices that can store 12TB of data. The result is that your topology might end up looking like Figure 7.19.

Figure 7.17
A fabric-based topology that has hubs is used to cluster the storage devices.

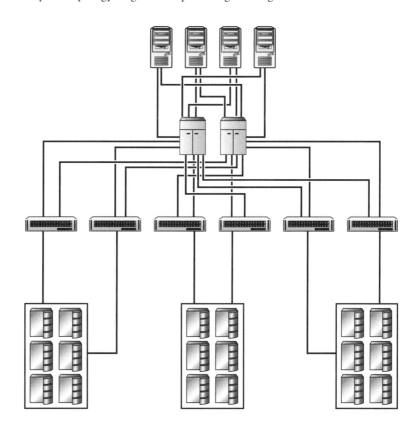

Although a number of SAN topologies have been illustrated here, which SAN topology you need also depends on the high-availability requirements and backup methodologies to be followed.

→ To learn more about implementing a high-availability SAN and different backup topologies, **see** "Implementing Storage Area Networks," **p. 191**

PART

III

CH

7

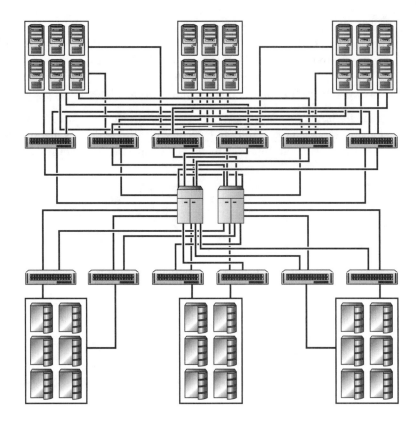

Figure 7.18
A fabric-based topology with clustered storage devices and servers.

BUILDING ON LEGACY SYSTEMS

When you are designing a SAN setup, in most cases you cannot just pick one of the topologies described here and implement it directly. It is not because the topologies wouldn't work, but rather because that in most cases you will not be building a SAN in a new network setup. You will have an existing setup that takes care of the organization's current storage requirements. You know that the organization is moving to a SAN because its current setup is inadequate, but this means that the company has some existing storage devices that it might want you to incorporate into the SAN setup.

The storage devices in the existing system are likely to be devices such as RAID storage or JBODs. The legacy storage devices are likely to be SCSI-based systems. There is also a likelihood that the organization has many different kinds of data and applications that contribute to its storage requirements. It would be ideal if you could transfer all the data to a SAN-based storage scheme. However, in most cases you would be required to hold some data on servers and other host systems.

Because a storage area network is a costly storage system, you should decide which applications need to be on the SAN and which are to be left out of it. On a general scale, you would want to shift all mission-critical data to the SAN storage devices. Applications such as e-mail, enterprise resource planning, and video streaming would benefit most from the features of the SAN.

Figure 7.19
The ideal switched topology for your high-end, complicated SAN.

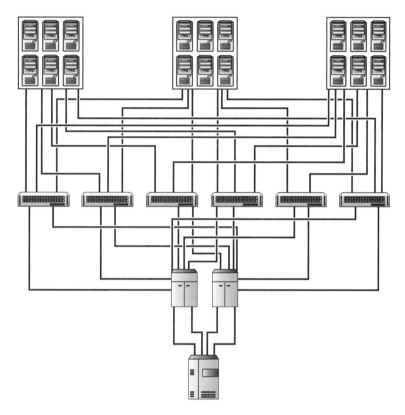

Consider an organization called Alternatives.com, which has a mainframe-based network setup. Alternatives.com has several SCSI-based storage devices that provide the organization's storage space. Because the total storage space, which is about 1TB, is insufficient, Alternatives.com wants to shift to a SAN.

As with any typical mainframe system, the mainframe is connected to multiple storage devices and linked distributed networks. It would involve a huge expenditure to replace the existing storage capacity and then add additional storage space in order to move to a Fibre Channel-based storage device. So it would be wise to retain the existing devices and add additional devices that are Fibre Channel-based.

The question now is how to decide what kind of data will be on what device and how to connect all the devices. Given the limitations of SCSI, it would be prudent to connect the SCSI-based storage devices in a small network that is contained in one location. To get the maximum results from your SCSI-based devices, ensure that the devices are placed within a

PART

III

CH

7

radius of 15 to 20 meters. These SCSI-based systems are ideal for the transmission of small amounts of data in short bursts. If you place all digital and multimedia files on the SCSI-based system, performance would take a beating.

It would be prudent to place such huge applications and files on a Fibre Channel-based connection system. Apart from their ability to handle large files and online streaming of files, Fibre Channel-based connections can transmit files across long distances. A Fibre Channel connection also gives you twice the bandwidth of a SCSI connection.

SCSI-based devices cannot be connected to an FC hub or switch directly because of compatibility issues. So what is the solution? A bridge helps you ensure that FC-based devices can coexist with SCSI-based devices.

→ To learn more about bridges, **see** "Bridges," **p. 94**

The simplest topology that you can adopt to connect your SCSI-based devices over Fibre Channel connections to the servers would be to connect the servers to the bridge, as shown in Figure 7.20.

Figure 7.20
A simple topology to connect the SCSI-based devices to the server through a bridge.

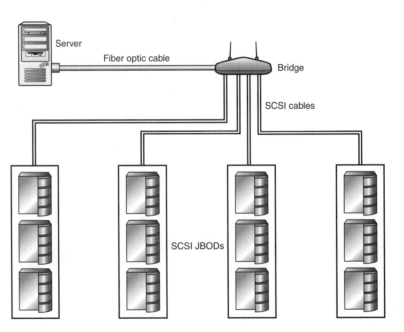

However, this topology does not give you a reliable set of connections. You can add additional equipment and configure the topology as shown in Figure 7.21 to ensure that there are no single points of failure.

You will not connect only one kind of storage device to the network. The best advantage of using bridges is that they can support multiple kinds of devices (unlike a hub). You can also use bridges to cluster the devices and connect them to switches, as shown in Figure 7.22.

Figure 7.21
A reliable method to connect the SCSI-based storage devices.

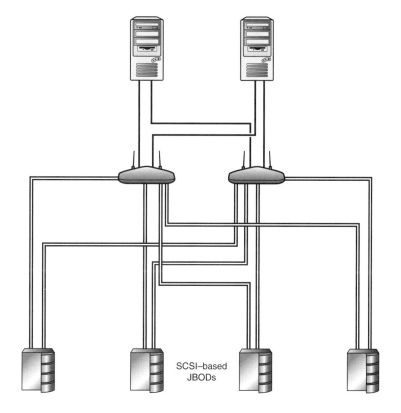

SCSI–based
JBODs

Many topologies are possible with SAN to connect legacy storage devices. You can mix and match the different topologies listed so far and arrive at a combination that will ideally suit your requirements. When you integrate a SAN into an existing network, you must iron out many issues before the actual implementation. You need to decide whether you want to use a Fibre Channel-based connection or continue with SCSI connections. You can still create a SAN that uses a switched SCSI fabric to give you greater performance. However, this limits the range of your SAN.

The topology that you want to adopt for the SAN depends, to a large extent, on the existing network setup. If you are following a centralized network setup, implementing the SAN might be easier, because all the storage is concentrated in one location. The different disparate storage devices present also affect the decision of the SAN setup. Other factors, such as cost and management, also affect the SAN topology.

The number of devices you have to connect also determines the topology you will adopt. Although a loop topology is said to support 127 devices, if you actually connect that many devices, the network's performance is bound to take a beating. As mentioned earlier, in a

PART

III

CH

7

loop topology, even if a section of the loop has high latency, the performance of the entire loop is affected. If you have to configure a loop topology, the ideal number of devices that you connect to a single loop is about 12. If you want to connect a larger number of devices, create separate loops and then link the loops through a switch or hub. However, if you want more than 12 devices in one logical namespace (that is, within one loop), use switches to link the different sections of the loop. This ensures that the loop can contain a number of devices without compromising bandwidth. It is still recommended that the number of devices in such a loop be kept under 50 to ensure that the loop's performance does not deteriorate.

Figure 7.22
Connecting a cluster of different SCSI-based storage devices.

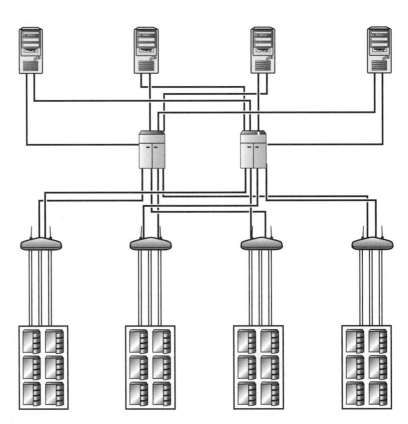

The cable type to be used to connect the different devices also has to be chosen based on what is already available. The basic types of cables can be classified into two groups: copper cables and optical cables.

→ To learn more about different cables, **see** "Types of Primary Cables," **p. 22**

If given a choice, everyone would want to have the backbone of every network on fiber-optic cables. However, because of the number of limitations of fiber-optic cables (in terms of cost and installation), you might have to settle for copper cables. In fact, it actually is simpler to implement copper cables as interconnects because a number of SAN devices provide for only copper interfaces. For simple cost constraints, even some Fibre Channel HBAs and hubs provide for only copper interfaces.

Cabling is an important aspect to consider when designing a SAN, because the speed of a SAN depends to a large extent on the cable and interface (SCSI, Fibre Channel, and so on). Copper cables, however, cannot span long distances.

If you intend to have a section of the network on fiber-optic cables and another on copper cables, ensure that the necessary external media adapters are used to connect the fiber-optic cables to the copper interfaces of the SAN devices.

Note

Some vendors can give you hubs that have a few ports for copper cables and a few for fiber-optic cables.

COST-BASED SAN DESIGN

SANs provide an enormous opportunity for you to create a scalable and fast storage network. You can create a setup that uses the fastest and latest set of storage technologies. Everyone wants to have the best interconnect (which would be a director), the best storage devices (high-end magnetic disk devices), and the best topology with a highly redundant setup. However, all of these might not be feasible for two reasons: They would not exactly suit your requirements, and they would cost you a lot of money, without equivalent returns.

Apart from analyzing what is the best system to implement a SAN technically, you also have to analyze the most cost-effective method of implementation. In an effort to make sure that data is available across the network, large enterprises tend to make multiple copies of the data. The problem with that is the cost of ensuring that all the data is updated and consistent.

The ideal storage solution is one in which storage is consolidated and optimal availability is ensured. What constitutes optimal availability depends, of course, on your requirements. For example, if you need to stream data and do video editing, you would want to deploy a SAN over a network that provides you with a faster mechanism to read and transfer data.

To design an ideal SAN setup that will be technically effective and cost-effective to maintain, you need to do a cost analysis (as in management) and arrive at the most cost-effective alternative that suits your requirements. Note that the emphasis is on an effective system and not on the cheapest system. You need to analyze the cost of ownership over the short and long term.

Note

Although a detailed study of cost of ownership is outside the scope of this book, this section contains some important points that you need to keep in mind while designing your SAN setup.

COST CONTRIBUTORS

The major contributors to the cost of establishing and maintaining a SAN architecture are as follows:

- Equipment: You must purchase the additional hardware and software required to set up a SAN. This includes the interconnects, cables, and other devices to upgrade or modify the existing setup.

- Space: Typically, a SAN is set up to cater to storage needs that exceed 1TB. This requires some floor space for the equipment, power, and so on.

- Management: A SAN is another network—and a special kind, too. Additional manpower is required to oversee and manage it. This also involves training personnel about the nitty-gritty of management.

- Establishment: The cost of setting up a SAN could in some cases be even more than the cost of acquiring the equipment. Designing a SAN also involves test-running the SAN setup to ensure that you can at least revert to the old setup without too much of a hassle.

The cost of creating and maintaining the SAN architecture depends on which features of a SAN you want to implement. For example, if you want a highly scalable SAN setup, your equipment cost could be high. This is because you would have to use switches and directors to provide the ability to expand in the future.

For the ABC company from Case Study 3, a stable and simple SAN is what the company requires. In such cases, making the SAN stable would be expensive, and you would need to provide for redundancy. The cost of other factors is not zero, because you cannot have a SAN working through repeaters and still expect it to be functional and stable. The primary idea here is to identify the area that contributes the most to cost and find an effective way to optimize it.

COST ANALYSIS

The best way to decide on the perfect SAN setup is to analyze the total cost involved in each SAN alternative that can satisfy your organization's basic requirements. The cost of ownership of each alternative is the sum total of the various costs involved, in terms of setting the architecture, the equipment, the personnel, disaster recovery costs, and other indirect costs. The idea is not to pick the cheapest alternative, but to study the different alternatives and pick one that best suits your long-term objectives. To decide on the best alternative for you, you need to analyze various factors and decide on the topology to use and how best to utilize the existing resources. The results of your study will be of no use if you choose an alternative that doesn't satisfy the basic requirements.

Consider HT Industries from Case Study 2, which requires its SAN to be set up at a distant location. The amount of data to be handled is huge—more than 5TB. Even more important is the fact that the storage needs are predicted to almost triple. Added to this is the time constraint, which means that more human resources will be required over a short period.

The alternative for HT Industries could be in terms of the topology it uses. Ideally, HT Industries would adopt either a loop-based topology (as shown in Figure 7.13) or a fabric-based topology (as shown in Figure 7.19). You could even have a mixture of the two topologies to get at the ideal design for HT Industries. The cabling to be used must be fiber-optic or better because of the distance between the locations. The cost of fiber-optic cables compared to an ATM connection is low. However, setting up a fiber-optic connection could be expensive, depending on what is between the locations (bare fields or the city center!).

The selection of each device affects the total cost, so each device must be selected after a cost analysis among similar devices and vendors. SAN's storage capacity is expandable and is only limited by the number of servers and storage devices connected to it. However, in real terms, to have a truly scalable SAN, you need to ensure that the components of a SAN are integrated in a manner that lets you actually scale the storage. The interconnects and interfaces must be capable of supporting additional load and delivering the expected levels of throughput. Therefore, when selecting the devices, you must consider the long-term perspective.

Integrating Storage

There are basically two approaches to storing data: the distributed approach and the centralized approach. The distributed approach to storing data involves multiple copies of data and, in most cases, multiple locations. Consider XYZ.com from Case Study 1, which services members at different locations. Assume that XYZ.com decides to personalize its content for each location (something like what Yahoo.com has done). This would mean presenting the data in different formats, depending on from where you are trying to access their site. If you are connecting from Location A, you would get a different home page than a person accessing the same site from Location B.

Usually, a distributed storage setup is maintained to speed up access to the site. The only snag is that most of the base content emerges from the parent site. This means that the content at Location D must be replicated to the other locations.

The costs involved in maintaining a distributed storage setup are very high. You need multiple storage devices and redundant connections to maintain availability from the redundant storage devices. Your storage architecture would look like Figure 7.23. You would also need more personnel to manage the system. The most expensive element in a distributed setup are the high-speed, high-bandwidth long-distance connections, which involve overhead to maintain consistency among the different locations.

A simpler and more cost-effective method is to consolidate the storage (the centralized approach). Many huge enterprises are now moving to a centralized, consolidated storage management system. In a centralized model, it is easier to share data and still maintain separate segments for different applications.

PART

III

Ch

7

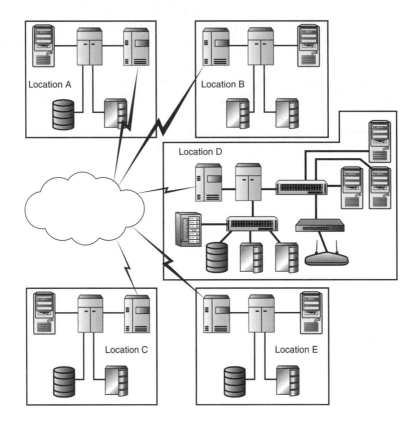

Figure 7.23
A complicated distributed setup alternative for XYZ.com.

The advantages of following a centralized storage management scheme are many:

- You have a common management interface for all the storage tasks across the network.
- It enables high-speed access, because more resources can be pooled at one logical location. Load balancing and sharing are far more efficient than in a distributed model.
- You can control storage utilization more effectively and administer a smoother scaling of the storage resources.
- You can monitor the frequency of access to data and base your decisions on what kind of data is to be on the more expensive storage medium and what can be shifted out.

Before implementing a SAN on your network, be sure to conduct a detailed study of the existing resources and identify the compatibility of the resources with SAN. Ensure that you check with different vendors about the compatibility of the devices with SAN technologies.

RAID SELECTION

Different storage devices and different technologies are involved in each device. Tape devices are still in use but are not used as the medium for primary storage. Tape devices are primarily used to back up large volumes of data. Magnetic disks are the preferred device for primary storage. The problem with magnetic devices is that a drive can fail at any point. It might sound as if magnetic devices are unreliable, but they are stable devices. However, a drive's failure would result in a considerable amount of downtime.

RAID lets you provide a fault-tolerant array of drives.

RAID lets you set up a simplified system to maintain and manage the storage environment. It creates an impression of a combined large storage device from small individual devices. A single large virtual drive is created. This eliminates the need for the operating system to recognize multiple drives. In a RAID implementation, data is generally stored across the different drives. The different levels of RAID offer different levels of redundancy and performance. RAID 0 is the most basic level, which offers no redundancy. This is not a recommended level at which to store data.

→ To learn more about RAID, **see** "Redundant Array of Inexpensive Disks," **p. 42**

The primary issue in implementing RAID is the problem of selecting which RAID level to implement. The best level is one that offers a very high mean time between failures and a low-cost option. Table 7.1 shows a comparative analysis of the different RAID levels you are likely to use when you design your storage area network.

TABLE 7.1   A COMPARATIVE ANALYSIS OF THE DIFFERENT RAID LEVELS AND THEIR APPLICABILITY

RAID Level	Description	When to Use	Disadvantages
0	This level uses a simple level of disk *striping*. Data is stored on all the drives.	The ideal use for this level is when all you want is high throughput at minimum cost.	It offers no redundancy of data.
1	This level uses a simple concept of mirroring. It replicates data on one drive to another.	You can use this level when high availability and high reliability are your prime requirements.	The cost is considerable because you have to provide double the storage capacity.
3	This level uses a parity concept and stores the parity value on a separate drive.	You can use this level in cases where high data transfer rates are required. It costs less than other RAID levels.	The write performance on these drives is low. It is unsuitable for frequent transactions that use small data transfers.
5	This level uses the parity concept. It stores the Parity values across the different drives.	It can provide you with a high read rate and is reliable. It can withstand single drive failures. It is suitable for multiple applications.	The performance of this RAID level goes down when the drive fails.

PART

III

CH

7

RAID Level	Description	When to Use	Disadvantages
TABLE 7.1	**CONTINUED**		
6	The parity information is stored on striped drives, along with the data.	The reliability and read speeds are high. It can be used when high availablity and data security are the requirements.	The costs are high. The write speed is slower than RAID 5.This level is not offered by all vendors.

RAID technology is suitable for even large database operations. The level of redundancy offered by a single virtual disk ensures that your data is protected from drive failures. With present-day high-end storage devices, RAID also lets you hot-swap damaged drives without disrupting the functioning of the network. RAID 5 and RAID 3 are the most popular choices for large databases.

The write speeds of RAID systems have been seen to be slow when software implementation of RAID is adopted. The primary reason for the loss of speed is that the host system must calculate the parity values and perform additional I/O operations to ensure that these values get stored. To eliminate or minimize host processing, fast RAID arrays come with additional hardware such as cache, multiple buses, and striping schemes. The cache on the I/O controller can be used to immediately commit a write as soon as the data is written to the cache. This means that while the drive is processing to write on the disks, the processor assumes that the write job has been executed. A word of caution: Be sure to analyze the requirements carefully. If you're in doubt, contact the vendor.

Note

Given the fact that the method the cache uses determines the speed of data writes, no vendor is likely to divulge such information. Cache on RAID systems could range from anywhere between 16MB and 4GB. This does not necessarily mean that the larger the cache, the faster the speed.

When you have a RAID-based system, especially one with a *write-back cache*, be sure that you have a backup power supply that ensures that the disk cache is kept alive. If the disk array precommits data writes, and a power failure occurs before the actual write, you could lose the entire contents. Some vendors offer disk arrays that have enough power supply to ensure that the contents of the cache are dumped to the disk before shutting down.

SAN is a highly scalable network. However, if you want to add more storage space to the existing setup, ensure that your RAID setup allows you to expand the number of ports through *daisy-chaining*. To ensure that you can manage the RAID devices easily, most vendors let you create Logical Units (LUNs) of the entire RAID system. LUNs are useful to partition the RAID storage space among multiple systems or applications.

→ To learn more about LUN and LUN management, **see** "LUN Host Masking," **p. 226**

SUMMARY

SANs are a technology that is gaining popularity and becoming a part of networks of large enterprises. A storage network's complexity depends on your organization's requirements.

Identifying the different goals of your business is the first step in designing a SAN on your network. The well-known maxim "If it ain't broke, don't fix it" is very true in the case of SANs. Your goals can be classified into business goals and policies, and technical goals and requirements. You need to carefully analyze these to ascertain exactly what you want your SAN setup to do for you.

There are many applications in which SAN can be used. You generally want a SAN setup to consolidate and externalize storage to enable scalability. You can use different SAN topologies on your network. The simplest is a point-to-point connection. You can also use a loop-based topology or a fabric-based topology. When selecting a topology for your organization, be sure to select one that does not have any single points of failure.

You also must ensure that you take the existing network into consideration. An ideal SAN design attempts to make maximum use of the existing storage resources on the network.

The topology you use on your network also depends on how much it will cost you and how much you can spend. You need to do a cost analysis before selecting the topology, components, and SAN design.

When you are designing your SAN, also ensure that you plan for the RAID level that you will implement on the storage devices. This will also help you see the redundancy levels you should plan for.

PRODUCTS ARENA

Media Area Network (MAN) from Grass Valley offers the perfect answer to all your shared storage needs. This company provides you with a real-time, high-availability infrastructure that lets you share more than 40 channels of video and 300 channels of audio. Built on a Fibre Channel-based connection, MAN from Grass Valley gives you a shared RAID-protected storage network that can store thousands of hours of video and audio files. The company states that its architecture can support future applications, such as video streaming over the Internet and interactive television. The product is highly suitable for broadcasters and content and animation creators.

PFC 500/E, another product from the Profile XP series of Grass Valley Group, is a high-performance RAID storage system. It comes with either a 36GB or 73GB Fibre Channel drive. Most critical components are hot-swappable. This product comes with an optional redundant RAID controller to ensure that if one fails, the other can take over. It also comes with a preconfigured RAID level of RAID 3, which is configured as 4 data/1 parity. It also provides you with remote SNMP-based error monitoring and configuring capability.

PART

III

CH

7

IMPLEMENTING STORAGE AREA NETWORKS

In this chapter

SAN IMPLEMENTATION GUIDELINES

SANs are not merely a theoretical concept; it can be implemented in your organization. It is also a technological solution to your storage-related problems, so you need to formulate an implementation plan. Every company or organization has its own set of requirements and networking limitations to a certain extent. The solution of what kind of implementation needs to be adopted by any company is not universally applicable.

Each company, based on its specifications, requires a different implementation solution. On a general scale, a few questions need to be considered before you decide on a feasible implementation. For example, what is the company's current status? What are its requirements and what kinds of developments are anticipated in the near future?

When you are thinking about how to implement a storage area network, you can ask several sets of basic questions:

- Speed: What is the rate at which the data needs to be accessed?
- Sharing: How many servers need to share or access data?
- Distance: What is the distance required between the computers and the storage devices?
- Continuous data availability: Are the computers and databases expected to process 24/7?

IMPLEMENTING BACKUP SOLUTIONS

Backup is a means of duplicating or copying data to a secondary location apart from the original storage device. A backup is generally done for data that is important and that is required for future reference.

Backup started with storage devices such as tapes, which are inexpensive and physically compact and that have high density. The drawbacks associated with tapes are that storing data on tapes can be error-prone, the process of recording or writing data on tapes is slow, and tapes are prone to getting damaged.

In the earlier period of storage, data from mainframes was stored on primary storage devices and was then copied to secondary storage devices. A user couldn't have a number of tape drives, because it was difficult to manage a number of individual tape disks or cartridges. The user was generally provided with a couple of disk drives that he used to obtain data from the disks. Currently, tape drives are being used with the same concept, but the size of the equipment has changed. Tape drives now can store more data, but disk drives have the advantage of being easily accessible, and you can use them to store data that needs to be stored for a long time.

Network administrators still use tape drives, but they have to store all the data on the backup media in the shortest possible period. Tape drives have greatly shrunk in size, and the tape capacity has increased, but the disk drives are still bigger in terms of capacity. In an enterprise network or a large organization, you are likely to use many servers, so disks would be better for backups, because the transfer rate between disks is much faster than tapes. The tape backup process still has its drawbacks, but the density and the length of the tapes are improving.

The larger the organization, the greater the volume of data that needs to be backed up. With companies growing exponentially, the need for backup is directly proportional, but the backup process is time-consuming. Generally, backups could be carried out in the middle of the night, but now, with companies working around the clock, it is increasingly difficult to create a minimum downtime or backup window. The backup process is generally considered to be a tension-filled task that cuts into a network's productive time, but the outcome is beneficial and absolutely necessary if you have a data-centric organization.

In the current situation, with data being available from various sources such as an intranet and the Internet, you have an immeasurable need for storing as well as securing data. LANs have bandwidth congestion, because many clients send requests to access the data stored on the server. SANs come into the picture as a network most appropriate for the enterprise. SANs came to rescue LANs that were expanding to include more users and hence were suffering a plunge in network performance. SANs are constructed so as to consolidate servers such as file and print servers, along with the storage devices, to form a different network. In this manner, SANs relieve LANs from the congestion caused by requests for data sent to the server.

In the current situation, with networks moving toward working in mission-critical environments, there is significant growth in the need for storage, along with a minimum downtime for backups. This minimum downtime also implies that errors in making backups need to be avoided.

SANs also help consolidate hard disk storage, in comparison to assigning individual drives to a specific server and ensuring that the servers can share these disk drives. It is also possible to partition the disk drives so that they can support servers with multiple operating systems.

In the field of tape and disk storage, developers can provide high performance apart from an appreciable increase in the data transfer rate. The implementation of SANs promises an integrated backup architecture that offers the following features:

- The concept of tape mirroring promises reliability in terms of tape backups. A mirroring controller can drive a number of tape units and offer fail-safe solutions during the process of restoring data.

- Servers, when clustered, provide improved availability and performance. To meet the requirements of daily backup, you can use the SCSI multiplexers on a common tape library that is shared among multiple servers. These multiplexers manage the backup operation for the entire cluster without affecting network performance.

- SAN devices also let you make remote backups. With the aid of Fibre Channel, you can create an online link between two devices across locations, which can be separated by a large distance. Consider the use of a Fibre Channel-SCSI bridge to serve as a backup on a tape library at a remote site. The mirroring technique allows you to ensure that

the local and remote backup processes can happen simultaneously, as shown in
Figure 8.1.

Note

Multiplexers are devices that combine multiple signals and then transmit them as one
signal over the transmission medium.

Figure 8.1
Mirroring lets you
automate backups
concurrently at the
local and remote
sites.

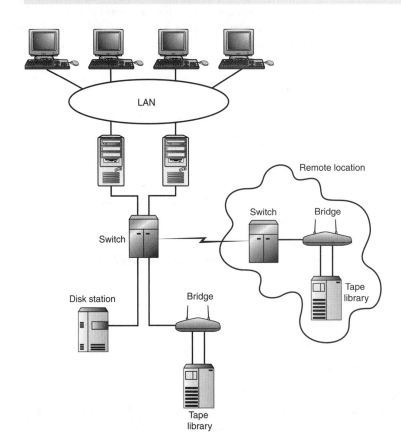

STORAGE AREA NETWORKS FOR BACKUP

The three features just discussed state that SANs provide a suitable backup for networks.
These features let SANs work toward the following plus points:

- The mirroring controller can make use of Fibre Channel bridges to support local and
  remote backups.
- The servers that are a part of a SAN can use a SCSI multiplexer to share a common
  tape library, and the latest devices can benefit from an increase in data transfer rates
  and the tapes' storage capacity.
- SANs succeed in providing an improved performance rate.

Consider the following scenario: A company called Grax Limited has 100 employees. Over a period of five years, the company grows to a large enterprise with 600 employees. Its need for backup also grows proportionately. In such a case, the backup strategy that was created five years ago might no longer be appropriate. You need to change the backup strategy after considering the following conditions:

- The most important factor is the ability to manage the backup process.
- The backup process needs to be automated to ensure ease and simplicity in terms of management.
- The backup process should be scalable enough to be able to adapt with the increase in the need for storage.
- The backup servers as well as the clients need to be easily deployed.

After these conditions are considered, a consolidated backup strategy is to be designed. This backup strategy should attempt to maximize the backup resources and automate the backup. Assuming that the backup needs have grown five-fold and are almost choking your system, you need to ensure that your backup topology is scalable. With the rate at which the company is growing, it seems that you should be planning to make sure that Fibre Channel connections are used to ensure that they can be linked to remote locations if needed.

WHY AND WHEN TO PERFORM A BACKUP

Loss of data, whether significant or insignificant, can happen at any time and in any manner. Data loss can occur in various forms. A printout of program code can be misplaced, the file or document can get corrupted, the floppy disk containing the entire day's work can get infected, or the record can be deleted accidentally or on purpose. The list of reasons for making a backup is endless. The main reason why a backup is important is that when data is lost, especially a large volume of data, it can never be reproduced in the same manner again.

A backup operation should never be left for tomorrow. Neither should you wait for a panic call to begin thinking about backing up. You must be prepared with the right backup technique and ensure its success. Before designing a backup technique, study the volume of data that is currently being generated in the organization, as well the organization's future growth. This study helps you prepare a backup technique for the worst situations, in terms of the need to store a large volume of data. Each enterprise that uses data demands high-speed access as well as reliability with an insignificant downtime. This results in the need for a well-structured backup. You need to implement a system that lets you separate your backup environment from your disaster recovery environment.

In the current environment, manufacturers of the devices used for backups are concentrating more on primary storage devices instead of secondary storage devices. Manufacturers are working on increasing the storage capacity of disks. As far as the development of devices used for SANs is concerned, Fibre Channel products are being given priority, with a 4Gbps Fibre Channel being evolved. With these types of developments, data storage and retrieval are simplified, and there is an increase in bandwidth.

THE BACKUP RETRIEVAL PROCESS

The backup retrieval or restoration process involves copying the data that was backed up to the secondary storage device, such as tape drives, and restoring it to the primary storage devices. This is handy when the primary storage device that originally held the data malfunctions. In such a case, the secondary storage device serves as a "lifesaver" with its backup data.

You can basically put backups into two categories: full and incremental. Consider a situation in which in you create a set of Word documents. At the end of the day, you back up these documents to a central storage system (which could be your server's shared space). The next day, you create more documents and also edit one of the earlier documents. At the end of the day, when you make a backup, all the files are copied to the storage device. This is called a *full backup*. You can alternatively use the *incremental backup* process, in which only new and modified files are copied to the storage device. With incremental backup, the modifications to a file are generally copied to the backed-up version on the storage device.

A full backup, although more secure, consumes more time than an incremental backup. After an incremental backup, the data that is created and stored only on the primary storage device has the risk of being lost. So, if the backup process is not carried out on a 24/7/365 basis, it has the risk of being incomplete.

Consider the example of a bank that carries out a large number of transactions on an hourly basis. If its primary storage devices became corrupted, the bank would rely on the secondary storage devices. However, the risk of not having done a backup for all the data affects the bank's transactions drastically. The only precautionary measure in such cases is to employ the most suitable and reliable primary storage devices, such as high-availability disk arrays, using redundant power supplies, redundant controllers, the RAID technology, and hot spares. (See the section "Hot Spares for Unassigned Drive Groups" for more information on hot spares.)

Another method of data protection is high-speed disk-to-disk copies. In this method, the transfer of data to tapes happens along with the transfer of data to secondary disks, as shown in Figure 8.2. This process involves the copying of data from disk to disk continuously and at a very high speed.

In SAN configurations, a high-end disk array is used as shown in Figure 8.2. The copying of data from disk to disk implies transferring data from the source volume, which is the X RAID system, to the target volume, which is the Y RAID/tape system. To restore data, the content of the target volume can be copied back to the tape with no interference with the working of the source volume. In real-time environments, there is rarely a need to restore backup data in ideal situations. This kind of configuration is ideally suited for the XYZ.com example (introduced in Chapter 9, "Designing Storage Area Networks"), because it ensures that the system can function properly without shutting down. This kind of backup system ensures that you can provide seamless access to the data.

→ To learn more about the example of XYZ.com, **see** "Case Study 1," **p. 162**

Figure 8.2
Disk-to-disk copies
with tape backup.

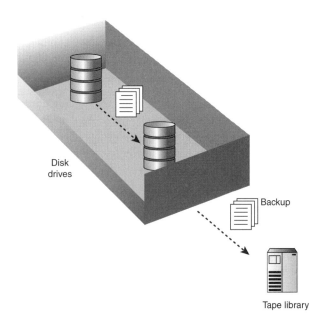

Disk
drives

Backup

Tape library

The loss of data can happen in multiple ways. In the IT environment, loss of data can occur due to hard disk drive corruption, hardware malfunction, or the user's unintended deletion of a program or file.

The volume of data that needs to be stored can vary proportionately with the organization's size. In large enterprises, a greater number of people access the stored data, and the volume of data accessed is also large, in terms of gigabytes to terabytes. The capacity of servers designed for large enterprises is also high. The risk of data loss also increases in parallel with the volume of data that needs to be stored in these enterprise servers.

Data loss is often related to hardware failure. It can also happen when another user intends to destroy data. The Internet is another location where data loss often happens. A number of users hack Web sites and impede access to data or information. With the Internet being used on a global scale, any kind of data loss can be a disaster.

With such risks of losing data, it is a good idea to schedule backups to be carried out regularly. Consider the hypothetical case of HT Industries (introduced in Chapter 9), whose new building will be located at a distance from the main administration building. All data access is distributed between the two locations. In such large-scale enterprise network topologies, it is advisable to do incremental backups every day and do full backups at the end of the week (if needed). This ensures that you do not put a lot of load on the network with backup traffic.

→ To learn more about the example of HT Industries, **see** "Case Study 2," **p. 163**

BACKUP CRITERIA FOR STORAGE AREA NETWORKS

SANs are a feasible solution for enterprises, because it offers better flexibility and capacity, but it has a drawback. Backing up data on SANs is similar to making a backup on conventional storage devices, but SANs have the advantage of storing more data.

You should design a backup process keeping in mind the volume of data that needs to be stored. You must be sure that your backup device has more than enough space. This ensures that in case of modifications or additions to the backed-up files or folders, you can copy them using incremental backup to the same device. In a company such as a software development company, the amount of data used increases on a daily basis, with a corresponding effect on the capacity of the disk drives. The enterprise servers in companies like these will always contain embedded storage in the servers, whether SANs are implemented or not. Increasing disk capacity at all times is not the best idea. This is where SANs play an important role, because SANs are scalable. You can increase SAN scalability by adding JBODs, applying different RAID levels, and attaching disk arrays to SANs. The volume of data that needs to be backed up never stagnates, so you should design your SAN backup strategy with this fact in mind.

In an enterprise, the fact that a large volume of data can be accessed is not the only criterion. The problem that accompanies the process of backing up data is the time taken to back up the data, resulting in machine downtime. SAN aims at bringing the downtime to a minimum (zero downtime is the target). SAN makes use of software and devices allowing disk-to-disk copies to ensure that downtime due to backup processes is reduced.

Another reason why the speed of the backup process is a point of serious consideration is that the speed of processing is also affected by the backup speed. The backup strategies that enable the transfer of data over LANs to the servers and the transfer of data from the attached storage devices to tape libraries over LANs eventually slow down the performance of LANs. For this reason, a LANless backup is preferred. Because the backup process also involves servers, a serverless backup also is preferred. One of the reasons why SANs are preferred for backups instead of DAS is that the task of the network administrators is reduced due to automatic backups. SANs, with the aid of management software, also ensure that the effort involved in making complex backups is less.

Apart from the issues of the volume of data that needs to be backed up and the high speed of the backup process, another issue of importance is reliability. Reliability involves two factors: the backup must be carried out for the entire volume of data that requires a backup, and the write processes to the backup device must not be error-prone. The first factor is achieved by using backup software that increases the storage capacity and that handles storage management issues. The second factor is achieved by making use of a medium that has the least error rate. Few SAN configurations, where the tape write process is performed, can cause problems in terms of reliability. Consider a typical FC-AL-based topology, shown in Figure 8.3.

Figure 8.3
The FC-AL-based topology.

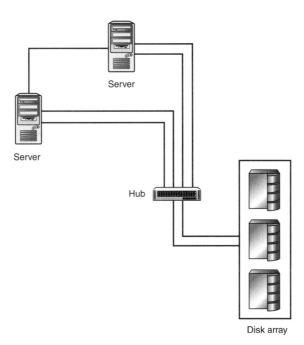

Server

Server

Hub

Disk array

Because this is a loop-based topology, the FC-AL protocol that is used on this topology could prove counterproductive to your backup process. The main reason is that in a loop topology, it is possible that some devices generate a Loop Initialization (LIP) that could cause your backup process to abort. An aborted backup is never trustworthy and might require that you redo the whole backup. The simplest solution to avoid such complications is to use a switch-based topology. This also allows you to make full use of the bandwidth supported by the connection.

SANs, including their components, provide the benefit of working with heterogeneous storage devices. A SAN is suitable in any type of processor environment such as Windows NT, Windows 2000, and HP-UX servers, implying that a SAN can be used in a heterogeneous environment. This suitability does not imply that any particular operating system can carry out the backups for LUNs that are used by a different operating system. (LUN is covered in more detail in the section "LUN Host Masking.")

TYPES OF BACKUP

With the never-ending increase in the volume of data that needs to be backed up, IT and network administrators take care of storage management issues at a high price. They still encounter the problem of storing more and more data at a nonstop rate.

There are two conventional methods of backing up data on a set of clients: distributed backup and centralized backup. In the *distributed backup* method, also known as *local backup*, a backup device is directly attached to every server. In the *centralized backup* method, the backup device is not connected to each machine. Instead, a central backup device is connected to the main machine. The server and the backups for the remaining clients are then directed over the LAN by passing through the server to reach the central backup device.

A third type of backup method is the LANless or LAN-free backup. In this method, a central backup device is attached to a SAN. All the servers attached to a SAN share this backup device.

THE DISTRIBUTED BACKUP METHOD

If a backup device is directly connected to the server, this is the quickest way to back up the server's internal disk drives. The distributed backup configuration uses the concept of distributed architecture, as shown in Figure 8.4.

Figure 8.4
The distributed backup configuration with the backup devices attached directly.

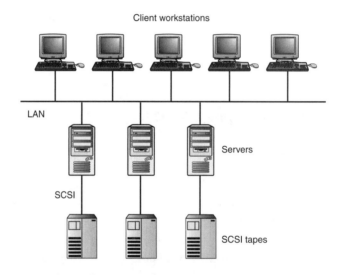

This distributed backup model is most suitable for small network environments. In a small network with few servers, backup can be carried out easily. But as more servers are added, the distributed backup process becomes tedious and creates problems. Also, employing more and more tape drives with the additional servers becomes expensive.

Another area of concern with employing distributed backup is managing the process. The technical person also comes into the picture when the data in the server is more than what a tape can store. The backup operations need to be constantly monitored, and the tapes need to be changed as and when required by the technical person. Considering the monetary angle of using this backup process, the administration costs would sum up to a very large estimate.

THE CENTRALIZED BACKUP METHOD

In the centralized backup method, an IP network serves as a data path with a centralized backup repository, as shown in Figure 8.5.

Figure 8.5
The centralized backup model containing a central data repository in the form of the SCSI tapes.

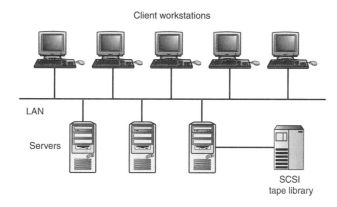

Client workstations

LAN

Servers

SCSI tape library

The difficulty with this kind of backup is that the TCP/IP processing that is related to transferring the complete volume of data consumes the server CPU to the maximum extent. This complete consumption causes the backup cycles to be long enough to go beyond the planned downtime. This results in very poor server performance.

In Figure 8.5, the Ethernet LAN is the means of transport for the backup data. In this method, the data needs to move through two servers before it actually gets transferred to the tape library. This passing of data twice is the centralized backup copy problem.

Ease of management is the main benefit of using the centralized backup method. Multiple backups can also be scheduled by using advanced management products. These backups can be carried out without any operator assistance.

The issues that arise with this backup strategy in a shared LAN environment are poor transfer rates and very low LAN performance. The time taken to back up data is also very high, excluding the incremental backup time. The centralized backup method is most appropriate and cost-effective for network environments in which the LAN load is not very large.

THE STORAGE AREA NETWORK TYPES OF BACKUP METHOD

Conventional backup procedures make use of a structure in which the application server, the backup server, and the LAN are all a part of the data path adopted. As the volume of data to be backed up increases, there is a proportional increase in network resources and the amount of time that needs to be spent performing the backup. With enterprises and companies working round the clock, the time that can be afforded to perform backup at the expense of the server is minimal.

In the SAN type of backup method, the storage process is performed using a dedicated storage network. The SAN-based backup method provides all the management benefits that are offered by the centralized backup method. This method also gains a point on centralized backup by providing a high data transfer rate.

SANs not only increase the efficiency of backup operations but also succeed in performing storage without involving the server. Due to the server's isolation, users can control the storage resources with greater efficiency. The SAN-based configuration is shown in Figure 8.6. The Fibre Channel interconnect is commonly used in SANs.

Figure 8.6
The Fibre Channel SAN-based configuration using bridges to perform LANless backups.

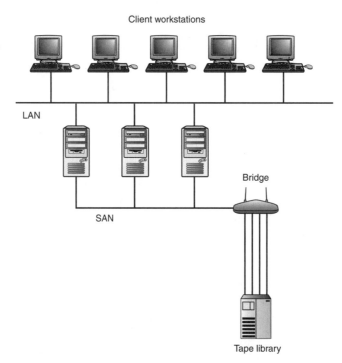

As shown in Figure 8.6, the data is copied from the storage of the internal server and is then written to the tape unit to complete the backup process. In this method, because the data does not travel through two paths, as is the case in a centralized backup topology, the server is not exploited.

Consider the case of a 1GB Fibre Channel that has a data transfer rate of 100MBps. In such a situation, the only area of concern is the tape drive's low transfer rate. The benefit of using a Fibre Channel SAN is that if the number of tape drives in the tape library is increased, the backup speed can be increased substantially. In the scenario just mentioned, it would take you 30 hours to back up 1000GB of storage to a tape that has two drives. If the number of drives in the tape library were increased to six, the time taken would be cut down to almost 10 hours. SANs are considered a cost-effective and time-saving solution, because they remove the load of performing the backup process from the servers—and the LANs.

Note

If you keep adding drives to the tape library, beyond a certain point you will not be able to reduce the total time to back up.

In a LAN-free backup operation, the load of backup data and data retrieval is no longer a part of the LAN, but the administering server is still involved in the flow of data between the backup and storage devices. The LAN-free backup with the help of Fibre Channel carries out backups in an environment where the LAN is congested, without affecting the LAN's performance.

In the serverless type of backup operation, the servers are no longer in the data path and are responsible only for supervising the backup operations, with no involvement in transferring the data, as shown in Figure 8.7.

Figure 8.7
The serverless backup topology.

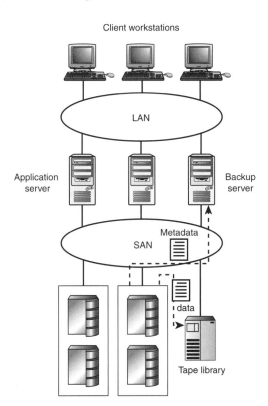

> **Note**
>
> *Metadata* is data about data. It is used to track movement of data or files.

The storage devices ensure that the data is copied directly from disk to disk or disk to tape with the help of the intelligence integrated into the storage devices. This type of intelligence can also be integrated within Fibre Channel switches or Fibre Channel hubs, which are again SAN components.

With LANless and serverless backup techniques, the amount of bandwidth that is provided to the client users during the backup process increases significantly. Serverless backups further enhance the performance value of backup operations by offloading backup administration overhead and easing the task of moving data from the backup server. By making use of these SAN-based techniques, server and network performance are utilized to the fullest extent.

The concept of serverless backup could be best utilized by the example of ABC company introduced in Chapter 7.

→ To learn more about the ABC example, **see** "Case Study 3," **p. 164**

ABC has a small network setup with a minimal number of servers. The company also works on the shift system and therefore cannot afford to shut down its servers to LAN operations. In this kind of situation, serverless backups prove useful. The storage on the RAID subsystem can be transferred to a tape drive through the switch (the interconnect on the SAN setup).

DATA REPLICATION: A SERVERLESS BACKUP TECHNIQUE

Data replication is a way to back up data by using the serverless backup concept. Data replication is the copying and storing of data in different forms. In the IT environment, data replication offers numerous advantages. In a global enterprise, data replication allows multiple copies of the data or information to be stored in different divisions of the enterprise. Typically, organizations such as XYZ.com (Case Study 1 from Chapter 9), which are spread across locations, want to use this concept to maintain local copies of data. This ensures that end-users' seek time is kept to a minimum. A single location or branch could then hold a consolidated backup of all the locations.

Replication of data enables disaster recovery solutions and also enables a correlation between globally spread-out companies with regular updates of their business-critical data. In the world of the Internet, replication ensures that the information on the file server can be copied and distributed. In some cases, replication can also provide the benefit of improving the host's processing speed, because the data can be transferred to the secondary servers for the purpose of backups. The high data availability feature that again works on data replication highlights the currently used SAN architecture.

Data replication (the copying of data from one type of storage system to another or between servers) can be done by different methods. Tapes are the commonly used devices for distributing information, but they are very slow in terms of data access. Replication is generally performed by either storage replication or application-level replication.

STORAGE REPLICATION

Storage replication is the bulk transfer of data as files (or blocks) that belong to one application from one server to another server or to multiple servers (storage devices). The storage replication technique performs replication irrespective of the application it replicates, so it allows multiple applications to run on a server and also allows replication to a secondary server.

APPLICATION-LEVEL REPLICATION

The application replication technique, in contrast to the storage replication technique, works only on a particular application, such as a Web server. This process is performed at the transaction level by the application on its own. In cases where multiple applications are used on a single server, each application requires an application-specific replication.

It is possible to implement remote storage application at the host level or data storage array. With array-based replication, data can be copied from one array to another with the condition that both the disk arrays are of the same type. In a SAN environment, ESCON is one type of channel that is generally used to connect disk arrays and other storage devices. The implementation of host-level storage replication is carried out in the software at the CPU level, with no influence in terms of the disk arrays employed. This type of replication is performed with the help of standard protocols such as TCP/IP across an existing network (such as ATM). Storage replication is implemented in either synchronous or asynchronous mode.

→ To learn more about ESCON, **see** "Enterprise Systems Connection," **p. 81**

SYNCHRONOUS REPLICATION

In synchronous replication mode, the process of writing the data to the target needs to be completed faster because the writing process that is carried out on the host needs to wait until its completion. This increment in speed ensures that data at the target is the replica of the data at the source. The drawback of synchronous replication is that it introduces performance delays at the host, especially when the network connection is slow.

ASYNCHRONOUS REPLICATION

In asynchronous replication mode, the writing process on the source is carried out without the need for a signal of completion from the target. Certain operations make use of both synchronous and asynchronous replication, so that when a communication problem is encountered with synchronous replication, the operation can switch to asynchronous mode and return to synchronous when the communication problem is resolved.

THE APPLICATIONS OF REPLICATION

Storage replication is applicable for different uses. The solution selected varies, based on the organization's replication requirements. These uses can be broadly classified into two functions.

The first function is disaster recovery or off-host processing. Disaster recovery involves the need to maintain an up-to-date copy of mission-critical data at a location apart from the original location. These locations are mostly situated at distant places, and some kind of connectivity is established using WANs. With off-host processing, critical data is transferred to a replicated server. The replicated server is the server that carries out tasks such as reporting and performing backups. You can use these types of operations when the production data is required to be backed up but the performance of the production system is not to be affected.

This kind of processing is ideal for companies such as HT Industries because the disaster recovery setup is at a remote location. Moreover, the processing unit is also located elsewhere. Therefore, to ensure that production does not get affected, you can use this kind of processing to copy data to another storage device and then transfer over Fibre Channel to the tapes at the distant location.

The second function is content distribution. It groups data sharing, data consolidation, and follow-the-sun processing. In *data sharing*, a pool of data is commonly shared by multiple servers. In *data consolidation*, the data is copied from a number of distributed locations to a central location. In *follow-the-sun processing*, multiple copies of critical data are maintained with the idea of supporting a global-scale enterprise.

BACKUP MEDIA CHOICES

When a backup medium needs to be selected for the storage system, the thought that comes to mind is that the volume of data that can be transferred to the tape needs to be very high, and performance should be improved. The volume of data is significant because if much data can be placed on the tapes, the administrator's task of changing tapes frequently is reduced. Of course, this is not exactly true in the case of modern tape drives, which can store up to 120TB. Many people believe that tape devices have no limits on storage.

> **Tip**
>
> The rule of thumb to use is this: The higher the storage, the higher the expense.

In cases where the system must be offline during backups, the demand is for a high data transfer rate. If the backups are performed quicker, the backup window is reduced. This benefit is very significant to a company or organization.

The two types of tape commonly employed are digital linear tape (DLT) and digital audio tape (DAT). Over the years, tape's density and compression rate have been on the rise.

Currently, the capacity of 8mm DAT is scaled to 24 to 28GB native capacity per tape, with a data transfer rate of 2.2 to 4MBps. With compression, DAT can scale up to 40GB. DLT is believed to have a leading edge over DAT in terms of performance and capacity. DLT has a native capacity of nearly 45GB per tape (and 80GB with compression), with a data transfer rate of 6MBps. The transfer rates in the DLT-IV level tapes can reach as high as 12MBps. These factors of measurement are still improving, with the promise of greater capacity and a higher data transfer rate for DLT in the future. Another kind of tape used for backups are Advanced Intelligent Tapes (AIT). AIT has a native capacity of 25-30GB and can scale up to 50-70GB with compression. The sustainable data transfer rates are 6MBps and can reach a peak of up to 12MBps.

A magneto-optical type of backup device or an optical technology-based CD-ROM is becoming popular backup media. However, when the data that needs to be backed up is very large, writable CDs or DVDs become an expensive choice. Nevertheless, the optical media is suitable for environments that require high performance. These devices face a significant increase in terms of their capacity, and the cost per megabyte of storage also differs.

HIERARCHICAL STORAGE MANAGEMENT

The basic crisis faced in terms of data storage is that the data environment continues to increase in volume at an alarming rate. With the unpredictable growth in the volume of data to be stored, at times the hardware employed to store the data is insufficient. The fastest answer to this type of problem is to delete files that don't seem important or to add more storage devices to increase the capacity, but these are temporary solutions and cannot always be used in the long run. A large organization needs to adopt a well-developed and advanced type of storage technology.

You can control data growth by employing the technique of automatic file grooming. In advanced data packages, certain files that are not accessed during a specified period are automatically removed. The backup system removes these files and stores them on multiple tapes that are archived. If a user needs to access these groomed files, they can be manually retrieved. This technique does free some file space, but the users can't be sure which files were removed, and the manual retrieval process involved can be cumbersome.

A more feasible method of data storage is hierarchical storage management (HSM). In HSM, files that are used infrequently or that remain unused for a long time are automatically transferred to secondary and tertiary storage devices. The users are unaware of their files being moved, because the moved files remain listed in the file directory. HSM works on the assumption that if the files remain idle for a long time, they are unlikely to be used. These files are stored in the secondary and tertiary storage systems for an affordable cost. This storage also results in freeing the space in the primary storage system to accommodate more active files.

A number of hardware and software components are required to implement HSM. In terms of hardware, equipment used for secondary storage, such as an optical disc changer or a tape drive with a media changer, is required. A tape drive with media changer is used only when a longer period for retrieval of files is permissible. In most HSM implementations, the secondary storage is not accessed directly by the user. When certain moved files are required, the HSM software communicates with the secondary storage to transfer the required files back to the primary storage system. In cases where an additional backup is required to carry out backups for the primary and secondary storage systems, a tertiary storage system such as a magnetic tape is used.

In terms of storage management, a complex set of operations needs to be performed, so specialized software is used. The HSM application needs to be incorporated securely with the server's operating system. The HSM software also ensures that files moved to a different location are still visible by name to the user and that there is a technique to retrieve these files if required. The HSM software is responsible for storage problems associated with the primary and secondary storage systems.

The implementation of HSM would prove useful in most SAN topologies. It is of particular relevance in companies, such as the fictitious Oil Expo Corporation introduced in Chapter 9, that use RAID-based substrategies. HSM is ideal when you have storage devices of varying capabilities (in terms of speed) or you are connected through different types of cables and connectors.

➔ To learn more about OEC, **see** "Case Study 4," **p. 165**

In the case of OEC, due to the additional storage requirements, the company installed a new storage subsystem to handle the additional load. Because the new device has more capacity and is faster, it would be prudent to make it the primary storage medium. HSM helps you ensure that the data is transparently managed between two devices and thus ensures that the objectives of faster data retrieval and streaming are ensured.

THE BACKUP TOPOLOGIES OF STORAGE AREA NETWORKS

With the tape library in mind, different kinds of topologies are available under SANs, but they have a few restrictions that can be overcome with the change in technologies over time.

One such restriction involves connectivity. In general, most tape libraries are SCSI-based devices. These devices can be incorporated into SANs using Fibre Channel or SCSI bridges.

Note

Even in the so-called native Fibre Channel-enabled types, the tape internally uses a bridge because tape drives are still more or less SCSI-based. However, things are changing. By the time this book is published, you could be using a Fibre Channel-based tape library.

Another restriction involves hubs. Tape libraries are not very functional when connected with an FC-AL hub, but they are well-suited to FC-AL switches. In relation to hubs, the drawback is in terms of bandwidth. FC-AL provides connections up to 126 node ports on the loop. One connection is always present between a pair of ports. Consider that all the loop's active ports share the loop's bandwidth, so each port is given only a small portion of the loop bandwidth.

→ To learn more about Fibre Channel, **see** "What Is Fibre Channel?," **p. 110**

Now consider the Fibre Channel switched-fabric type of topology, in which the ports that are on the fabric make use of the entire bandwidth without the need to share the bandwidth.

The other issue that arises with FC-AL is that it can interfere with the backup process. To explain this point, consider the fact that FC-AL can interrupt the tape backup procedure in a situation when LIP is generated.

Note

Loop Initialization (LIP) is a protocol used in FC-AL networks to initialize the network on power-up or recovery. All the nodes in the network obtain valid addresses on the loop for communication. During a LIP, no data communication can be performed.

To avoid any type of data loss or to recover a command that has failed, you must be prepared in terms of error handling. The backup application software that you use should be able to recover from any change in the loop so as to avoid any backup operation failure. LIPs can occur due to a number of FC-AL activities, such as hot-plugging devices. The creation of LIPs needs to be avoided to the maximum extent, because it can also result in backup failure by causing a SCSI command to fail. When a tape operation fails, the administrator is informed about it by means of the application. An administrator needs to prevent or completely avoid such failures. To do so, the administrator needs to use applications that can bring up error recovery. The following types of backup connections can be employed to result in a stable (system) environment:

- The tape library can be connected directly to the server.
- The tape library can be connected directly to the server using a bridge.
- The tape library can be connected to a hub.
- The tape library can be connected to a fabric switch.

SERVER-TO-TAPE LIBRARY BACKUP

In cases where another server needs to be backed up, the data is transferred from the server through the backup server and then over the LAN, as shown in Figure 8.8.

In LAN's conventional backup method, the data that is stored on embedded disks is moved to the tape library over the LAN connection. The throughput for the backup is slow, and there is bandwidth consumption in terms of the network, resulting in performance bottlenecks.

Consider a backup server connected directly to a tape library using a SCSI interconnect, as shown in Figure 8.9.

Figure 8.8
The backup from the servers to a tape library is performed using the LAN.

Backup server

Tape library

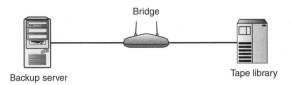

Bridge

Backup server

Tape library

Figure 8.9
A direct backup using a SCSI interconnect and another backup using a Fibre Channel connection.

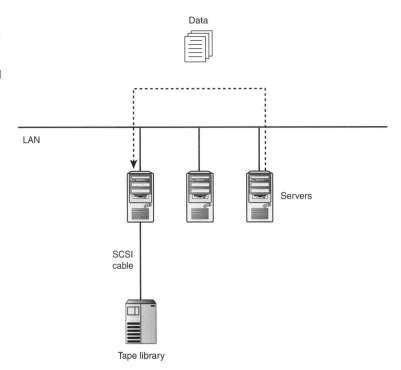

Data

LAN

Servers

SCSI
cable

Tape library

In Figure 8.9, another backup server is connected to a tape library through a Fibre Channel bridge. The Fibre Channel bridge is connected to the backup server, which is placed at a distant location using a Fibre Channel connection. The bridge is then connected to the tape library using a SCSI cable.

STORAGE DEVICE SHARING

Consider a case in which two servers need to access data from a common tape library, as shown in Figure 8.10.

Figure 8.10
Two servers sharing a common tape library using a bridge to perform a LANless backup.

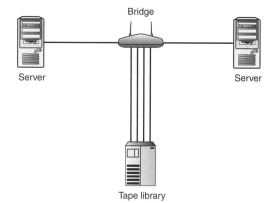

In Figure 8.10, two servers use a Fibre Channel bridge to share a tape library and eventually help you improve the backup. In this kind of setup, both the servers can back up data, and no data moves over the LAN.

> **Note**
>
> The remaining servers that are not using the Fibre Channel bridge are still backed up using the LAN.

Consider the case of Oil Expo Corporation (OEC), which has six servers. If you decide to share a tape library through a dedicated SAN connection (negating all other issues), you need to connect the servers to the tape library. Assuming that you use a Fibre Channel bridge, you need to use three bridges to connect the six servers, as shown in Figure 8.11.

Three pairs of servers are connected to the tape library using one Fibre Channel bridge for each pair.

Consider a case in which the backup is offloaded from the LAN, as shown in Figure 8.12.

The four servers use two Fibre Channel bridges. These servers are also connected to the disk array by a switch or hub. This type of strategy is a high-performance backup solution, and there is no congestion on the LAN.

VAULTING SECONDARY STORAGE DEVICES

Consider the case of HT Industries, whose data center is located at a distance from the main administration building. The disaster recovery site is also located at a distance from the new data center. To connect the new data center to the remote backup location, you would need to use switches to link the locations, as shown in Figure 8.13. The ideal system would be to use broadband connections between the switches connecting the two locations.

Figure 8.11
The six servers of OEC sharing a tape library using three bridges.

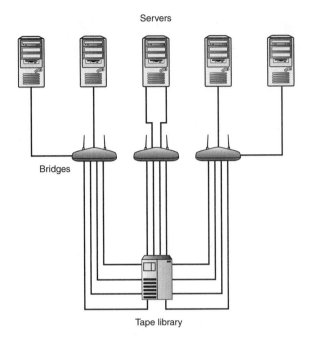

Figure 8.12
The backup offloaded from the LAN due to the SAN connection.

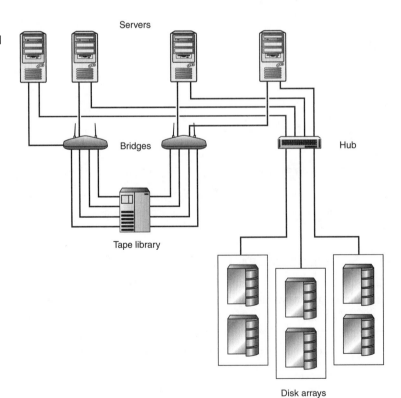

Figure 8.13
The new data center is connected over a large distance to the tape libraries at the remote backup location.

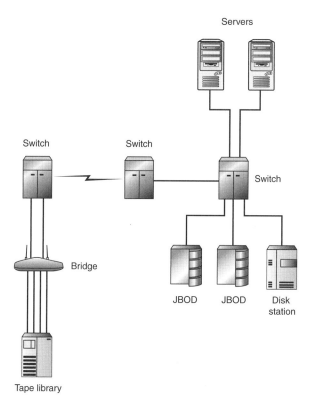

The system of vaulting ensures that you can use maximum bandwidth to cater to exclusive backup needs. All data in the data center can be pushed across the broadband connection to the tape libraries. In case you need some data held natively in the administration building, you can transfer it through the data center to the tape libraries.

> **Note**
>
> This type of arrangement, with the servers in one location and the storage devices in another, is called *vaulting*.

> **Tip**
>
> In such a case, the best course is to copy data from the devices at the data center and then transfer it. This increases the speed of transfers.

ZERO DOWNTIME FOR BACKUP

A high-end disk array can be used to achieve the least downtime that is required for enhancing backups. The zero downtime backup can be considered for a database scenario, as shown in Figure 8.14.

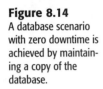

Figure 8.14
A database scenario with zero downtime is achieved by maintaining a copy of the database.

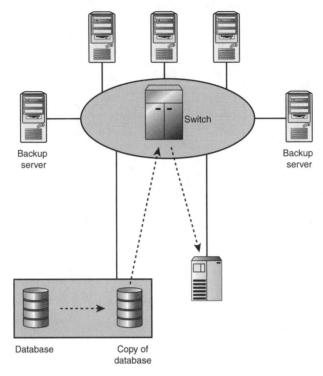

In this type of setup, users can access the data even while the backup process is being carried out. This setup might also reduce the databases' performance loss.

Figure 8.15 shows the comprehensive split-mirror type of backup. The production environment is separated from the backup and recovery environment.

The data from the production database is copied and maintained as another database, from which the data is then copied to the tape library. This kind of setup ensures that a backup is carried out regularly to the copy database without affecting the database applications. Hence, there is no performance degradation for the application. A zero downtime backup can be made possible by following these steps:

1. Put the database in backup mode, and enable a regularly updated copy of the data on the copy database.

2. The mirroring of data needs to be split between the source volume and the target volume by the backup server.

3. After the data is split, the database can be removed from backup mode. When the database is in backup mode, it is still possible for the application to access the data. The only drawback is that performance is reduced slightly during that phase.

4. The backup server can carry out the backup from the copy database.

5. The mirroring can be continued as soon as the backup is complete.

Figure 8.15
The backup environment that provides a separate backup and disaster recovery medium, ensuring zero downtime.

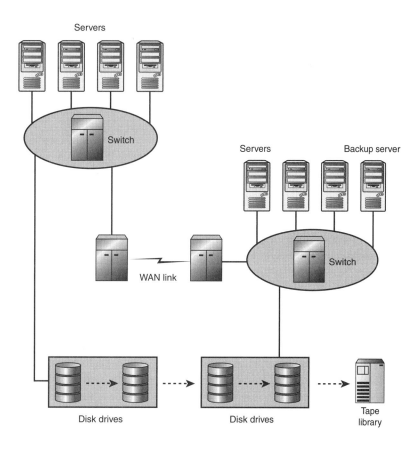

In the disaster recovery method of backup, the software used enables the mirroring of data transactions from the source disks to the target disks. In this type of backup, the target database consists of the copy disks that will serve as the data source for remote locations.

This kind of disaster recovery system works well with companies such as XYZ.com that need to make backups without affecting their functioning. XYZ.com runs 24 hours a day, 7 days a week and is accessed by people across time zones. Shutting down the system to create a backup window or slowing down performance is unacceptable. Therefore, the concept of mirroring ensures that you can back up all critical data from a database that holds replicated information.

The software used ensures that the backup is carried out on disk array 1 at the site of disaster recovery. Full performance along with maximum throughput is obtained by the application situated locally as well as at the remote location.

IMPLEMENTING A HIGH-AVAILABILITY PLAN

SAN technology has gained recognition in terms of being a suitable storage network and also for its deployment in mainstream data centers. With high availability turning out to be a crucial factor, the SAN interconnects carefully-selected technology needs to achieve minimal downtime and a high level of balanced availability of the SAN structure.

The SAN solutions, in terms of high availability, are mainly implemented using interconnects such as 16-port fabric switches and 32-port directors.

RELIABILITY FEATURE

In the case of SANs, the redundancy factor is very important, because SANs are the main connection between the storage devices and servers. If the SAN section is removed from its location and the remaining connections are damaged in some way, the applications will fail. To avoid such a disaster and to provide a high redundancy value, each server and storage device must have two connections to a SAN to ensure that there are no single points of failure. In the case of high-volume traffic, the number of independent connections can be more than two for storage devices. Another essential point is that the backup devices must also have two connections so that the backup operation can be carried out without any interference. The redundancy factor ensures some form of continuity in SAN's physical connections to a certain extent.

In the case of interconnects, directors and fabric switches are the two types of SAN interconnects. A fabric switch offers eight or more ports to connect servers with storage. A fabric switch offers you very few features in terms of redundancy. A director-class switch provides 32 or more ports. They are embedded throughout the fabric design and provide high availability and redundancy features. If SANs are to be designed for the purpose of redundancy, fabric switches and directors are employed to provide availability and reliability in different values.

> **Note**
>
> There are a number of methods in which you can combine switches and directors to suit your requirements. You'll read more about high-availability topologies later in this chapter.

→ To learn more about switches and directors, **see** "Switches," **p. 103**

A director-oriented SAN can offer connections from four to 32 ports or more. A *director* is a type of interconnect that provides built-in redundancy and continuous serviceability of all the components involved. It is possible to increase the port counts by interconnecting a number of directors. Multiple directors do not affect redundancy.

Consider a case in which an essential component of a fabric switch malfunctions. In such a situation, the switch must be replaced completely, causing a drastic downtime. Therefore, multiple fabric switches are utilized to obtain fault tolerance. To avoid such a type of downtime, ensure that each storage device and server is connected to two different switches.

> **Note**
>
> The latest range of switches comes with a lot of functionality, including hot-swappable components.

Now consider a scenario in which each storage device is connected to two fabric switches, and one of the switches fails. In such a case, a different data path through the second switch is adopted, and no connection is broken for the servers or the storage devices. The inter-switch links that connect the multiple switches also need to be redundant to maintain conti-nuity and allow the traffic between the switches. The disadvantages of using ISLs are that the number of switch ports available for connecting the servers is less, and the aggregate bandwidth available for applications is reduced. Another precautionary measure for a failed switch situation is to have a spare switch in order to replace the failed switch immediately.

PERFORMANCE BOTTLENECKS IN STORAGE AREA NETWORKS

Fibre Channel-based SANs initially came into the market with the idea of replacing the SCSI interconnects between the storage devices and CPU. The initial SAN setup lacked management and capacity-planning features.

A director-based SAN has an advantage over a switch-based SAN because of the fact that a director can offer high-speed data throughput to every port and increase performance. Consider a situation in which a three-switch SAN is built with fabric switches (eight-port or 16-port). In this situation, the traffic that is available across the ISLs is reduced to 9Gbps, in comparison to the 30Gbps offered by the attached devices and servers, resulting in a delay to correlate with the remaining SAN devices. This type of delay is known as *blocking*. In this configuration, the assumption is that the corrections are based on 1Gbps Fibre Channel connections. This means that if 10 devices connect to a switch, they represent a total capac-ity of 10Gbps (assuming simultaneous communication from all devices). In the three-switch configuration shown in Figure 8.16, there are nine ISLs, which means a 9Gbps capacity. In contrast to the number of devices supported, this represents one-third of the total capacity. This results in a new delay.

The chance for blocking is minimal, because SANs do not carry a level of sustained traffic flow that might approach blocking. Blocking can occur when a large amount of traffic is directed by the servers and the storage devices across ISLs.

Blocking can have different effects. In some applications, blocking causes an increase in queuing delays that the application might interpret as a device failure.

The problem of interswitch blocking can be overcome by creating a multiswitch configura-tion in which the storage devices and servers can connect to a common switch so that an interswitch blocking will not occur. This type of configuration is complex to design. If a device is changed or removed or a switch fails, the configuration will need another approach. This approach eliminates the advantage of any-to-any connectivity that SANs offer.

THE OBJECTIVES OF HIGH AVAILABILITY

Any crucial data should be stored and backed up. You also need to be able to access the data. The general issue is when a number of users (spread out globally) try to access data simulta-neously and, due to heavy traffic or systems being temporarily unavailable due to some backup process, the users are unable to access the data. This issue is identified as data unavailability in correlation with high downtime.

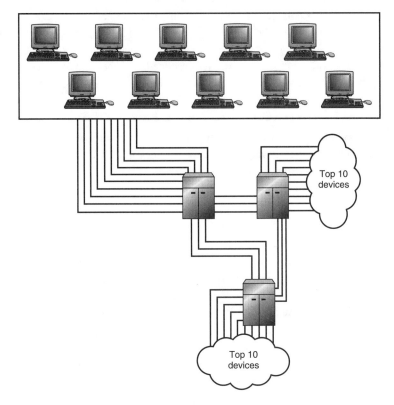

Figure 8.16
A three-switch configuration that could lead to blocking due to ISLs. Note that not all the connections are displayed.

Downtime can prove to be expensive in different ways. Downtime can result in revenue losses for large-scale enterprises that survive on data. For example, a significant amount of downtime on the Internet can affect the field of e-commerce, in which users regularly access the Internet and require updated information. In the arena of businesses that run on computers worldwide, end-users are helpless when they face any amount of downtime. If ATMs are shut down temporarily, customers are unable to perform any kind of transaction. In today's field of tough competition, if suppliers face any kind of problem in delivering their order, there can be a heavy loss in terms of reputation, and share prices can fall. To summarize, the greater the downtime, the less the production in any field, and the more the expenses to overcome the issues.

To overcome data unavailability, use high-availability systems. High-availability systems should be able to meet the following requirements:

- This system needs to provide minimal downtime with the concept of planned maintenance.

- The system needs to be designed so that it is not affected by unpredictable hardware and software failures.
- Finally, the system should be designed to be able to work efficiently during natural calamities, which means that you should have a disaster recovery plan.

In general, a fault-tolerant setup is assumed to be the answer to high-availability needs. The reason is that in a fault-tolerant setup, if a switch or any redundant device fails, work can continue on the alternative set of devices provided to ensure a minimum downtime, as shown in Figure 8.17.

Figure 8.17
A fault-tolerant system with redundant paths for data storage.

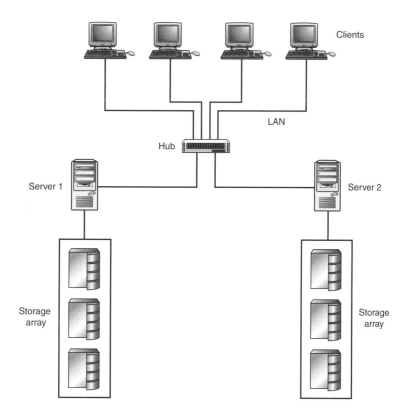

Figure 8.17 shows multiple clients connected to servers 1 and 2 through the hub. Generally, operations are carried out on only one of the servers, while the mirroring of operations is performed on the other. If the active section malfunctions, the secondary system enters the picture. This type of fault-tolerant system is considerably more expensive than systems that offer no redundancy. The risk factors in implementing this type of fault-tolerant systems are as follows:

- The setup (all the equipment) is placed in one location, which actually increases the risk of disaster.

- Due to the fact that these systems are redundant with only one section active, one section is always inactive.
- When some updates from the client need to happen on both the systems, certain complicated software issues might arise.
- In case one of the systems fails, a certain amount of downtime is involved in order to bring the system up-to-date with the other system that is online. This problem results in a drastic increase in maintenance downtime.

These risk factors are related to the initial systems used for high availability. In the current technologies, computers are widespread over remote locations, and data availability is not limited to the central system but is required by all the users who are connected. In the current setup, multiple computers are connected. These computers are not only linked with each other for data but also link with the globally located repository for data. This type of setup led to the usage of SANs for data availability.

The basis of SAN's high-availability design is stated in a few aspects. The high-availability design needs to be implemented throughout the fabric. Another requirement is that the end nodes also need to support the high-availability features.

In terms of the solution design for SANs, the fabric and the nodes need to be one design. You design SAN solutions by trying to solve only a specific problem. When a SAN is designed for specific solutions, the fabric is designed in coordination with the storage devices and the server. In this design, the server and the storage nodes are equidistant from each other. This type of design allows multiple servers to be connected to the same set of storage devices.

SANs promise redundancy in their configurations by ensuring that operations are carried out uninterrupted, even if a connection fails. But SANs need to find a solution to the problem of downtime that occurs when there is performance degradation. SANs are not the ideal solution if true high availability is not fully achieved.

With true high availability, applications can run smoothly even when there are unpredictable operation failures, such as the problem of blocking due to a switch or director failure.

Servers that have redundant connections to SANs make use of path fail-over software that can identify a path failure and ensure that the traffic is offloaded from the broken path and transferred to the other connections. This type of software is not implemented in all types of situations, such as multiple applications operating on the same server simultaneously. Fail-over software requires about 60 to 90 seconds to work on its reconfiguration and to redirect the traffic to a safe path. In this span of time, it is possible that few applications will fail. It is suggested that the path fail-over software be rigidly tested in heterogeneous operating environments before implementation.

Performance degradation in SANs can also occur due to port card failure. The port card is a component within the director that has four SAN cables attached. This is the only nonredundant component. When a port card fails, it affects the four servers attached to it. This in turn reduces SAN throughput by almost 4Gbps, with a downtime of nearly a minute to replace the port card. To avoid this kind of problem, you must ensure that the connections are distributed across more than one port card.

A fabric switch in a SAN is redundant, but its internal active components are not. If one of the internal components fails, the switch needs to be changed (assuming that critical components that are not hot-swappable fail). This changing process has a drastic effect on the storage devices and servers that are connected to the switch. It also affects the servers that follow a data path by passing ISL to that switch. To summarize, a single switch failure affects the working of many servers (causing path fail-overs) apart from limiting access to the storage device that is connected to the failed switch.

Switch failure reduces data throughput and introduces the possibility of blocking, because the traffic is completely loaded on the other functioning ports.

HIGH-AVAILABILITY NETWORKING TOPOLOGIES

High-availability systems can be built on different types of topologies. The shared storage loop is one type of commonly used topology. It is used to attach multiple clients connected over the LAN and across two servers to the storage systems, as shown in Figure 8.18.

Figure 8.18
Clients connected in a shared topology to a common storage system through a Fibre Channel switch.

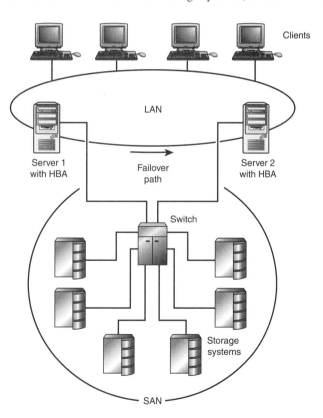

In Figure 8.18, multiple clients are connected over the LAN to both the servers, where HBAs from each server are connected to a common Fibre Channel switch. This switch is then connected over Fibre Channel to the set of storage devices, such as disk arrays. Consider a case in which server 1 fails or the connection between server 1 and the switch is broken. Due to the path fail-over strategy, server 2 takes over the control, and the operation of storage is carried out with the assurance of high availability.

In the shared storage loop, if the sole switch fails, the setup collapses. To overcome this problem, the cascaded storage type of topology is used. In this topology, the setup is similar to the shared storage loop, with the addition of another switch, as shown in Figure 8.19.

Figure 8.19
Two servers connected across two Fibre Channel switches with the switches cascaded.

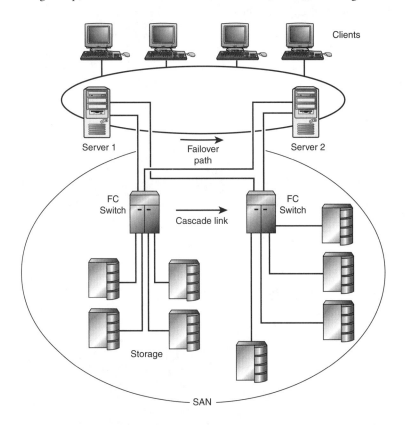

Figure 8.19 depicts the client setup over the LAN and connected to the two servers. The HBAs from these two servers are connected to both the switches, with each switch attached to storage devices across a SAN. The two switches are also attached to each other by means of a cascade link. Consider a scenario in which one of the switches fails. The operations can be carried out through the other switch without any downtime. The cascade links also ensure that both the storage devices are updated through either of the switches.

Clustering in IT terminology refers to connecting a few computers in such a manner that the linked computers function as a single computer. Clustering is another fault-tolerant solution that offers high availability and is suited for load balancing.

In the SAN environment, clustering is generally used to join servers to improve performance. Server clustering also serves as security in the event of any server's failing. This failover strategy works perfectly. Server clustering promises continuity in terms of data availability that is most beneficial to the SAN architecture.

Clustering would be the ideal solution for ABC (Case Study 3 from Chapter 9). Clustering would allow ABC to share the SAN storage across all servers. Each server in the scenario is currently controlling a storage device. All these storage devices can be aggregated to form a SAN, which would enable all the servers to have access to the entire storage space. Therefore, if you implement clustering, the topology of ABC would be as shown in Figure 8.20.

Figure 8.20
The modified topology of ABC after clustering the servers using a hub.

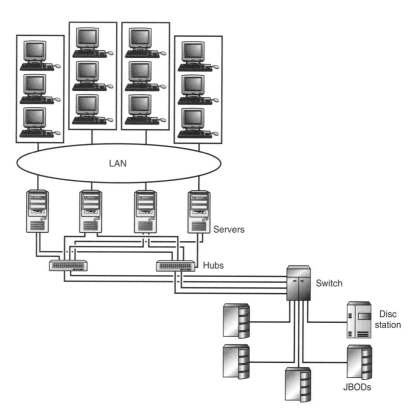

This clustering in a SAN lets you share disks and backup devices and improve scalability in terms of storage resources to offer high availability. Clustering also makes use of specialized fail-over software that provides the solution of using another server when any functioning server fails and requires repair. Server clustering is a suitable choice in terms of disaster recovery. For example, clustered servers spread out globally (in distant locations) can be linked by means of a WAN connection.

VIRTUALIZATION IN STORAGE AREA NETWORKS

Most storage devices (especially JBODs and RAIDs) are made by combining multiple sets of disks. In such cases, you have a number of devices and drives on your SAN. If you attempt to map these drives directly, it is very possible that you could run out of drive letters. You would also need to ensure that you could work out some means to share the total space among the different devices or operating systems. This space-sharing conflict is taken care of by a set of SAN virtualization products. These products combine SAN's physical disks into a pool. The application servers can access this pool without needing to map a number of devices to the SAN.

Five varying techniques share SAN's virtual disk capacity:

- Multihost storage arrays
- Dedicated storage domain servers
- Host-based LUN masking filters
- File system redirectors via outboard metadata controllers
- Specialized in-band virtualization engines

These techniques vary in terms of their application, performance, and price. The efficient utilization of these techniques is decided by the location in the SAN where the technique is to be applied and also according to the platform being used to provide the service.

THE STUDY OF VIRTUALIZATION SCHEMES

The criteria for selecting a virtualization scheme have been outlined. Now it is necessary to study each virtualization scheme and decide which scheme is appropriate under which circumstances.

MULTIHOST STORAGE ARRAYS

In a multihost array, the pooling responsibility is carried out at the storage subsystem level, along with the RAID controller firmware, as shown in Figure 8.21. The benefit of this scheme is that it provides a high level of performance along with high-availability configurations.

The multihost storage array offers connectivity with different hosts, but the disks are available only as a part of the array. The disadvantage of this method is in terms of the restriction over the size of the pool due to the array's enclosures. Adding more pools would result in the risk of losing the centralization and storage allocation option. A number of vendors suggest centralized management for multiple arrays, but multivendor support has its own disadvantages.

Figure 8.21
A common storage array for multiple hosts.

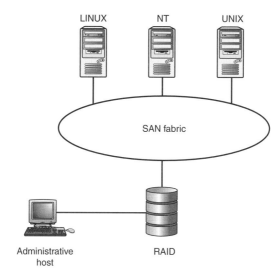

STORAGE DOMAIN SERVERS

A storage domain server is a commercial server platform that is dedicated to allocating disk storage to multiple hosts and to the virtualization of the SAN. The process of virtualization is implemented in software, which runs as a network storage control layer on top of the platform's operating system. The storage domain server is depicted in Figure 8.22.

Figure 8.22
The storage domain server with multiple hosts.

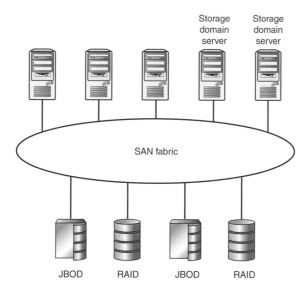

This virtualization enables the control of device interoperability and security features, the networking of the operating system, and volume management. Few storage domain servers are designed to collaborate over a SAN. In such a manner, the centralized administration factor is controlled, and the load as well as management tasks are distributed for a large storage pool. The number of storage domain servers that you need to have on your network and the configurations for I/O performance can be optimized on the basis of the demands or requirements of your topology.

The storage domain servers carry out functions such as in-band performance and load monitoring, remote mirroring services, and optionally performing storage device or host-independent caching to add value to the I/O stream. With these features, it becomes easier to implement serverless and LAN-free backups, disaster recovery programs, and decision support practices carried across the entire storage pool, irrespective of the supplier of the physical storage components. Finally, the outcome is a significant reduction in administrative and upgrade costs, along with a significant *return on investment* (ROI) for the SAN environment.

→   To learn more about in-band management, **see** "In-Band Management," **p. 246**

The specialized virtualization engines relate to storage domain servers, because a number of specialized products are a combination of storage domain servers with additional hardware and software. These specialized products might lack the flexibility of a storage domain server, but they serve as a plug-and-play device and are priced reasonably. Storage domain servers offer the most significant benefits of disk virtualization for SANs, just as network domain servers promise great advancement for LANs.

LUN HOST MASKING

It is possible to enable storage pooling by installing specialized device drivers on each host so that the host is restricted to accessing the storage resources that belong to the other servers. A central management application that is either host-based or an outboard is used to configure the LUN masking drivers, as shown in Figure 8.23.

This option is feasible for small configurations, but it is largely inapplicable in enterprise SANs, where it brings up a lot of complications and is expensive. LUN masking support needs to be spread over multiple server platforms, which is an arduous task for the vendor in terms of maintenance. The compulsion that each host needs to have the LUN masking driver is a problem in terms of performance for the host, indirectly to the network. The main drawback is that a rogue host with improper LUN masking software can overcome the security controls of the shared resources and can eventually end up corrupting the remaining disks that are in the storage pool.

SPECIALIZED IN-BAND VIRTUALIZATION ENGINES

Specialized in-band virtualization engines consolidate the storage allocation and the security functions on dedicated platforms that are present between the physical storage and the hosts—hence the term in-*band*. There is no need for additional software on the host for these virtualization engines. This permits the engine to work with different servers. A varied set of components with different features can be added to this engine. The products that deal with simple storage pooling, along with storage devices and switches, form the virtualization engines, as shown in Figure 8.24. The option of including disks is also available. This is similar to multihost arrays, with the difference being a reasonable price and better flexibility in terms of configuration.

Figure 8.23
Central management with LUN masking.

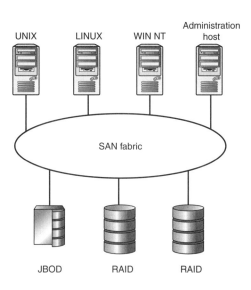

Figure 8.24
Storage pooling with storage devices to form a virtualization engine.

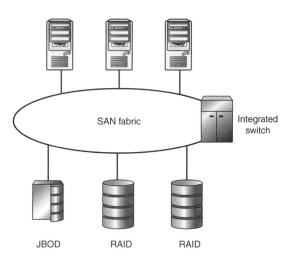

There is a debate over in-band and out-of-band virtualization products. Some people believe that in-band products reduce the speed of data access. Certain storage control suppliers have succeeded in proving that caching and alternative paths, when used, enable high performance and availability. When you use virtualization engines along with RAID arrays and JBODs, you can significantly increase I/O throughput. Configuring alternative paths is a means of achieving continuous availability that helps in implementing storage networks.

Which appliance to choose and how to use in-band virtualization schemes depends on how you implement the concept and how the implementation can cope with the technical challenges. If your implementation is imperfect, there will be single points of failure. An intelligent implementation will provide you with alternative paths and multinode redundancy. If your virtualization solution is weak, performance will decrease as data travels through the product. However, in case of sophisticated solutions, data throughput will improve externally because of the use of robust caching algorithms. These systems also enhance the virtualization of the cache on the storage device (usually disk arrays).

FILE SYSTEM REDIRECTORS VIA METADATA CONTROLLERS

The file system redirector is a type of pooling method in which file access control moves over the LAN, with the disk data I/O traveling over SAN. Each host that is a part of SAN needs software to assist in the mapping of filenames to block addresses with an external metadata controller or file system manager acting as the mediator, as shown in Figure 8.25.

Figure 8.25
File system redirection using a metadata controller.

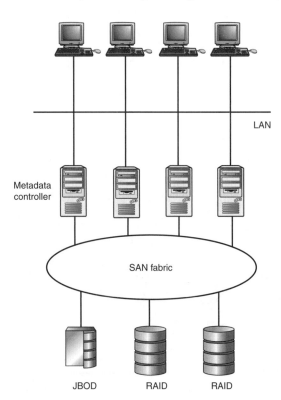

> **Note**
>
> The main purpose of these products is to offload disk I/O traffic from the LANs and not actually enable virtualized storage pooling.

→ To learn more about metadata, **see** "Network Data Management Protocol," **p. 257**

The level of storage abstraction in the design of the redirectors is the reason behind their inclusion as a virtualization scheme. File system redirection, similar to the LUN masking software, is part of a specific operating system, with the need for the components to be installed on each host. The file system redirector is not the perfect answer to storage management and SAN virtualization.

CREATING A LUN

A LUN is a section that represents a certain amount of storage from an assigned drive group. The RAID then portrays the LUN as a physical disk to the host. It is possible to create LUNs by using two different approaches.

> **Note**
>
> An assigned drive group contains disks that are ready to be allocated into LUNs. An unassigned drive group is the set of disks that are a part of a subsystem. This subsystem is the one that has not been assigned to a specific drive group for the purpose of allocation into a LUN.

A new LUN can be created from disks that are a part of the unassigned drive group. This mode enables the creation of a new drive group. It also provides freedom toward specifying the RAID level as well as the number of drives in that group. A new LUN can also be created by allocating the unused space of an existing drive group. In this mode, the RAID level and the number of drives in the drive group cannot be specified. The drive group determines which RAID levels are not specific to a LUN.

You need to consider multiple factors when you decide to create a LUN:

1. Before creating a LUN from an unassigned drive group, ensure that some drives are available in the unassigned drive group.

> **Note**
>
> When the Configuration application is run for the first time, a 10MB LUN is created as the default LUN during the installation phase in some LUN management applications.

2. Select the appropriate RAID level based on the performance requirements and availability. Which RAID level you choose might be affected by the number of drives that are available. Consider the case of RAID 5, which requires a minimum of three disk

drives, while only two drives are available in the unassigned drive group. You need to specify the capacity that is required for the initial LUNs in megabytes.

3. Select the number of LUNs that are needed for the new LUN.

> **Note**
>
> A default value is set for the drives. You can change this value later.

4. Set the value for the number of LUNs that need to be created initially. If a value is not entered, by default, the LUN will occupy the available space in the drive group.

5. Ensure that a value is set for the capacity of the initial LUNs.

6. Select the number of drives. This number needs to equal the number of drives required for the LUNs that was mentioned earlier.

7. Select the required segment size based on the type of data you require.

8. Decide on the specification of the controllers that can access the LUNs.

9. Select the option required to cache the write transactions or to mirror the cache of the other controller. The Cache Without Batteries option decides whether the controller uses the cache while the battery is either not charged or not installed.

10. As soon as you confirm the options selected, the new LUNs are created.

CREATING A LUN FROM A PREVIOUSLY CREATED DRIVE GROUP

A new LUN can be created from an existing drive group using the same steps you followed for an unassigned drive group. It is not possible to select the number of drives that are required to create the LUN and the details regarding which controller has access to the LUNs. The reason is that the settings for the number of drives and controller access are the same as those for the drive group selected.

HOT SPARES FOR UNASSIGNED DRIVE GROUPS

Hot spare is a configuration that keeps a drive for use in case anything goes wrong with the existing drives. If a drive is assigned as a hot spare, that drive is kept reserved and is not used to store data. The main reason for using a hot spare is to replace a malfunctioning disk that is a part of the LUN. When you reserve a hot spare, any drive failures can be resolved immediately, with the advantage of minimizing the period during which the disk array is not fault-tolerant. Hot spares serve as additional protection for the data on the RAID modules.

> **Caution**
>
> Hot spares cannot be used to replace drives that have a capacity greater than their own. If the existing system consists of drives of varying capacities, the LUN must be a drive of greater capacity.

You can allocate a hot spare by following these steps:

1. Select the unassigned drive group for which you want to create a hot spare.
2. Specify the number of spares you want to create.

Tip

The number of spares that you can create is restricted by the number of unassigned drives present in the system.

3. Select the drive that is to be the hot spare.

ALTERING THE DRIVE GROUP AND THE LUN ATTRIBUTES

You can change the characteristics of an existing LUN or drive group using the following methods:

- One option is to change the RAID level, because the LUNs present within the drive group all share the same RAID level. The difference that might occur when you change the RAID level is that the number of available drives in the drive group might vary based on the RAID level.
- The cache parameters can be changed.
- The reconstruction rate that is assigned to the LUNs can be changed for individual LUNs.
- Another option is to change (increase) the number of disks in the drive group. Increasing the number of disks does not increase the capacity of the existing LUN, but it does serve as a benefit for new LUNs to make use of the increased capacity of the drive group.
- It is possible to change the segment size of an individual LUN. A LUN's segment size can be modified only by a factor of 2 per conversion. For example, if you want to increase a segment's size from 64KB to 256KB, you have to increase it to 128KB first and then to 256KB.
- The LUNs of the drive group can be defragmented to increase the total capacity.

Certain features cannot be affected unless a LUN is deleted and re-created, such as changing the LUN capacity and removing certain drives in the drive group.

Note

When you want to modify groups or group capacity, be sure that you select the proper drive group. Select the drives you want, ensuring that the drive you select is the same size as the existing drives in the drive group.

When a LUN is deleted, the data that is stored in it is lost. When all the LUNs in a drive group are deleted, the drives again become a part of the unassigned drive group.

Caution

> If all the LUNs in the RAID module are deleted, it is necessary to create at least one LUN before exiting the configuration. If a LUN is not present, there is a risk of losing communication with the RAID module.

To delete a LUN, you need to open the application and select the LUN you want to delete. As soon as the LUN is deleted, you need to delete the drive. This might involve rebooting the system and rerunning the configuration utilities.

RESETTING THE CONFIGURATION

When you reset the configuration, which happens in extreme cases of complete inaccessibility of the configuration, the RAID module, the drive groups, and the LUNs are reset to the default configuration. You might have to take certain measures when resetting a configuration.

Note

> For an IBM LUN product, the default configuration is a six-drive group with a 10MB LUN.

The deletion of LUNs results in data loss, so you need to back up the data that is present on all the drive groups or LUNs. When LUNs are deleted, the file systems that are mounted on them are also deleted.

All the I/O processes in relation to the RAID module need to be stopped, and there should be no users on the system.

It is not possible to reset a configuration on the module with an independent configuration.

If the storage management software is unable to gain exclusive access to the drive group or LUNs, this operation could fail.

Caution

> Keep in mind that as soon as a configuration is reset, it is not possible to regain the data that was stored on the LUNs.

It is important to note that to complete the configuration, your operating system might have additional requirements to identify the new LUNs. These requirements can include restarting the system and adding drives.

CONDITIONS TO CHECK FOR SOFTWARE SELECTION

You can check certain conditions to help you decide which is the most suitable virtualization software to adopt:

- The amount of independence offered by these products varies, depending on the host's operating system and which file system you are using.

- Consider the range of support that the software can offer for a mixture of storage hardware. The higher the vendor independence, the better the benefits that will be derived.

- Consider the technology's ability to reduce to a minimum losses that occur due to planned and unplanned downtime.

- The protection or flexibility that the software allows should be able to accommodate the legacy storage devices on the network.

- The virtualization scheme should allow you to share the storage resources without compromising on security issues.

- The system should be able to influence the storage devices to ensure improved performance and functionality, but not at a high price.

The main criteria for selecting a virtualized SAN are that it needs to offer high reliability, scalability, and availability. The virtualized SAN needs to serve as the foundation for advanced storage services.

HOST INDEPENDENCE   The virtualization software, provided by the vendors and suppliers, should be suitable for each type of host. Engineers, to qualify the software to be compatible with every operating system, spend a substantial amount of money and effort. This approach is not really feasible, because it is known that across multiple-host environments, the system's version changes frequently. The other issue is that you need IT staff to install the software on each host as well as deal with any technical complexities. Things get difficult for a network administrator every time there is an update or upgrade of the system in a host-based situation.

A MIXTURE OF STORAGE HARDWARE   Vendors generally indicate that interoperability is not a good idea, and that you should buy from a sole vendor. It is easier and less problematic from your viewpoint to purchase products from a single vendor, but this approach is impractical. The reason is that as technologies change, you might realize that your product is not compatible enough with the change.

Ensure that the product you select provides you with the freedom to add any hardware. The main reason for ensuring this is because you might need to make sure you can expand your SAN and connect it with other networks. The simplest method to do this is to ensure that all (or at least most) the Fibre Channel-based devices are compatible with your virtualization scheme.

THE QUESTION OF SECURITY   Host independence and security are interrelated, because the implementation of a security layer for shared access control over a SAN depends on the host-based software and hardware. It is possible for the host to read and write to the disks in the pool; this might result in corrupting data that belongs to other hosts. It is necessary to adopt an *outboard security* implementation, which results in centralizing access control. This implementation is also useful in terms of privacy in the world of e-commerce.

INVESTMENT PROTECTION   A question to put a lot of thought into is whether the current disk is Fibre Channel-compatible. If the system is a combination of interfaces, such as SCSI or SSA drives, the chances of SAN virtualization are much less. Fibre Channel bridges and routers might be a small and complex solution, but at a cost. Buying a product that has built-in support for the existing interfaces would be a suitable alternative. A proper virtualization implementation would ensure that the interface differences are hidden. The host system would not be able to distinguish between a Fibre Channel drive and a SCSI drive and therefore would perform intermittently.

OUTAGE RESILIENCY   It might sound feasible to buy devices in pairs to guard against failure, but this is impractical. The appropriate and practical choice is to buy only one additional piece. For example, if there are 10 units, you can purchase 11 of them, not 20, to serve the purpose of availability and save money.

Note

Not all the virtualization solutions can support this feature. This might result in an unexpected hike in terms of ownership cost.

PRICE WITH PERFORMANCE CONTROL OF THE VIRTUALIZATION PLATFORM   Because the virtualization product needs to be outboarded, the virtualization platform becomes an important factor to consider. In some cases, vendors sell products in which some hardware or software is required to offer virtualization. This factor of additional products increases development costs on the end-user's side. The end-user also needs to face the risk in terms of the system's performance and reliability. A better option for the end-user could be to utilize existing technologies such as processors, operating systems, and storage devices that are cost-effective, easily upgradeable, and easy to work with. It is appropriate to consider these factors and then plan on improving performance, storage capacity, and redundancy, keeping the budget as well as the business requirements in mind.

TASKS INVOLVED IN REMOTE NETWORK MANAGEMENT

You must perform a set of tasks before installing the storage management software. You need to be certain that the components on the network are correctly set up and are in working condition. The controller information that is required to ensure that the software runs properly should be available. The tasks are as follows:

- All the hardware components, such as RAID modules, that you want to connect to the network need to be installed, because the network hardware is preset.
- Choose the hardware Ethernet address for each controller in all the RAID modules that are connected to the network. It is necessary to carry out this task to configure the BOOTP (UNIX) server on the network.

- Fix and record a naming scheme for all the RAID modules, as well as for the controllers in the RAID module that are connected to the network. This naming scheme is helpful when names are assigned to the controllers and host machines.

- Get the IP addresses for each controller in all the RAID modules from the network administrator so that the BOOTP server on the network can be configured and the host can be set up.

- Configure the IP and the hardware addresses on the BOOTP server on the network. This enables the setup of the network address information for the BOOTP server.

- Verify that the TCP/IP protocol is installed and the host table or DNS is set up. This process is necessary to verify whether the Windows machine is configured to be able to access all the controllers over the network.

- Ensure that the components that are connected to the network are powered up so that all the links and devices are set to be operational.

Note

Refer to the Installation Guide that is specific to your hardware components for more information.

The hardware Ethernet address for each controller in all the RAID modules can be referred to only after the power to all these modules is switched off. The address is displayed on the label of each RAID controller.

When a storage management application is run for the first time, the information about the controllers in each RAID module is required to allow the software to identify them. You can determine unique names for each module as well as for the RAID controller.

You can name a RAID module as you choose, but the software has a name restriction of 16 characters. When you do not want to assign a name, the default name of Net Module *xxx* (where *xxx* is a sequential number) is accepted. If you decide to rename the module, it is possible to include the name of the host machine, a unique number, and an indication of its location.

There are no restrictions on names for controllers, but the first eight characters of the name are significant, because the software can display only the first eight characters in its device-name display.

Certain settings are required to configure a BOOTP or a DHCP (Windows NT) server:

- The subnet mask is used to route data packets to the defined subnets. Their format in the BOOTP server uses dot notation, such as sm=2555.255.255.0.

- The router is the IP address of a machine that enables routing of packets to other networks or locations. It uses dot notation, such as gw=8.56.15.3.

- The controller name is the name you assigned to the controller. It uses a character format, such as mach_3x.

- IP address refers to the controller's IP address. It is in dot notation, such as ip=8.45.13.42.
- Ethernet address is the controller's hardware Ethernet address. It is in hexadecimal notation, such as ha=00a0b456574c.
- Tag 164 is the remote management station or RMS tag, which includes a tag along with the IP address of each Windows station where the storage management software is to be installed. The format in BOOTP server is a hexadecimal notation, such as T164=0x45813621.

Note

You can have a maximum of only four remote management and SNMP management stations.

The next step after configuring the DHCP or BOOTP server is to check whether the FC-RSS is on the network. To do so, follow these steps:

1. Install the storage management software on the Windows NT or Windows 95 system.
2. Check whether the Disk Array Monitor Service is functioning.

Tip

In the case of a Windows NT machine, choose Start, Settings, Control Panel. In the Control Panel window, double-click Services, and observe the status of Disk Array Monitor. In the case of a Windows 95 machine, if you move the cursor over an icon in the service tray, you see a message stating that the Disk Array Monitor is running.

3. Add the required number of RAID modules.
4. Enter the names of the RAID modules. If the controller names differ from the IP host-names, you need to use the IP hostnames. If your machine is on an IP subnet that is different from the Fibre Channel-RSS, your machine's IP settings need to be altered to enable searching multiple subnets.

Note

The AIX software makes use of terminologies that vary from the software that is used to configure the FC-RSS under Windows NT, Solaris, and HP-UX. The terminologies assigned for AIX and the renaming are as follows:

Array	Drive Group
FC RAIDiant Disk Array Manager	IBM FC Storage Manager
Spare	Unassigned drive group
Disk Array Controller (DAC)	Fibre Channel-RSS Controller
Disk Array Router (DAR)	Not applicable
Fast load caching	Write cache mirroring

SUMMARY

Having designed the base topology for a SAN, you also need to optimize the design to suit specific backup and high-availability criteria. The backup implementation strategy needs to be in line with the requirements and the current setup of the SAN. Backup begins with tape devices that are still in use. The backup strategy is broadly classified into two types: incremental and full. Different types of backup topologies can be used to implement the backup system. The most important feature of a robust backup system is that it should provide maximum data security without leading to performance drops or network downtime.

While implementing the high-availability setup for your SAN, ensure that you do not overdo the redundancy factor. All high-availability systems should have no single points of failure. Also be sure that the high-availability factor is prevalent throughout the SAN.

SANs adopt storage virtualization to increase the virtual disk capacity. In addition to the virtualization of storage, you can use advanced features such as LUN masking to ensure that data on a pool of disks is adequately secure from unauthorized access.

PRODUCTS ARENA

IBM has introduced a tape library product called the Magstar 3575 Tape Library. The Magstar MP (multipurpose) 3575 family is designed to meet the requirements of network servers and midrange systems. This product is based on the multipath architecture, which enables multihost sharing of homogeneous and heterogeneous systems in user-defined libraries. The Magstar product provides online data access of nearly 6.8TB, and it has two to six drives. This product offers a backup time that is nearly 50% better across a wide industry.

Gadzoox Networks Inc. has introduced the Gadzoox Capellix 2000 series switch product, which enables clustering with SANs. Consider a case in which a two-node cluster is used that enables the addition of servers and storage devices. In a two-node cluster, a Gadzoox Capellix 2000 series stackable SAN switch is the main component of the cluster, with two servers connected to the storage devices through the switch. The Capellix 2000 switch is scalable up to 11 nodes and offers a high-speed connection between the devices. This product offers high-performance storage throughput and can connect distant components (up to 10km).

CHAPTER

9

MANAGING STORAGE AREA NETWORKS

In this chapter

THE WHYS AND HOWS OF SAN MANAGEMENT

In today's world, it is more important to connect to a network and stay connected. To stay connected, you must have available the network's resources, including storage. When you run mission-critical applications and store crucial data, it is not enough to install redundant devices to ensure high availability. It is equally important to manage the network, especially when the network has a high level of redundancy. The primary reason is that because of amazing features such as automatic fail-over, you would never know when a drive or hub has stopped functioning.

AN INTRODUCTION TO SAN MANAGEMENT

The design and implementation of a SAN will not be very effective if these are not backed by efficient SAN management. The vendors of different devices provide SAN management tools. As organizations continue to expand, the number and kinds of devices that make up a SAN will vary. Even a simple setup might have 30 to 40 HBAs connected over different kinds of wires and that follow different technologies to connect. Therefore, you need a management tool that integrates the tasks of management.

SAN management is required to ensure that a common standard can be implemented across the different devices to enable centralized management. SAN management lets you have a truly heterogeneous storage environment that can be managed easily.

A SAN is storage on a network; therefore, SAN management involves a combination of network management and storage management. The SAN management solutions provided by different vendors vary in the manner in which the different components are integrated. More about this is covered later in this chapter.

Data is regarded as the wealth of modern organizations. In such conditions, effective use of data results in profits for the company. This does not mean selling data (although that is a business in itself!), but rather the proper management and study of data to add value to the organization's processes. Consider a typical online shopping portal that deals in many types of products. For such a company, it would not make much sense to simply collect postal addresses and information about visitors and buyers. The company would gain much more if information about buyers' preferences and buying patterns could be trapped.

Centralizing and managing storage in a manner in which the required data can be analyzed is becoming a problem because of nonavailability of many high-end tools required to manage databases. SAN management can help you ensure that data stored in different formats and sources can be collated so that the data analysis software has access to all available data.

DATA ORGANIZATION

Availability and maintenance data for mission-critical applications and tasks can be handled better if data is organized. SAN management is not only about correcting errors but also about adding value to the existing SAN setup. If stored data is structured well, this automatically helps ensure that you do not have too many redundant copies and unnecessary files.

In an organization, there are two perspectives from which data organization must be planned for. At the workstations on the network (with the advent of client/server applications), large amounts of crucial data are being generated across platforms and applications. It is now normal to expect your file servers and database servers to generate huge backup requirements. At the enterprise level, centralizing storage from the distributed isles of information is gaining popularity. What this popularity implies is that the data across platforms and locations would have to be consolidated—and this is a major task. In addition, the data should be managed in a manner that ensures that data reliability and easy access are as high as they were in a traditional data center.

PART
III
CH
9

The key to ensuring that data is organized and consistent is to ensure that there is consistent and reliable data protection. The structure of data storage must be highly scalable. A hierarchical storage system helps ensure that data is organized and traceable. How you ultimately structure your data storage depends on the following factors:

- Storage policy: If your organization has a policy to maintain a distributed storage architecture, the upper division of storage could be in terms of the locations from which storage originates.

- Application-based storage: In case your organization has a number of applications and most storage and backup requirements are generated by the different applications, you can classify the storage according to the application from which the data originates.

- Criticality: You can categorize storage into different sections and store it on different devices according to its importance.

DATA QUALITY

One of the key factors in ensuring improved data management is maintaining the quality of data. Quality of data does not refer to what the data contains (although that is also important) but how accurate it is. In an enterprise network setup, multiple users might want to update the data kept on the centralized storage device. When multiple users attempt to access and modify data, data errors are likely to occur.

The management system must ensure that data writes are controlled in a manner that ensures that data integrity is maintained. Data errors can also occur because of the interaction of various platforms. SAN management tools are available to ensure consistency of data across platforms and control data updating through the deployment of various protocols.

The data entry process must be streamlined to ensure that corrections will not be necessary. In addition, data management methods help ensure data quality and network security. Data can be assigned owners, and those people can be made responsible for ensuring that only valid data gets put on the SAN storage devices. Generally, when people are asked to make a backup, they tend to copy a lot of files that might not be required. In addition, data management helps ensure that replicated versions of files aren't stored on the SAN storage devices.

The function of data owners is only to put required data on the storage devices. The manipulation of the different data to be stored is carried out by another set of people—usually administrators. Data is sorted and managed according to company policy.

You must ensure that the strategy to manage data is fixed after a careful analysis of the network and the requirements. Changes to the data management strategy are more difficult to implement than the most complex data management strategy itself. Having said that, ensure that you leave enough scope to modify your data management strategy, because the one thing that is constant is change. Requirements are bound to change over the years, so ensure that you have a flexible, well-documented plan.

SAN MANAGEMENT STRATEGIES

In a traditional network, the task of storage management has been the forte of the host servers to which the storage devices are connected. In a storage area network, storage is made independent of the servers on the network. Also, storage resources on a SAN are now shared among multiple platforms. This has necessitated that storage management also be made independent of the operating system.

In a traditional setup, the operating system is used to perform only in-band management of the different storage subsystems. SANs are typically meant for high-availability setups, so most SAN management systems provide support for in-band and out-band management.

Note

In-band management is the process of directly communicating management information between the storage and the processor.

Out-band management is the process of communicating management information without completely relying on the topology. You'll read more about in-band and out-band management later in this chapter.

Three main storage subsystems constitute a SAN: servers, infrastructure, and storage devices. The SAN infrastructure, which encompasses the interconnects, provides some information about the state of the SAN devices. The problem is that although some information is good, it's not good enough. Therefore, it is important for the management system to obtain information from the end devices, in addition to the interconnects, to ensure that end-to-end connectivity can be maintained and optimized.

The SAN management system must be capable of making system decisions on the basis of management data being collected. This means that the management system must have a huge knowledge base that lets it make those decisions. This involves collecting low-level system information and analyzing the relationships among the different entities. Analyzing and separating the entities lets the management system decide on the appropriate corrective actions.

The management system handles three basic tasks: failure notification, prediction, and prevention. The SAN management system must be able to notify you of any system or device failure on the network. It is quite possible that you would not notice the failure because of redundant configurations. Most SAN management systems have a simple method to accomplish this. The SAN management system has a display of all the operational devices. If any of the devices fails, the display helps you notice.

However, because disaster management is a costly system of management, you want your management system to be able to predict errors. The management system collects performance information from the different devices on the network. It uses this data to analyze and catch any drops in the device's performance. If the performance of any devices is dropping, the management system notifies you about the problem so that you can replace the component before its additional load falls on the rest of the network.

SAN MANAGEMENT LAYERS

Because a SAN is a heterogeneous storage environment, individual vendor solutions to manage the devices would only add to the problems. The primary reason is that interoperability might become a problem. Storage Networks Industry Association (SNIA) has set up a working group for creating an open standard for storage network management. The Storage Network Management Working Group (SNMWG) is working to define a standard that will ensure reliable transfer of data and management of data and resources.

The task of a storage management system can be broadly classified into five sections, as shown in Figure 9.1.

Figure 9.1
The SAN management layers enable the management of truly heterogeneous environments.

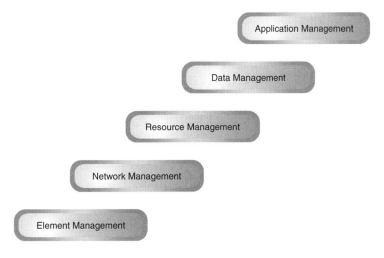

Application Management

Data Management

Resource Management

Network Management

Element Management

APPLICATION MANAGEMENT

An enterprise network has a wide variety of applications that might be running on various platforms. *Application management* is concerned with the availability and performance of the applications running on the network. The purview of application management is that even if devices fail, if the applications can function properly, everything is fine. However, having said that, it is also important that the data be placed in the correct location to enable the application to function properly.

The perspective of the application management console is to allow you to monitor, control, and manage the applications on the network through a consolidated graphical interface. SAN management software such as IBM Tivoli and Gadzoox Ventana let you group related applications and then base decisions on management information from these applications.

DATA MANAGEMENT

Data, the reason why storage management exists, must obviously be managed to ensure its optimal use. Data management is more concerned about the quality of data being delivered and stored. The main function of data management is to ensure that data is available and accessible across the network. Data management also ensures that the way data is stored is secure and that data recovery would be smooth.

The data management layer takes care of certain functions, such as backup and HSM. All movement and management of data originate from this layer. This layer lets you combine the different storage devices, including tapes. The data management system lets you achieve LAN-free and server-free backups.

The data management layer ensures that automated storage management happens on the basis of certain predetermined criteria. The policy-based data management system lets you decide how to distribute your data. In most data management software, you can predetermine the criticality levels of the data that is likely to get stored. This information is used by the data management software to place the data on different devices according to their reliability and availability levels.

Some data managers are intelligent enough to analyze old data that is no longer accessed and move it to cheaper storage devices. The typical concept used here is that of Hierarchical Storage Management (HSM). Server-free data transfers are used to accomplish the required results.

→ To learn more about HSM, **see** "Hierarchical Storage Management," **p. 207**

RESOURCE MANAGEMENT

Resource management is all about managing the different devices in a manner that results in optimal utilization of all resources. In an enterprise network, there are likely to be many interconnects and other resources, such as fabrics. These resources have a panel display attached to them that gives you some basic information about the device's status. However, the devices are likely to be spread across the network; therefore, you would require a system that can be used to centrally manage the resources.

The resource manager provides you with a single console from which you can monitor all the devices that form a part of your SAN. The resource manager maps all the resources on the SAN and provides you with graphical and chart-based information about the different devices and the network's overall performance.

The resource management layer lets you share the devices across different applications. By placing the different devices on one common console, the resource management layer lets you reduce the effort of managing devices on different platforms. Some advanced resource managers also allow the creation of secure connections between disk LUNs and host systems.

The major advantage of using a SAN resource management system is that you can create host-to-LUN masking. In fact, the resource management layer lets you create LUN segments on the disk that form a part of the SAN. The advantage of the resource management layer is that it lets you create LUN masking even on JBODs. With hardware-based LUN masking, you can create LUNs only for RAID-based subsystems. The other problem with hardware-based LUN masking is that it is proprietary to the maker of the devices. This means that LUN masking on an IBM subsystem differs from that on a Legato subsystem.

→ To learn more about LUN and LUN masking, **see** "LUN Host Masking," **p. 226**

NETWORK MANAGEMENT

Networks have become so pervasive that enterprises cannot function if network connections go down. With enterprise networks, things have become so complex that it's becoming more difficult to isolate problems. To ensure that downtime is kept to a minimum, you need to use network management tools.

The same concept is applicable to SANs, where you need to use certain network management tools to ensure that the SAN is always available. The network management layer maps all the physical components of a SAN, gives you a view of the SAN topology, and lets you manage it.

The network management layer performs both in-band and out-band monitoring and management of all the devices attached to a SAN. This information is used to construct the SAN's topology. The network manager lets you create zones and group related entities. The entities do not need to be directly connected devices.

Note

Zoning is the process of logically segmenting the network according to the relationships between the entities. You'll read more about zoning later in this chapter.

The difference between network management and the other management layers seen up to this point is that network management ensures that SAN is available around the clock (if that's a requirement). Optimization of resources from the topology level is the focus of network management. For example, suppose you have a couple of switches on the network as SAN interconnects. Resource management would concentrate on whether the devices are working. Network management would be more concerned with making optimal utilization

PART

III

CH

9

of the resources. This means that if the load on one switch were more than the other, network management would try to balance the load. Crucial decisions about topological and physical changes to the network structure are made on the basis of network management analysis.

ELEMENT MANAGEMENT

Elements in a SAN include disk subsystems, removable media, and interconnects such as switches, hubs, and so on. Vendors of these components provide individual proprietary management consoles. These management consoles can provide only management information about the particular devices. Information about fabrics is not given by interconnects that support the fabric. Fabric management is one of the primary tasks of element management. Two basic techniques are used to manage fabrics: in-band management and out-band management.

IN-BAND MANAGEMENT   In-band management is concerned with the direct transmission of management information between the devices and the management facility. The transmission occurs across the Fibre Channel connection using a protocol called *SCSI Enclosure Services* (SES). In-band management occurs between the storage devices and the switch. In-band management helps the switch obtain crucial topology-based information to help it route information and requests in an intelligent manner. The drawback of in-band management is that if the Fibre Channel connection fails, there is no way to obtain management information. Without information, problem isolation would be a problem in itself, and access to the devices would be lost. The simplest way to address this issue is to have redundant lines configured among the devices and switches.

In-band management lets you query for specific attribute-based information. This allows you to plan your error correction for specific errors and analyze the interdependencies of the different attributes. In-band management occurs over SAN and therefore does not require any additional configurations. Communication with the LAN is not required.

OUT-BAND MANAGEMENT   Out-band management gathers management information over TCP/IP-based connections. SNMP is the protocol used to achieve communication between the devices and the management facility. Out-band management lets you get management information without relying on the fabric topology completely. However, the problem with out-band management is that it does not automatically generate SAN topology mapping.

You would need to use additional MIBs to ensure that out-band management information can be monitored. The problem with the implementation of out-band management is that the devices might not be directly connected to the LAN. However, given all the limitations, it is advisable to use out-band management as well as in-band management. This will ensure that you will always be able to get the required management information to ensure that the network is monitored continuously.

Note

In some cases, certain devices might not support out-band monitoring.

STAGES OF SAN MANAGEMENT

The SAN management process starts before the actual implementation of the SAN on the network and continues until the SAN stays on the network. Device installation and configuration are the first step in SAN management. However, many argue that installation is a part of the implementation process. The installation process is said to be a part of SAN management because the configuration of the devices determines the management strategy to be followed.

SAN management, like any other modern management system, aims to render itself obsolete. That is, the management system is in place to ensure that there is no failure of devices and resultant downtime. However, because electronic devices are the subjects under consideration, it is unlikely that SAN management will be done away with. Therefore, constant monitoring of the devices is required.

A SAN management strategy constantly monitors the devices that constitute a SAN. Here are the stages that the management strategy goes through:

- Resource management deals with monitoring and managing the different devices on a SAN.
- Problem detection deals with monitoring device failures.
- Problem isolation deals with preparing a temporary fix for the problem and identifying the exact cause of the problem.
- Problem diagnosis deals with conducting a detailed study of the factors that led to the problem and solving it.
- Prediction and prevention refer to monitoring the network for deviations in attributes that could signal possible future problems. This is a kind of preventive management.

MANAGING A STORAGE AREA NETWORK AT DIFFERENT LEVELS

Managing a SAN is a crucial factor, ensuring that your storage area network provides you with optimal utilization of resources. This means that you not only need to manage the various processes for which you use a SAN, such as backup, data movement, and data sharing, but you also need to manage the devices that make up the SAN. The management of devices is done from different angles. SAN management is divided into storage-level management, network-level management, and enterprise-level management.

STORAGE-LEVEL MANAGEMENT

SAN storage-level management is concerned with the management of storage resources. The aim of this level of management is to ensure optimal utilization of storage resources. Storage-level management is also concerned with optimizing the connections between the storage subsystems and the hosts or interconnects.

SANs provide you with a highly scalable environment. This means that you can add devices to the network and expand the storage capacity. However, having said that, when you add a device, the network does not automatically recognize it. Generally, in a scalable environment, the storage devices are likely to be a RAID storage system or JBODs. When you add a new device (especially a RAID), the system recognizes that additional storage capacity is being added. However, the file system does not recognize the availability of the additional bytes of storage space. Although the clients and operating system recognize the additional storage space, they do not do anything about it. To make the file system recognize the additional storage space, you need to use a volume and file management system.

Note

If your storage system is comprised of JBODs or you are adding JBODs, you need to use a file management system to ensure that the additional space is utilized.

When a new device is added, you must use the file management system to create new file systems or LUN spaces (in the case of RAID) on the devices or add the devices to existing file systems. Note that in most operating systems, when you attempt to add space to the existing file system, the existing file system must be erased and rewritten. However, modern file system management software lets you add additional space without tampering with the existing file system.

With file and volume management systems, you can segment the storage space according to the different operating systems that the storage system will service. When you add a new device, you can partition or segment it to service different operating system environments.

Note

The storage space on existing and new devices can be segmented to service different operating system environments. However, only the free space on the devices can be used for this. The existing data cannot be reallocated.

Most file and volume management systems also let you modify the RAID levels and create RAID volumes on JBODs, apart from many other functionalities. The file management system also lets you create zones. This topic is covered later in this chapter.

STORAGE PERFORMANCE TUNING

To optimize the storage environment, you need to optimize the components that constitute a SAN. You need to optimize the performance of the interface (Fibre Channel), the cache used by the storage devices, and the disk groups.

If your storage system configuration consists of a single host or switch attached to a single port on the storage subsystem, there will probably be problems in case of Fibre Channel connection or loop failure. The most basic step to ensure that this does not happen is to configure a redundant connection.

Unlike topologies such as token ring and other shared media, the transactions on a Fibre Channel-Arbitrated Loop topology are not transparent to all the devices connected to the loop. You might be wondering, "So what's wrong with that? Isn't that better?" The answer is that this is definitely a better system compared to the token ring topology; however, when it comes to network management, this complicates things a little. In a token ring topology, the token or data packet is sent from the source to the destination device. The destination device copies the data frame and sends it back to the source device to verify the completeness of the data frame received. The advantage of this topology is that the data frame traverses the entire length of the loop and is visible to the other devices on the loop. This lets you "sniff" the message (through the use of management systems) to observe the network traffic.

In the Fibre Channel-Arbitrated Loop topology, the source sends the data frame to the destination, which removes the frame from the loop after saving the data. This means that each port must be monitored and analyzed to troubleshoot any errors. Comprehensive management software is required to ensure that the monitoring and troubleshooting process can happen without adding to the load of each port.

The management system must identify the problem port and remove it from the loop. This would ensure that the rest of the loop could function normally while troubleshooting on the problem port is being carried out. In most arbitrated loop topologies, if a port loses valid signals, it is automatically removed from the loop. However, the management system should also consider other forms of errors, such as invalid Fibre Channel characters. These kinds of errors are more likely. The management system must be able to monitor the port's activities and trigger appropriate actions (which initially in most cases would be to take the port off the loop).

Loop recovery is the most immediate concern when a port goes down. However, bypassing the problem node might not be the ideal solution when the problem node is the center of your activities, such as the RAID storage subsystem. An intelligent management system should also allow you to automate port recovery.

For example, consider a situation in which a port attempts to reinitialize into the loop. The port attempts to stream LIP F8 sequences to get the loop to reinitialize. The port continues to stream the sequence until it joins the loop. This could bring the loop down; therefore, the management system must attempt to initialize the problem port. If the attempt to recover the problem port fails, only then does the management system take the port off the loop. This ensures the automatic recovery and continuous uptime of all the ports and devices.

ZONING

The utilization of the storage subsystem's disk drives needs be optimized. In some storage subsystems, the drives are divided into drive groups. These drive groups are controlled by the controllers. Typically, there are two controllers, with each controller controlling a set of drive groups. Each drive group can be controlled by only one of the two controllers. This implies that one controller could receive a lot more load than the other. Most subsystems come with a management tool that has a LUN balancing tool, which lets you reallocate the drive groups among the different controllers to ensure that the load is balanced.

You can also logically partition the storage devices to cater to different segments of the network. Zoning is not a physical division of the storage network but rather a software-based division. Zoning is a software feature that is used to manage devices on a SAN. You can restrict access to devices by configuring ports that are allowed to access the devices.

Zoning is done for two primary reasons: security of the storage system and ease of management. SAN makes data on the storage devices highly available across the network. However, you might not want all the devices on your network to access all the data on all the devices. Zoning gives you an efficient system to manage and control access to the data. It lets you truly provide for a heterogeneous storage environment, which is still secure. Zoning lets you group devices and storage space on the basis of the operating system platform.

The base components of zoning are

- Zones
- Zone sets
- Default zone
- Zone members

A *zone* is a set of devices that can access each other through port-to-port connections. When you create a zone with a certain number of devices, only those devices are permitted to communicate with each other. This means that a device that is not a member of the zone cannot access devices that belong to the zone.

Consider a situation in which seven servers are connected to four JBODs and two RAID subsystems through a switch (see Figure 9.2). Of the seven servers, two of them (A and B) are Windows NT-based systems. Another two servers (C and D) are Linux-based systems. The remaining servers (E, F, and G) are UNIX-based systems.

You want to group the storage devices on the basis of the operating system they will service, as shown in Figure 9.2. Three zones are configured—Zones A, B, and C. Server A cannot see or communicate with the RAID subsystems, which form a part of Zone C.

Zones can be grouped into zone sets. These help you administer zones easily by allowing you to enable or disable all zones in a zone set. The maximum number of zone sets that you can create is limited, and it varies from product to product.

Note

For example, MC DATA products let you configure and save 16 zone sets. Each zone set can contain a maximum of 256 zones.

In the Figure 9.2 scenario, you can also configure each zone as a zone set. However, in all practical scenarios of an enterprise network, you could have more than three zones, and you would not want to configure each zone also as a zone set. Typically, zone sets are used to combine two or more zones. However, if you have three zone sets (or more), only one zone set can be active at a time.

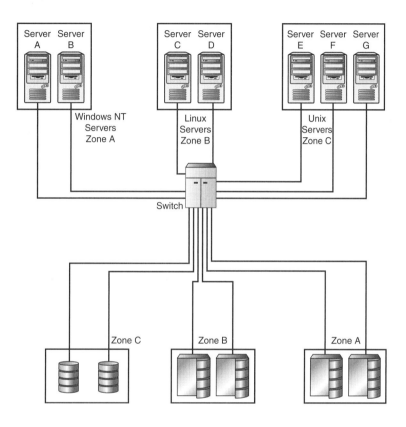

Figure 9.2
The concept of zoning on the basis of the platform to be serviced by the different storage devices enables the different platforms to share the same storage device.

When you enable a particular zone set, all the devices that do not form a part of the zones in the active zone set are included in the default zone. In the Figure 9.2 scenario, if Zone Set A is enabled, the devices under Zone Sets B and C are included in the default zone, as shown in Figure 9.3. The advantage of the default zone is that it can be enabled or disabled separately from the active zone set. This means that while Zone Set A is active, you do not have to shut down or inactivate the remaining ports on the network. The remaining devices would be a port on the default zone, which can also be active. If no zone set is active, all devices are considered to be in the default zone. Ensure that at least one zone set or the default zone is active to allow the devices connected through the director/switch to communicate.

In the Figure 9.2 scenario, assume that the RAID subsystems contain an RDBMS application and database. All users across platforms on the network need to access this database for their operations. This means that the device must be on a port that is a member of every zone on the network, as shown in Figure 9.4.

Figure 9.3
While Zone Set A is active, all devices that are not a part of it are combined to form the default zone.

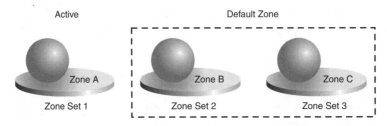

Figure 9.4
The RAID subsystem that contains the database is made a part of every zone to ensure that all the users have access to the database.

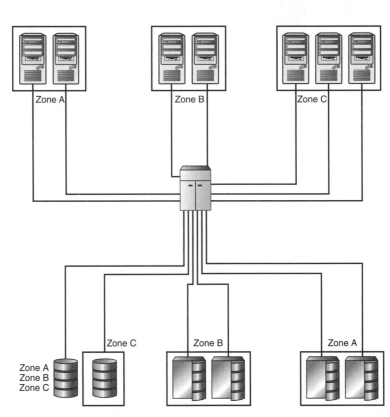

If you also want to ensure that the UNIX-based users and devices are always active, you can include the UNIX zone in both zone sets, as shown in Figure 9.5.

When you add devices or members to the zone, there are two ways in which you can identify the device: by port number or worldwide name (WWN). The port number is the port ID to which the device is connected. WWN refers to a unique 64-bit number that identifies the devices to the switch or director across the network (even global networks). The WWN is a 16-digit number in the form XX:XX:XX:XX:XX:XX:XX:XX.

The method you use to identify the device is crucial in the management of zones. If you use port numbers to identify the devices, you can add a replacement device if the original device fails without having to reconfigure the zones. This is useful when you have a problem. You can attach a temporary device until the hardware or software is sorted out. Typically, such situations are possible only with interconnects such as hubs and repeaters. It is unlikely that you would want to plug in a new JBOD as a replacement for an old one, because it would not contain the data held on the old one.

Figure 9.5
The devices in the UNIX zone (Zone C) will always be activated when either zone set is activated.

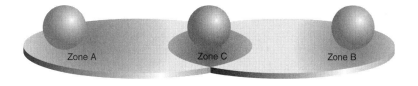

WWN identification is a far more useful way to identify devices, because it identifies the device itself. If you have a device A that belongs to zone B connected to a port X, and you shift the connection to another port Y, you do not have to reconfigure the zones. Furthermore, if you add a new device or move an existing device to port x, it does not automatically become a port of zone A (not unless the device was already part of zone A). You are allowed to use a combination of both name identification systems for members of a zone. In other words, you can refer device A through its port number and device B through WWN and configure both as part of a single zone.

TYPES OF ZONING   As soon as you have planned exactly how you will configure network and device zones, you should identify the type of zoning you want to use. You can choose between soft zoning and hard zoning.

Soft zoning is done using the name server database on the director or switch. This process is also known as *name server zoning*. The name server database stores the devices' port number or WWN. In soft zoning, the device identification method can be mixed, as mentioned before. The only problem (or, rather, the major problem) with soft zoning is that some HBAs do not support it. These HBAs would not abide by the zoning restrictions, and this could result in problems.

In such cases, you must use hard zoning. *Hard zoning* uses a route table to specify the WWNs that are included in a zone. The route table is located in the director or switch. In hard zoning, all devices have to be referenced in the route table and have to pass through the route table. This lets the director or switch regulate the data transfers and validate zones. The problem with hard zoning is that it does not offer you the flexibility of replacing devices. It accepts only WWNs and cannot reference devices through their port numbers.

BENEFITS OF ZONING   Zoning lets you regulate access to devices by configuring logical routes or zones. More than creating zones to limit access to certain devices, you can use zones to restrict nonmembers from accessing the devices on the zone. Zones can also be used to create user subgroups, which can be assigned special access rights. You (as an administrator) can grant specific user subgroups access rights to a specific zone or zones.

Only these users would have rights to access and modify (if permitted) data on the storage device that forms a part of the zone.

Zoning is also used to segment the storage space to cater to the different platforms on the network. In a truly heterogeneous environment, this helps ensure that a Windows NT system cannot alter any information that was stored in a UNIX file system format. The simplest system would be to segment the different storage devices into groups that form a part of a zone created on the basis of the platforms on the network. However, you might not have too many devices. You are more likely to have one or two massive storage subsystems (probably RAID-based systems). Even in such cases, zoning can help you separate storage areas for each zone, as shown in Figure 9.5. This feature, coupled with LUNs, creates a secure system to segregate storage within a subsystem. You would, however, need at least as many controllers as the number of base zone classification (on the basis of platforms) you will have.

Zoning can sometimes prevent you from making network backups across the network. In such cases, you as an administrator can create temporary access to all devices and ensure that enterprise backups can be made. Alternatively, you can configure a new zone set that will group all zones. You can have this disabled by default. Only when you need to make backups, you need to configure or activate the particular zone set.

A PRACTICAL PERSPECTIVE   Consider the organization ABC (Case Study 3 from Chapter 9), which has six servers—three Windows NT-based systems and three UNIX-based systems. The storage resources include a 3TB RAID-based storage subsystem and four JBODs. It also has a TB tape device. All the devices are connected through a high-availability topology, as shown in Figure 9.6.

ABC wants to equally distribute the storage in the RAID subsystem and use JBODs as a database file system. Ideally, you would want to create zones to segregate the ports that connect to the controllers of the RAID subsystem.

To configure a zone, you can go through the network management software, which lets you create, modify, or delete zones. To create a zone, you need to add the members (devices) that are to be a part of the zone. The recommended method in the current scenario would be to use WWNs of each device and perform hard zoning. Hard zoning is recommended because it is safer compared to soft zoning and prevents the UNIX servers from accidentally modifying data on the Windows NT portion of the RAID subsystem. Moreover, it is unlikely that you would want to replace devices on the ports (it is unlikely that you would even want to shift ports). Generally, your management software would display a list of all the WWNs (one for each device or connection) available or connected to your SAN. You can choose the devices and ports that you want to configure as parts of each zone.

Note

The same process is applicable to zone sets, except that you select zones instead of devices. Ensure that when you create zone sets, at least one zone set is activated.

Figure 9.6
The topology of ABC, where servers of the same platform are clustered through hubs to form a true high-availability network.

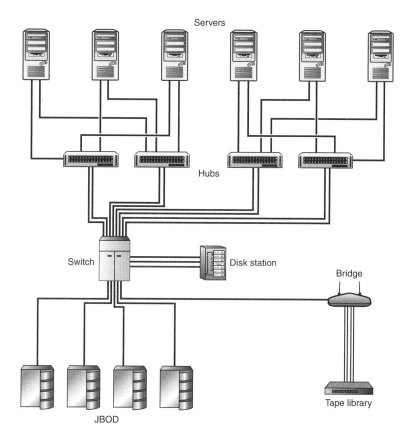

In the preceding scenario, to create a zone for the UNIX systems, you would have to add the WWNs of all the three UNIX servers. You can do this either by selecting the WWNs of the end devices (the servers) or by including the hubs that are used to cluster the servers. You would also need to add the controllers of the RAID subsystem that will monitor the storage space dedicated to the UNIX-based systems.

> **Note**
>
> To ensure that the implementation of zoning is correct and that there is equal alloca-tion (as required), ensure that LUN segmentation is implemented correctly.

→ To learn more about LUN and implementing LUN segmentation, **see** "Altering the Drive Group and the LUN Attributes," **p. 231**

NETWORK-LEVEL MANAGEMENT

In a small network, which often has single-vendor installations, you cannot afford a lot of time to troubleshoot and rectify errors on the SAN. You are also unlikely to have the luxury of having a separate set of networking professionals to manage the SAN setup. In such cases, you would want to set up your SAN in a manner that will allow you to manage it with the least difficulty.

The method to make administration of the network relatively easy is to use protocols and management systems that are commonly used in normal networks (LANs). In most LANs, the TCP/IP protocol is used for communication and SNMP (a part of the TCP/IP suite) is specifically used for network management. However, in a SAN, the connections are based on Fibre Channel connections. The Fibre Channel connection lets you communicate using specific protocols.

→ To learn more about Fibre Channel and its functioning, **see** "What Is Fibre Channel?," **p. 110**

In a Fibre Channel-based connection, it is possible for you to enable support for a number of protocols, because the Fibre Channel header provides protocol information. It is therefore possible to build support for multiple protocols over Fibre Channel connections. The Fibre Channel controllers can then be used to perform segmentation and reassembly of IP datagrams. Standardization already exists for the use of SCSI over Fibre Channel and IP over Fibre Channel.

IP over Fibre Channel is an IETF standard—RFC 2625. According to this standard, each IP datagram is mapped to a single FC sequence. The IP datagrams have their own headers. The Fibre Channel network header is added to the IP datagram to complete the Fibre Channel frame. The frames are then transmitted as one or more frames in a sequence. These frames are received by the destination, which reassembles the IP datagrams from the frames. The IP datagrams are then passed on to the IP module on the network adapter. The Fibre Channel network headers are removed before the transfer to the IP module. Because an IP datagram is fragmented to be transported over Fibre Channel, one interrupt per datagram is sent over Fibre Channel. The use of IP over Fibre Channel lets you manage a SAN in a manner that is similar to managing a LAN.

SIMPLE NETWORK MANAGEMENT PROTOCOL

Simple Network Management Protocol (SNMP) is an IP-based protocol that lets you obtain management information from devices. It is designed to manage a heterogeneous network platform of TCP/IP and IPX-based networks. SNMP has a set of commands that let you get status and parameter information from devices and also set values for the variables. Network management is crucial for an organization to audit and manage its system resources efficiently. SNMP enables management of network computers, routers, bridges, and hubs from a central computer that runs the network management software. SNMP helps you monitor and manage all the components of a SAN (the interconnects, interfaces, and storage devices). SNMP manages the network by using a distributed architecture consisting of management systems and agents.

Most SAN devices come with support for SNMP. The SNMP management system runs SNMP management and agent software. The management system sends information and update requests to an SNMP agent. The agent software responds to information requested by one or more management systems. The SNMP service lets you remotely manage systems and utilize Performance Monitor counters.

The SNMP service is divided into two parts: the management station and the agent. The SNMP management station is the server, which controls the querying of information from the agents. There should be at least one management system for you to be able to use the SNMP service. The management system can either query specific agents or send a general query to all the agents and other servers.

Note

> The SNMP manager is allowed to request information from the SNMP agent. The agent cannot, under normal circumstances, send management information about the devices to the SNMP manager.

The SNMP agent is allowed to send certain critical information to the SNMP manager under specified circumstances. Typically, the SNMP agent sends messages called *trap messages* to the SNMP manager when certain special events occur:

- Link up or link down
- Authentication failure
- System startup or shutdown

Trap messages help you know immediately about any disruption in the normal activity of the devices. You can configure the agents (or, rather, the devices on the SAN) to trigger trap messages. This simplifies the management of a SAN and makes it easy for you to monitor the network.

NETWORK DATA MANAGEMENT PROTOCOL

The main purpose of a SAN is to provide a secure and efficient method to store and manage information on the network. To ensure that management is simplified, you need to centralize it. To do this, you have to centralize the segmentation and control of the information about exactly where and how data is stored (given that it is likely to be distributed across locations and storage devices). The current practice is to adapt the storage management system to the operating systems on the network. This results in layers with a dependency on the operating system.

Network Data Management Protocol (NDMP) is a network-based protocol that lets you communicate without OS dependencies for performing centralized backups. With the independence from operating system restrictions, NDMP lets you centralize backup at enterprise levels, thus creating a truly heterogeneous storage environment.

Intelliguard and Network Appliance pioneered NDMP. Many leading vendors have endorsed NDMP as a powerful protocol that simplifies the management of critical data. NDMP is used as an embedded protocol and therefore separates the data path and the control path. This feature lets you centrally manage backups that could have been locally backed up at different locations.

NDMP provides you with a common interface for controlling the data flow during backups. In a general backup architecture, the backup software controls the data that is being backed up. The backup software maintains a catalog of the data. To implement this architecture, different vendors use different protocols to control the data flow. With NDMP, vendors do not have to incorporate separate interfaces. They can use the common interface provided by NDMP. Furthermore, the interface can be used across platforms. This brings down the total cost of ownership.

The data to be backed up flows from the file system to the backup device directly, over NDMP, regardless of the platform. The control information (metadata) is passed to and from the backup software, as shown in Figure 9.7.

Figure 9.7
Using NDMP to transfer data and metadata using a standardized interface across platforms brings down the total costs.

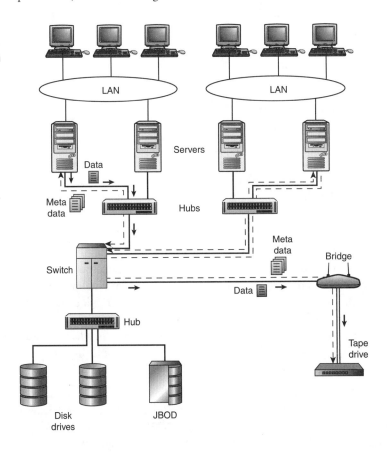

Few vendors currently support NDMP. The NDMP protocol is still not fully deployed in all devices. It was submitted to IETF in October 1996. There have been modifications and improvements to the protocol, and it is still developing.

ENTERPRISE-LEVEL MANAGEMENT

You have seen how to manage the SAN setup at different levels. However, these are the finer points of SAN management. From a truly practical perspective, you need to study and use only the management software that will help you manage a SAN. A typical SAN environment has a number of devices spread out over different locations. When trying to manage an enterprise SAN topology, you need enterprise management tools that can provide you with data in a manner that is easy to understand.

An enterprise SAN topology has multiple SAN devices that contribute status data and other management data to your centralized management application. It is likely that the individual devices are from different vendors and also run their own management applications. The enterprise management system that you will deploy on your network must be capable of collecting management data from each management system (for each device) or directly from the devices and consolidating the data.

PART

III

CH

9

> **Note**
>
> There are several enterprise management system software products, such as the StorWatch family of products from IBM, Unicenter from CA, Openview from HP, and the NetWorker family of products from Legato.

Given that management of actual data is important, it is also important to manage the management data that is a part of every network. Management information on the network is present in various forms and comes from various devices. Consolidating this assortment of information requires the management system to decipher the information available. *Common Interface Model* (CIM) helps the management system integrate data from different management applications. CIM lets you have distributed management of systems and networks.

The advantage of using an enterprise management system is that the total cost of ownership and administration costs are reduced. It lets you automate most management tasks and eases the load on management. It also lets you consolidate the backup platforms on the enterprise network. The most important feature of an enterprise management system is that it transcends the different operating systems to provide a truly platform-independent and consistent management system.

The emergence of Web-based solutions on normal networks (LANs) has also moved into SANs. Industry-wide initiatives are being taken to create a simplified system that lets you truly manage your SAN from a remote location. Web-based enterprise management systems are being created, and a few vendors have already started providing such functionality in their management software. Currently, Web-based enterprise management lets you provide Web access to the managed elements and data.

Enterprise management systems let you standardize backup procedures across platforms. The management system comes with support for a number of platforms and ensures interoperability between the various platforms.

This standardization helps ensure that a single support model for the entire network is created. Enterprise management systems also let you consolidate operations and centralize controls.

Note

NetWorker from Legato provides support for as many as 42 different environments. The number of environments supported by a management system depends on the vendors and additional functionality installed.

SECURITY

In many cases, apart from scalability, the second-most important reason in many organizations for moving to SANs is to ensure data protection. On a small scale, SANs are very safe, but some critics have doubts about SAN's safety in a huge enterprise setup. A SAN is a network that permits many users to access data on storage devices. A security threat to data is perceived, because a SAN is a heterogeneous storage environment.

SANs are relatively well-protected from attackers on the client system on the network, because a SAN does not enable direct client access. Therefore, a SAN is safe as long as the servers connecting to it are not breached. Having said that, past experience tells us that servers, such as application servers or file servers, can be breached if security levels are low.

There are several things you can do to strengthen the basic security levels of your SAN:

- Partition data on the basis of its sensitivity and criticality.
- Secure the SAN management system and software by securing the servers that host those agents.
- Implement switch zoning to segment the storage space on the SAN.
- Implement LUN masking to ensure that even if an attacker enters, he does not have access to all the information or data.

A SAN is a very secure network. Effectively breaching a SAN to cause damage would require the attacker to write some driver-level code. Executing this code from a remote location could be tougher (especially if you are using LUN masking features).

SANs also help secure your network by ensuring that all local and remote systems on the network are properly backed up. Traditional backup utilities back up data on the basis of the operating systems' share access. In most modern enterprise management systems, client software can be used to ensure that complete and reliable data backups are made. In a traditional system, only normal data can be backed up. Critical system and security files cannot be backed up. This creates a problem when you want to restore the system after a crash. The client software ensures that you can back up the entire system and in effect create a mirror image of the system. This lets you restore data quickly.

→ To learn more about enterprise management system software and its applications, **see** "An Introduction to Available SAN Products," **p. 299**

Summary

A SAN is a secure network that is said to require the least management effort. However, because a SAN is a network, it is safer to have a sure management plan that helps you recover from errors and failures quickly. The focus of SAN management is optimizing the settings and handling of data. This helps you make your SAN a fast network and lets you use it to its maximum potential.

In SAN management, as in any network management, you can plan for disaster recovery, failure (or error) recovery, prediction of errors, and prevention of errors. SNMWG has defined a standard for all SAN management systems. According to this standard, there are five management layers or levels:

- Application management
- Data management
- Resource management
- Network management
- Element management

SAN management is basically divided from the perspective from which the management tasks are carried out. There are three broad classifications: storage-level management, network-level management, and enterprise-level management. Storage-level management is concerned with the management of storage devices. Because a SAN is primarily a storage network, optimizing storage is the primary concern of SAN management systems.

Storage performance tuning requires you to ensure that storage devices are available. When you have a heterogeneous environment, it is advisable to use zoning features to ensure that you can segment storage space.

Network-level management deals with the tasks of making management simpler. It attempts to deploy common LAN protocols to simplify management of the network. SNMP and NDMP are the two main protocols that are supposed to make the management of the network simpler.

Enterprise-level management deals with the overall management of an enterprise network. It makes enterprise network management simpler by using management software that gives you a simplified and consolidated method to view and manage all the devices.

Products Arena

In an enterprise network, you need network management software to efficiently manage your SAN. Pathlight's SAN gateway comes with a Pathlight SAN Director, which provides a complete remote management solution for configuring and managing a SAN.

SAN Director provides you with two views: a tree view and a front panel view. The tree view provides you with a consolidated structure that maps the entire set of devices on the network. The front panel view option gives you the real-time status of the LEDs on the front panel of the SAN gateways.

SAN gateways use SNMP as the protocol that is used to implement management, configuration, and remote notification capabilities. The SAN gateways are preconfigured to send trap messages to the server when certain specific events occur, such as reaching the threshold capacity. SAN Director also lets you modify the settings for trap messages and configure additional conditions, if necessary.

CHAPTER 10

The Future of Storage Area Networks

In this chapter

VIRTUAL INTERFACE ARCHITECTURE: THE FUTURE OF COMMUNICATIONS

The earlier chapters dealt with aspects of how SANs are instrumental in reducing the storage load on large networks, which demand high data transfer rates, high reliability, and scalability. This chapter deals with where SANs are headed. It deals with an efficient architecture called the Virtual Interface (VI) architecture. When implemented with storage area networks, VI improves the performance of SANs. This is because the VI architecture is more efficient than the traditional architecture in terms of factors such as bandwidth, latency, and host processing load.

In the traditional network architecture, the operating system (OS) logically divides the network hardware into a set of logical communication endpoints that are available to the network's consumers. Access to the hardware is multiplexed among these endpoints. The operating system performs this multiplexing. Mostly, the operating system also implements protocols that make communication between connected endpoints dependable. The shortcoming of this organization is that all communication operations require a call to the operating system kernel. This might be quite expensive to execute.

Note The process of *multiplexing* involves combining multiple signals to transmit over a single line or medium.

THE NEED FOR A CHANGE IN THE TRADITIONAL ARCHITECTURE

Traditional network architectures do not provide the performance required by distributed applications, which require fast and stable exchange of information across a network to synchronize operations and to share data. This constraint in the traditional network architecture is mainly due to the host-processing overhead of *kernel-based transport stacks*. This processing overhead has a negative performance impact in terms of bandwidth, latency and synchronization, and host processing load.

The overhead restricts the actual bandwidth that a given network can provide. Although network hardware bandwidths are increasing, the software overhead in available networking stacks is relatively constant. In order for distributed and network-based applications to be *scalable*, good synchronization is required. The overhead causes latency of messages used for synchronization. The overhead uses CPU cycles that could be used for other processing.

The VI architecture addresses these constraints by increasing the sustainable bandwidth between servers, workstations, and storage devices. It also lets applications perform most data transfer operations without the involvement of the host CPU. As a consequence, there is a significant reduction in processing overhead along the communication paths that are vital to performance.

Thus, because of the advantages that the VI architecture offers, it is gaining importance as the most sought-after interconnect mechanism that links servers in high-performance

SANs. The result of a number of proof-of-concept trials conducted by Intel only reiterates this fact. According to these trials, there is a significant reduction in message latency as well as an enormous increase in sustained bandwidth.

VI ARCHITECTURE

The VI architecture is a design in which the system software processing for exchanging messages is considerably reduced compared to traditional network interface architectures. The purpose of this architecture is to improve the functioning of distributed applications. Reducing the *latency* associated with critical message-passing operations does this.

ORIGINATION OF THE VI ARCHITECTURE

A number of industry-leading companies, such as Compaq Computer Corporation, Intel Corporation, and Microsoft Corporation, jointly specified the VI architecture. The VI architecture defines mechanisms to ensure low-latency, high-bandwidth message passing between interconnected nodes. Low latency and persistent high bandwidth are achieved by avoiding intermediary copies of data and bypassing the operating system when sending and receiving messages.

Existing LAN and WAN standards cannot address the requirement of interconnecting a group of servers, workstations, and I/O devices as a scalable computing cluster. VI was created to speed up the development and lower the cost of clustered servers, workstations, and I/O devices. Cluster area networks have distinct characteristics, such as short-distance, high-performance interprocess communications (IPCs) between multiple building blocks such as servers, workstations, and I/O subsystems connected directly to the network.

> **Note**
>
> *Clustering* is the process of connecting two or more computers in such a way that they behave like a single computer. Clustering is used for parallel processing, load balancing, and fault tolerance.

The VI architecture ensures the delivery of cost-effective, high-performance cluster solutions to end-users.

OVERVIEW OF VI ARCHITECTURE FUNCTIONS

The VI architecture excludes the system-processing overhead of the traditional model by giving each consumer process a protected and directly accessible interface to the network hardware. This is the Virtual Interface. Each communication endpoint, or network hardware, is represented by a VI. VI endpoint pairs can be logically connected to enable data transfer. The data transfer can be bidirectional or point-to-point in nature. It is possible for a process to own multiple VIs exported by one or more network adapters. A network adapter carries out the task of endpoint virtualization directly. It takes over the tasks of multiplexing, demultiplexing, and data transfer scheduling normally performed by an OS kernel and device driver. An adapter might completely ensure that the communication between connected VIs is reliable. The transport protocol software loaded into the application process can share this task.

COMPONENTS OF THE VI ARCHITECTURE

The VI architecture is comprised of four basic components: Virtual Interfaces, Completion queues, VI Providers, and VI Consumers. The organization of these components is illustrated in Figure 10.1.

Figure 10.1
The VI architecture model is organized in the form of the four basic components.

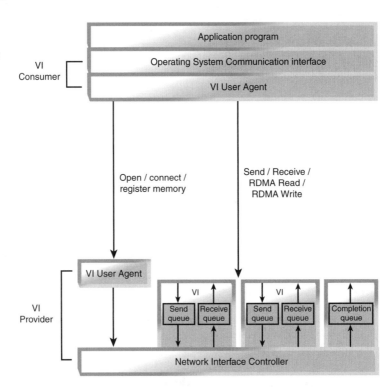

Each of these components is covered in detail in this chapter.

THE ROLE OF VI

A Virtual Interface is the mechanism by which a VI Consumer is permitted to directly access a VI Provider to perform data transfer operations. Figure 10.2 illustrates a Virtual Interface.

A VI comprises of a pair of Work queues, which include a Send queue and a Receive queue. VI Consumers post requests on the Work queues to send or receive data. These requests are in the form of Descriptors.

Figure 10.2
A Virtual Interface comprises the VI Provider and VI Consumer.

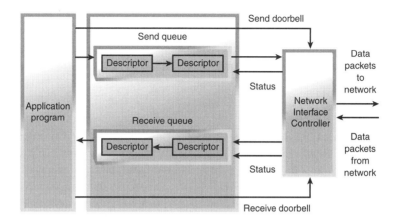

> **Note**
>
> A *Descriptor* is a memory structure that contains all the information that the VI Provider needs to process the request, such as pointers to data buffers.

VI Providers execute the posted Descriptors asynchronously. As soon as the execution is completed, the VI Providers mark the Descriptors with a status value. VI Consumers eliminate the completed Descriptors from the Work queues and use them for further requests. Each Work queue has a Doorbell associated with it. A Doorbell is used to inform the VI network adapter of a new Descriptor sent to a Work queue.

> **Note**
>
> A *Doorbell* is a mechanism used by a process to notify the Virtual Interface Network Interface Controller (VI NIC) that work has been placed on a Work queue.

The adapter directly implements the Doorbell. The adapter does not require any intervention from the operating system to operate. A Completion queue permits a VI Consumer to combine notification of Descriptor completions from the Work queues of multiple VIs in a single place. Completion queues are discussed in more detail later in this chapter.

THE ROLE OF VI PROVIDER

VI Provider is the set of hardware and software components that is in charge of instantiating a Virtual Interface. The VI Provider comprises a Network Interface Controller (NIC) and a Kernel Agent.

The VI NIC implements the Virtual Interfaces and Completion queues. It also directly carries out the functions of data transfer. The Kernel Agent is a driver that performs the setup and resource management functions needed to maintain a Virtual Interface between VI Consumers and VI NICs. These functions include the creation and destruction of VIs, VI connection setup and termination, interrupt management, interrupt processing, management of system memory used by the VI NIC, and error handling. VI Consumers use standard operating system mechanisms such as system calls to access the Kernel Agent. Kernel Agents interact with VI NICs by means of standard operating system device management mechanisms.

THE ROLE OF VI CONSUMER

VI Consumer refers to any user of a Virtual Interface. The VI Consumer is usually composed of an application and an operating system communication facility, such as Sockets, MPI, and so on. The operating system communication facility enables communication between the different processes and among the multicomputing clusters. An application is the final consumer of communication services. Applications access these services by using standard operating system programming interfaces such as Sockets and MPI. The OS facility is usually implemented as a library that is loaded into the application process. The OS facility makes system calls to the Kernel Agent to establish a connection between a local system and a remote system. This is done by creating a VI on the local system and connecting it to a VI on a remote system. When a connection is established, the OS facility sends the application's send and receive requests directly to the VI of the local system. The data transfer mechanism is discussed more in a moment.

The OS communication facility often loads a library that encapsulates the details of the underlying communication provider. In the case under consideration, the underlying communication provider is the VI and Kernel Agent. This component is shown as the VI User Agent in Figure 10.1.

REGISTERING MEMORY

In the case of traditional network transports, on every data transfer request, memory pages used to hold messages are locked down until the data transfer is complete. Also, the virtual addresses of the memory pages are translated into physical locations before a NIC can access them. This processing adds substantial overhead to the data transfer operation.

In the VI architecture, the VI Consumer is required to identify memory used for a data transfer even before a request is submitted. Only the memory that has been registered with the VI Provider can be used for data transfers. It is because of this memory registration process that the VI Consumer can reuse registered memory buffers. As a result, duplication of locking and translation operations is avoided. In addition to this, memory registration eliminates processing overhead from the data transfer path that is performance-critical.

In general, copies of data and management of buffers are a large component of overhead in communication and consume memory bandwidth. This problem is avoided when it comes to the VI architecture. Due to the memory registration, it is possible for the VI Provider to transfer data directly between the buffers of a VI Consumer and the network. Thus, copying any data to or from intermediate buffers is avoided. But this process of copying data between user buffers and intermediate kernel buffers happens in traditional network transports.

Memory registration involves the locking of pages of a virtually contiguous memory region into physical memory. It also involves providing the virtual-to-physical translations to the VI NIC. For every memory region registered, the VI Consumer gets an opaque handle. The VI Consumer can reference all registered memory by its virtual address and the handle associated with it.

MODELS OF DATA TRANSFER

Two types of data transfer facilities are offered by the VI architecture—the traditional Send/Receive messaging model and the Remote Direct Memory Access (RDMA) model.

THE SEND/RECEIVE MODEL

The Send/Receive model of the VI architecture follows a popular model of transferring data between two endpoints. In this model, the VI Consumer that is on the local node specifies the location of the data at all times. The memory regions that contain the data to be sent are specified by the sending process. The receiving process specifies the memory regions where the data will be placed. When there is a single connection, there is a one-to-one correspondence between send Descriptors on the transmitting side and receive Descriptors on the receiving side.

PART
III

CH
10

A Descriptor to the receive queue of a VI is preposted by the VI Consumer at the receiving end. After this, the VI Consumer at the sending end can post the message to the corresponding VI's send queue. In case of this Send/Receive model of data transfer, the VI Consumers need to be notified of the Descriptor completion at both ends of the transfer for synchronization purposes.

VI Consumers control flow on a connection. Even before the sender's data can arrive, the VI Consumer on the receiving side must post a Receive Descriptor of sufficient size. An error occurs if the Receive Descriptor at the head of the queue is not large enough to handle the incoming message or if the Receive queue is empty. If the connection is intended to be reliable, it might be broken. You will read about reliability levels in a few minutes.

THE REMOTE DIRECT MEMORY ACCESS MODEL

The source buffer and destination buffer of the data transfer are both specified by the initiator of the data transfer. There are two types of RDMA operations—RDMA Write and RDMA Read.

For the RDMA Write operation, the VI Consumer specifies the data transfer's source and destination. The source of the data transfer is specified in one of its local registered memory regions, and the destination of the data transfer is specified within a remote memory region that has been registered on the remote system. It is allowed to specify the source of an RDMA Write operation as a list of buffers that could be spread across noncontiguous regions. But the destination should necessarily be a single, virtually contiguous region. The implication in the RDMA Write operation is that even before a data transfer can happen, the VI Consumer at the remote end informs the initiator of the RDMA Write of the destination buffer's location. It is also implied that the buffer itself is RDMA Write-enabled. Its virtual address and the memory handle associated with it specify the remote location of the data.

Even for the RDMA Read operation, both source and destination are specified. The VI Consumer specifies the source of the data transfer at the remote end. The data transfer's destination is specified within a locally registered memory region. The source of an RDMA Read operation should necessarily be a single, virtually contiguous buffer. But it should be allowed to specify the destination of the data transfer as a scatter list of buffers. Similar to the RDMA Write operation, there is an implication for the RDMA Read operation also. The implication is that even before the data transfer can happen, the VI Consumer at the remote end informs the initiator of the RDMA Read of the source buffer's location, and the buffer itself is enabled for RDMA Read operations. Its virtual address and the memory handle associated with it specify the data's remote location.

The RDMA operations do not consume any Descriptor on the remote node's Receive queue. The remote node is not notified that the request is completed. But there is an exception to this rule, according to which it will consume a Descriptor on the remote end at the end of the data transfer if the type of data transfer is specified as *Immediate Data* by the initiator of an RDMA Write request. This process enables synchronization between the VI Consumer and VI Provider. Before the sender executes the RDMA Write, the VI Consumer on the receiving side must post a Receive Descriptor to receive the Immediate Data. An error occurs and the connection might be broken if no Descriptor is posted. Immediate Data can be used only on RDMA Writes. In the VI architecture, RDMA Write is a necessary feature. It is optional to have the support of VI Provider for an RDMA Read operation. It is necessary for the VI Provider to supply a mechanism by which a VI Consumer can determine whether the Provider supports RDMA Read operations.

THE ROLE OF THE COMPLETION QUEUE

For every VI work queue, notification of completed requests can be directed to a Completion queue (illustrated in Figure 10.3). Whenever a VI is created, this association is established. All the completion synchronization should necessarily take place on the Completion queue after a VI Work queue is associated with a Completion queue.

Similar to the case of VI Work queues, the VI NIC can place notification status into the Completion queue without an interrupt. Also, a VI Consumer can synchronize a Completion queue without having to go through the Kernel Agent.

In addition to the elements discussed earlier, VI architecture uses the VI User Agent and VI Kernel Agent in its data transfer function.

The VI User Agent is a software component with the help of which an operating system communication facility can make use of a VI Provider. Its function is to create, manage, and finally destroy VI instances that are under the control of the VI Kernel Agent. The VI User

Agent encapsulates the details of the VI NIC hardware according to an interface defined by the operating system communication facility.

Figure 10.3
A model of the Completion queue, which is a part of the VI work queue in the VI architecture model.

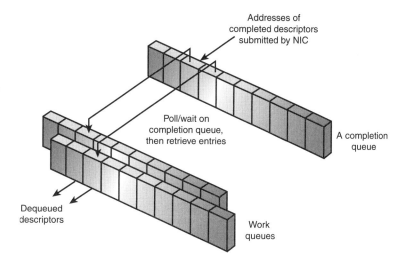

Addresses of completed descriptors submitted by NIC

Poll/wait on completion queue, then retrieve entries

A completion queue

Dequeued descriptors

Work queues

The VI Kernel Agent is a part of the operating system that performs the setup and resource management functions. These functions are needed to maintain a VI between VI Consumers and VI NICs.

These components work together to make the application programs use the VI to send and receive messages through the network fabric that joins the nodes in the SAN.

RELIABILITY LEVELS IN VI

A reliability level is a VI attribute. This is of prime importance in terms of data communication, because it is possible to connect Virtual Interfaces only if they have the same reliability level.

The VI architecture supports three levels of communication reliability at the NIC level—Unreliable Delivery, Reliable Delivery, and Reliable Reception. All the VI NICs must support the Unreliable Delivery level. It is optional to support Reliable Delivery and Reliable Reception. To enable lighter-weight Consumer software, support for one or both of the higher reliability levels is strongly recommended.

UNRELIABLE DELIVERY IN VI

The Unreliable Delivery VIs ensure that a Send or RDMA Write is delivered not more than once to the receiving VI. They also ensure that corrupted data transfers are always detected on the receiving side. For instance, if an incoming Send or RDMA Write consumes a Descriptor on the Receive queue, and the transferred data is corrupt, the corresponding error bit must be set in the status field of the Receive Descriptor.

Only in cases where late delivery or loss of data can be tolerated can RDMA Writes be used on Unreliable connections. RDMA Reads are not supported on an Unreliable VI connection. Hence, if an RDMA Read request is posted on an Unreliable VI, a Descriptor format error appears.

Because the Unreliable Delivery VIs would be used frequently for latency-sensitive operations, they must not excessively slow down the transmission of messages. Also, an Unreliable Delivery VI that allows very large transfers to hinder small transfers is also unacceptable.

RELIABLE DELIVERY IN VI

It is the responsibility of a Reliable Delivery VI to ensure that all data submitted for transfer arrives at its destination exactly once, unaltered, and in the same order as it was submitted, without any errors.

Errors might crop up for various reasons. When a transfer is lost, corrupted, or delivered out of order, the VI Provider transmits an error to the VI Consumer. Transport errors are considered the most dangerous error. Whenever an error is detected, the VI shifts to the Error state. Consequently, the connection is broken, and all posted Descriptors are completed with an error status.

→ To learn more about the Error state, **see** "Error State," **p. 295**

As soon as the associated data is successfully transmitted on the network, a Send or RDMA Write Descriptor is completed with a successful status. An RDMA Read Descriptor is completed with a successful status as soon as the data that is requested has been written to the target buffers on the initiator's system.

RELIABLE RECEPTION IN VI

The Reliable Reception VIs are similar to Reliable Delivery VIs—with a few differences. Here, a Descriptor is completed with a successful status only after the data reaches the target memory location. If an error occurs that prevents the successful delivery of the data into the target memory, it is reported through the Descriptor status. Successful delivery refers to in-sequence unaltered delivery that happens exactly once. In the event of an error, the Provider ensures that none of the subsequent Descriptors are processed after the Descriptor that caused the error.

In the case of errors such as disconnection and hardware errors, the asynchronous error-handling mechanism might be invoked. Similar to the Reliable Delivery connections, any error that happens breaks the connection, shifting the VI to the Error state, and all posted Descriptors are completed with the Error state.

→ To learn more about error-handling mechanisms, **see** "Error-Handling Mechanisms," **p. 295**

MANAGING COMPONENTS OF VI

We will now look at how the VI components are created, destroyed, and managed.

ACCESSING A VI NIC

By means of the standard operating system mechanisms, a VI Consumer gains access to the Kernel Agent of a VI Provider. Usually, opening a handle to the Kernel Agent, which represents the target VI NIC, does this. The VI Consumer performs general management functions using this handle, such as registering memory regions, creating Completion queues, and creating VIs. This mechanism retrieves information about the VI NIC, such as the reliability levels it supports and its transfer size limits.

MANAGING MEMORY

We will now look at registering and deregistering memory, and memory protection.

REGISTERING AND DEREGISTERING MEMORY

In the VI architecture, the memory used for data transfer must be registered with the VI Provider. Memory used for data transfers includes both buffers and Descriptors. One or more virtually contiguous physical pages are defined as a *memory region* by the memory registration process.

A memory region is registered with the Kernel Agent by the VI Consumer registers. The Kernel Agent returns a memory handle that, along with its virtual address, uniquely identifies the registered region. The VI Consumer must qualify any virtual address used in an operation on a VI with the corresponding memory handle. A VI Consumer should also deregister a memory region when the region is no longer in use.

> **Note**
>
> A *memory handle* is a programmatic construct that represents a process's approval to specify a memory region to the VI NIC.

Every page within the region is locked down in physical memory when a memory region is registered. This ensures that the memory region is not paged out. It also ensures that the translation from virtual to physical remains fixed when the NIC is processing requests that correspond to that region. The VI Kernel Agent manages the Page Table, which contains the mapping and protection information for registered memory regions.

Memory is registered for each *process* that happens. A *thread* in a process can access another thread in the same process. But this cannot happen across processes. In other words, a process cannot use another process's memory handle to access the same memory region. When such an action is performed, a memory protection error occurs.

Memory registration might fail if a NIC is unable to find a *Page Table entry* large enough to register the memory region. In such cases, memory is not registered. The memory registration either completely succeeds or completely fails.

When posted Descriptors reference memory that is deregistered, a protection violation results. This error is generated when the VI Provider attempts the memory reference.

PROTECTING MEMORY

Memory contents can get exchanged only among the two VI Consumer processes associated with a pair of connected VIs. The processes can also bring limitations in terms of access to specific regions of registered memory. Two mechanisms, *memory protection tags* and *memory protection attributes*, achieve this. These mechanisms are complementary to memory handles.

Unique IDs called *memory protection tags* are associated with both VIs and memory regions. On behalf of the VI Consumer, the VI Provider creates and destroys memory protection tags. Within a VI Provider, the memory protection tag should be unique. The VI Consumer assigns a memory protection tag to a memory region. This is done when the VI is created. It is the responsibility of the VI Provider to ensure that the memory protection tag that is associated with a VI or registered memory region is valid only for that VI Consumer. Only when the memory protection tag of the VI and the memory protection tag of the memory region involved are identical does a VI NIC allow a memory access. When accesses do not go by this rule, a memory protection error occurs, resulting in no data transfer. This validation applies for registered memory regions that are used to hold Descriptors, as well as memory regions that hold data. A VI Provider must be able to supply at least one memory protection tag for each VI instance it supports.

Memory protection attributes are used to control RDMA Read and RDMA Write access to a given memory region. They are associated with memory regions and VIs. RDMA Read Enable and RDMA Write Enable are the memory protection attributes. When they are created, these permissions are set for memory regions and VIs. When there is a discrepancy between the memory protection attributes of a VI and a memory region, the attribute providing the most protection is honored. A memory protection error occurs when an RDMA operation violates the permission settings. Consequently, no data is transferred.

CONNECTING AND DISCONNECTING VI

The VI architecture provides a connection-oriented data transfer service. When a VI is created for the first time, it is not associated with any other VI. It needs to be deliberately connected to another VI for any data transfer to happen. After the process of data transfer, the associated VI needs to be disconnected to ensure that the VI states are reset and the Descriptors are released.

CONNECTING VI

To establish a connection with a remote VI, a VI Consumer issues requests to its VI Provider. The VI Providers must implement robust and reliable connection protocols. The endpoint association model is of client-server model type. In this model, the server side waits for incoming connection requests. Then it either accepts them or rejects them based on the attributes associated with the remote VI. A VI architecture endpoint connection process is shown in Figure 10.4.

Figure 10.4
The endpoint connection process in VI architecture that enable the VI Providers to implement a robust connection system.

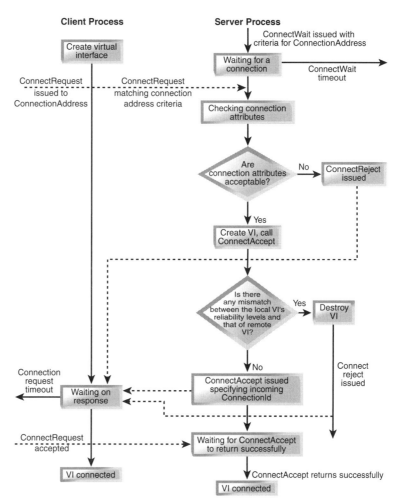

The VI connection model must allow two endpoints on the same node to be connected.

DISCONNECTING VI

To disconnect a connected VI, a VI Consumer issues a Disconnect request to a VI Provider. A Disconnect request completes all outstanding Descriptors on that VI endpoint with the appropriate error bit set.

The VI Provider must detect whether a VI is no longer connected and notify the VI Consumer. At a minimum, the Consumer should be notified after the first data transfer operation that follows the disconnection.

PART

III

CH

10

THE ROLE OF SANS ON THE WEB

There has been enormous growth of the Web in terms of access to its information and content. Access to information is currently universal in that any platform with an Internet connection and a browser can access information anywhere in the world. Content was previously text-based data. But now it is information in the form of text, graphics, sound, and video. Widespread access to knowledge bases has proven to be so successful that both the infrastructure of the Internet and its content generation have developed enormously.

This enormous growth is also accompanied by rapid growth in the number of Internet users. A critical problem faced by the designers of the Web infrastructure is helping the systems cope with the rapid growth in the number of Internet users and storage capacity. The following sections discuss current Web server scenarios and SAN solutions for storage on the Web.

CURRENT WEB SERVER SCENARIOS

The current design of Web servers has a limitation that stems from the fact that the storage is directly attached through the I/O channels to each server. Whenever the number of hits on a Web site increases, the site needs to be able to service user requests as and when they are posted. For this, Web sites must have *scalable* capacity. This is often accomplished through a technique called load balancing (see Figure 10.5).

Note

Load balancing involves evenly distributing processing and communications activity across a computer network so that no single device is overwhelmed.

When one Web server is flooded with requests, more Web servers are employed to handle further requests. The crucial aspect here is that all the Web data should be present in all the Web servers.

This would be a cumbersome process whenever Web data needs to be updated. When such a need arises, all the Web servers need to be updated so that all the user requests are serviced with the same information.

When the storage capacity of the entire site needs to expand, disks need to be added to the existing servers (see Figure 10.6). Disks cannot be added while the servers are operating. Hence, downtime occurs while the storage disks are added. This is another problem with the current Web server scenario.

By using load-balancing hardware, you can add additional CPUs. But the problem of replicating data remains. SAN technology when applied to the Web addresses all these issues. The following sections describe the distinct features of SAN that make it possible to provide a solution for the issues just described.

Figure 10.5
Load balancing in the current Web scenario.

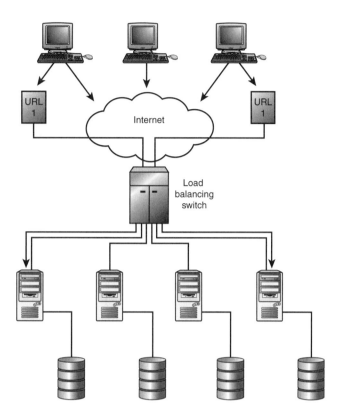

Figure 10.6
Storage is added to the directly attached storage system.

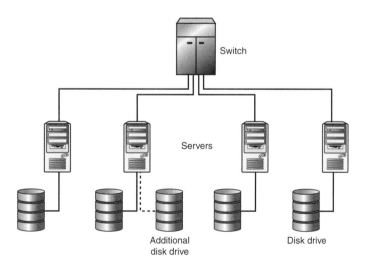

SANs in the Web Scenario

Fibre Channel-based SANs are an effective means of overcoming the constraints just discussed. Fibre Channel SANs have robust features, such as high *bandwidth*, hot-pluggability, high speed, low *latency*, and hardware error detection.

> **Note**
>
> *Hot plugging* is the ability to add and remove devices to and from a computer while the computer is running and have the operating system automatically recognize the change.

We will now look at some of the desirable features of SANs on the Web.

Efficient Storage Management

Unlike directly attached storage, in which each host is administered separately, the SAN environment aids in administering hosts simultaneously with other processes. Software tools such as Brocade Zoning, Veritas Volume Manager, and Transoft SANManager help with various processes, such as partitioning storage, allocating storage to hosts, replicating data, making backups of storage, and monitoring storage health. Because there are a number of servers, access to the data doesn't need to be restricted to one access point. Dual attachment to a single resource is possible in Fibre Channel disk arrays, because they provide primary and secondary ports (see Figure 10.7).

Figure 10.7
A dual data path ensures storage availability in the event that one path fails.

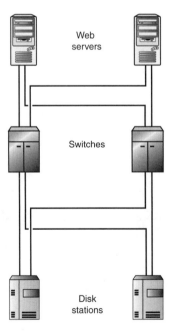

Web servers

Switches

Disk stations

SANs on the Web allow the addition of storage disks and servers as and when the need arises without interrupting the system. If more CPU cycles are required, servers can be added to the existing system with ease. Figure 10.8 shows the servers getting added.

Figure 10.8
Servers being added to the existing SAN without interrupting the working of the system.

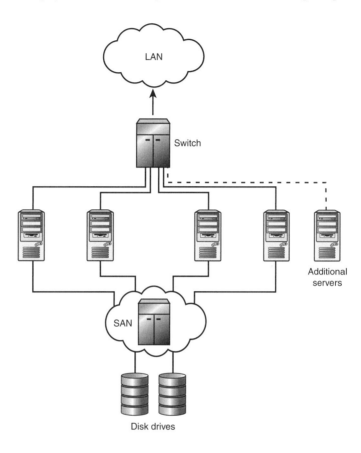

If more content needs to be accommodated, storage can also be attached to the SAN and associated with existing servers. Figure 10.9 shows storage getting added to the SAN.

MAKING SERVERS AVAILABLE WITHOUT DOWNTIME

You can remove specific servers from the SAN without halting the transactions that are taking place. Moreover, the data is not local to any server. Hence, the storage resources can be manipulated without disrupting the availability of storage at any point in time. SANs on the Web are made all the more reliable by using the fail-over software. This software ensures that the clustered servers take up the workload if a problem arises.

THE COST-EFFECTIVENESS OF SANs

SANs offer an Open Systems model for the server and storage infrastructure. This ensures that the site administrators will be comfortable choosing the best server both price-wise and performance-wise. It is also possible to grow the site without hassles by making complete use of the existing equipment.

Figure 10.9
Storage being added to the existing SAN enables you to increase the capacity without affecting the system.

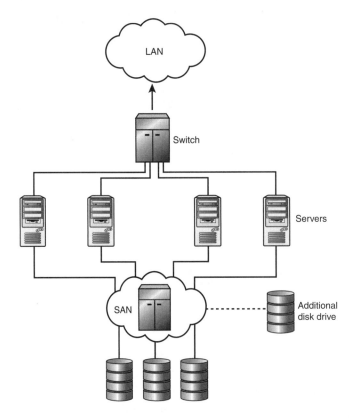

REMARKABLE PERFORMANCE

Fibre Channel fabrics offer a switched 100MBps full-duplex interconnect. Moreover, when compared to networking traffic, block-level I/O is handled with great efficiency. Many megabytes of data with minimal protocol overhead are transferred using a single SCSI command. Consequently, hosts and storage devices that are relatively inexpensive can gain good usage and throughput on the network.

SCALABLE NATURE

Sixteen million devices can be addressed as Fibre channel fabrics using a 24-bit address. Moreover, servers and storage can be increased indefinitely in case of switched Fibre

Channel SANs. This is due to the fact that when switches are added, switching capacity also increases. This is in contrast to shared-medium networks, in which performance deteriorates as the available bandwidth is shared among newly added attached nodes.

When the number of nodes in the network increases, the network administrator can manage the network just by adding switches to the network. The fabric learns the network's topology on its own as switches and nodes are added.

THE HOT-PLUGGABLE NATURE OF SAN ON THE WEB

One of the most common aspects of Internet sites is that when they become popular, their number of hits per day increases rapidly. The Internet infrastructure should therefore be able to scale quickly.

For this, switched Fibre Channel SANs permit the site administrator to manage the site's increased demand by bringing it online with a moderate investment in infrastructure. Thus, there is no need for expensive servers customized for built-in storage limits or built-in limits for handling the number of clients. The additional necessary storage can be installed and brought online without bringing the server down.

THE DISTANCE BETWEEN INTERCONNECTED SYSTEMS

Fibre Channel permits links between the hosts and storage units up to 10 kilometers. This is unlike traditional storage interconnects, which are restricted in the length of the cable connecting hosts and storage units.

SHIFTING WITH EASE

Shifting from the existing infrastructure to the SAN is not difficult. To do so, you need basic components such as Host Bus Adapters (HBAs), Fibre Channel storage, SCSI-FC bridge, and Fibre Channel switches. HBAs are used to connect servers to the SAN. Fibre Channel storage can be used to connect directly to the SAN.

When the SAN is implemented on the Web, it is efficient to use SAN-attached tape. Doing so allows backup to be done faster than network-based backup.

SHARED STORAGE IN SANs

In contrast to traditional approaches, SANs combine all the storage to create a larger pool of SAN attached storage. All the servers share it. In SANs, the servers use a software layer called a cluster file system or shared file system to share the pool of storage. Sharing storage has potential benefits. The main benefit is reduced cost of storage administration. The other benefit is a reduced number of potential points of failure. This is possible because larger disk arrays are substituted for individual disks. Shared storage is depicted in Figure 10.10.

Figure 10.10
Storage being shared in SAN using the shared file system.

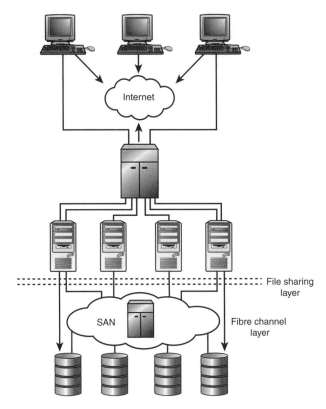

SUMMARY

Virtual Interface architecture is the latest interconnect mechanism, which, when combined with SANs, makes SANs more efficient. The VI architecture is more efficient than the traditional architecture in terms of factors such as bandwidth, latency, and host processing load. VI has been developed to address the needs of the cluster server environment. The VI architecture is comprised of four basic components: Virtual Interfaces, Completion queues, VI Providers, and VI Consumers. A notable feature of VI is the use of memory registration, which considerably reduces the processing overhead from the data-transfer path. Another notable feature of the VI architecture is the reliability afforded by the architecture. The security and memory management features of VI are also a major advantage that makes SANs more efficient.

SANs have found wide acceptance in a number of areas. The growth of the Web has also brought in the enormous storage requirement that makes it the ideal for SANs. With features that make SANs a reliable 24/7 system and the use of Fibre Channel, SANs are gaining acceptance in the world of the Internet. With VI and the growing Web scenario, it looks like SANs have just opened a new chapter in a story that is going to run a long time into the future.

PRODUCTS ARENA

IBM's Magstar MP 3570 tape subsystem was created for medium-sized storage needs. It can be used to make traditional backups and for applications that require fast access to voluminous data. Magstar MP offers high performance for backup and other tape applications. It retrieves data within a few seconds.

Regarding connectivity, it offers a storage solution that works optimally with systems such as IBM's AS/400, RS/6000, and Netfinity servers, as well as non-IBM hardware and software systems such as HP-UX, NT, Sun, and Windows 2000.

Magstar MP 3570 is made for automation, from its heavy-duty cartridge designed for repeated robotic handling to its broad family of library offerings that store from 140GB to 420GB.

The Magstar MP family of tape drives offers a modular solution that permits expansion and high performance for backup and I/O-intense operations.

PART
III

CH
10

PART IV

Appendixes

AN ADVANCED STUDY OF VIRTUAL INTERFACES

In this appendix

THE INTRICACIES OF VIRTUAL INTERFACE

This appendix describes the various states of a Virtual Interface (VI) and the Descriptor Processing model. It also discusses the error-handling mechanisms for the various types of connections, such as Unreliable, Reliable Delivery, and Reliable Reception connections. Finally, it mentions some strategies and scalability factors that those who implement SANs with the VI architecture should consider.

DESCRIPTOR PROCESSING MODEL

Any request for data transfer is given in the form of Descriptors. They have the required information to process a request. This information includes the type of transfer to make (inbound or outbound), the status of the transfer, information in the queue, and a scatter-gather-type pointer list.

The VI architecture has two Description Processing models—the Work queue model and the Completion queue model. In both these models, Descriptors are enqueued and dequeued from VI's Work queue. The sole difference between the two models lies in the way the VI Consumer is notified of Descriptor completion.

In case of the Work queue model, the VI Consumer polls for completions on a specific Work queue. The VI Consumer does this by examining the status of the Descriptor at the head of the queue. The VI Consumer dequeues it when the head Descriptor is completed. Figure A.1 depicts the Work queue model of the Description Processing models in the VI architecture.

In case of the Completion queue model, the VI Consumer polls for completions on a set of Work queues. The VI Consumer does this by examining the head of the Completion queue. The identity of a Descriptor is written to the Completion queue when the Descriptor completes. Figure A.2 depicts the Completion queue model of the Description Processing models in the VI architecture.

It is the role of the VI Consumer to dequeue a Descriptor from the appropriate Work queue as soon as it receives a notification from the Completion queue that a Descriptor has been completed. It is required that the VI Provider should provide a mechanism with which VI Consumers can wait for Descriptors to complete on a VI Work queue or wait for a notification to be posted to a Completion queue.

DESCRIPTOR FORMATION

Descriptors are of two types—Send/Receive and Remote Direct Memory Access (RDMA). They perform two different functions—namely, outbound data transfer and inbound data transfer. Outbound data transfer is the process of reading data from the storage devices and sending the information to the server that requested the read. Inbound data transfer is the process of accepting data packets that are transferred to the storage device for storing the data.

Figure A.1
The Work queue model depicting a specific VI Work queue being polled for completion.

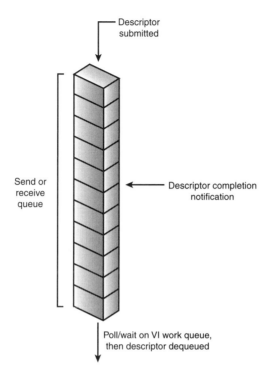

Descriptor submitted

Send or receive queue

Descriptor completion notification

Poll/wait on VI work queue, then descriptor dequeued

Figure A.2
The Completion queue model depicting a set of VI Work queues being polled for completion.

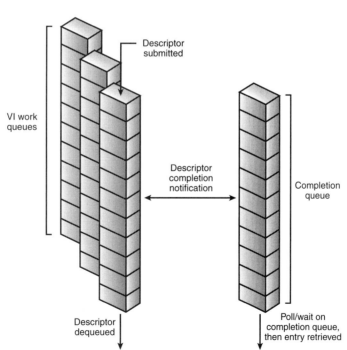

Descriptor submitted

VI work queues

Descriptor completion notification

Completion queue

Descriptor dequeued

Poll/wait on completion queue, then entry retrieved

A Descriptor occupies a variable-length, virtually contiguous region of a process's virtual address space. It is required that Descriptors be aligned on a 64-byte boundary. Memory regions registered by the VI Provider and the VI Consumer are the only place where Descriptors can reside. On the condition that a single Descriptor is located within a single memory, Descriptors are allowed to exceed physical page boundaries. A Descriptor must be accompanied by the memory handle associated with the memory where it lies. This needs to happen whenever it is used in a request to the VI Provider. The VI Consumer manages the allocation of Descriptors.

As soon as a Descriptor is posted to the Work queue, the VI Provider becomes the Descriptor's owner. If the VI Consumer modifies the Descriptor while it is posted, this results in unpredictable behavior. The VI Consumer becomes the Descriptor's owner when the VI Provider completes it. The completion of a Descriptor happens when a VI Provider writes a completion status to the Descriptor. When a Completion queue is in use, the VI Provider must write an entry to the associated Completion queue.

Segments constitute a Descriptor. The segments in a Descriptor are of three types—Control, Address, and Data.

The Control segment, which has the status information and reserved fields that are used for queuing, is always the beginning of the Descriptor.

The Address segment is present next to the Control segment and is meant only for RDMA operations. This segment has information about the remote buffer for the operations of RDMA Read and RDMA Write.

The final segment is the Data segment. Multiple Data segments might be present in a descriptor. Information such as local buffers of a Send, Receive, RDMA Read, or RDMA Write is present in the Data segment.

In the case of data transfers, two aspects must be taken into consideration—the scatter-gather list in each Descriptor and the size of the data that is getting transferred.

For the hardware to directly place or send the data, the Descriptor format permits the VI Consumer to specify a scatter-gather list in each Descriptor. It is possible for the VI Consumer to specify a scatter-gather list of a length up to the Network Interface Controller's (NIC) count limit, which refers to the maximum number of data segments the NIC can hold. The length of the scatter-gather list can even be zero. If the scatter-gather list is zero, Immediate Data can be transferred, or there might not be any data transfer at all. Scatter-gather elements of zero length are also acceptable. The VI NIC must support a segment count limit of at least 252 data segments.

There is no restriction on the length of data transfers, except that it should not be more than the Maximum Transmission Unit (MTU) of any VI Provider. The total length of the data would be the sum of the lengths of scatter-gather elements. The VI Consumer can be sure that any VI Provider can transmit a minimum of 32KB in one Descriptor, because the minimum MTU that is allowed is 32KB.

POSTING DESCRIPTORS

To process the Descriptors that are prepared, the VI Consumer submits them to the VI NIC by posting them to the appropriate Work queue and ringing the appropriate Work queue's Doorbell. A Doorbell's format and processing are specific to each VI Provider.

The respective Work queues get posted with the Send and Receive requests. Of the requests that get posted, the Read and Write Remote DMA requests get posted to the Send queue at all times. Sometimes, the Receive Descriptors might be posted before a connection is established. In such cases, they do not get completed until a connection is established and data is received. The exception to this is when Descriptors are completed in error. You can prevent errors that occur due to data's getting dropped or rejected because of a lack of Receive Descriptors by preposting the Descriptors.

Send and RDMA Descriptors are completed in error if they are submitted to VI before it is connected. They remain without being processed until a connection is established. The Descriptors that are already posted are processed without any hindrance, even if further Descriptors are posted.

PROCESSING THE POSTED DESCRIPTORS

A Descriptor is ready to get processed after it is posted to a Work queue. The VI NIC can start processing the Descriptor as soon as it is posted. The data transfer happens between two connected VIs during the time when VI NIC processes a Descriptor or when the data arrives on the network. Along with this, Immediate Data is also transferred. It is expected that the VI NIC will take necessary action if an error occurs while the Descriptor is processed.

ORDERING RULES AND BARRIERS IN PROCESSING DESCRIPTORS

The order in which the Descriptors are processed needs to be consistent across all the implementations of the VI architecture. These rules apply for the processing that happens on a single queue. The order in which the Descriptors are processed in multiple queues is not defined.

ORDERING RULES IN PROCESSING DESCRIPTORS   The type of order that is followed in Send and Receive queues is First In First Out (FIFO). The Descriptors follow an order in which they are enqueued and dequeued.

The Receive queues are purely FIFO queues. This is because when Descriptors are enqueued, they are processed, completed, and dequeued in the same FIFO order.

The Send queues are also FIFO queues but might not behave in the same manner when they get completed. The Descriptors first get enqueued and then get processed in FIFO order. But they might get completed in an order different from the order in which they were processed. Irrespective of the order in which the Descriptors get completed, they are dequeued only in FIFO order. With respect to Send and RDMA Write Descriptors, RDMA

Read Descriptors might complete out of order. With respect to one another, RDMA Reads complete in FIFO order.

A round-trip path is needed for RDMA Reads (unlike the case of Sends and RDMA Writes) to ensure optimal performance. Sends and RDMA Writes might start processing before the completion of RDMA Reads.

A Send Descriptor that bypasses an RDMA Read might write data to the receiving memory regions at any time prior to the completion of the RDMA Read. This might result in a loss of transmission, because the Receive queue on the remote VI that requested the information might not accept the data immediately. The contents of the receive buffer memory are volatile, so the transfer of data cannot be guaranteed until the associated remote Receive queue Descriptor is completed successfully. In a Reliable Delivery connection, a remote Receive queue Descriptor is consumed by the bypassing Send. This ensures that the Descriptor completes successfully prior to the completion of the RDMA Read.

The remote VI Consumer might successfully receive the bypassing Send before the RDMA Read is completed (or in the event of an error on the RDMA Read). In a Reliable Reception connection, the receiving VI Provider must not successfully complete the bypassing Send until all the RDMA Read data has been transmitted without error. In the event of an RDMA Read error, no remote Receive queue Descriptor is consumed. This allows the remote Receive queue to process the data from the Send.

Only in a Reliable Delivery connection might an RDMA Write that bypasses an RDMA Read write data to the remote memory region. In the event of an error on the RDMA Read, the bypassing RDMA Write operation could lead to some problems. The problem is that the issuing VI Consumer might dequeue all commands after the RDMA Read error. However, in a Reliable Reception connection, no such side effects are permitted. The remote VI Provider must not modify the contents of the remote memory region or, in the case of Immediate Data, consume a Receive queue Descriptor until after the RDMA Read has completed.

The VI Consumer is required to use a processing barrier to enforce a strict order in processing Descriptors.

BARRIERS IMPLEMENTED TO HANDLE DESCRIPTOR PROCESSING   This is a mechanism by which the VI NIC is notified that all the Descriptors posted before the designated Descriptor must complete before any processing can continue on that Descriptor. The VI Consumer ensures that this is achieved by setting the Queue Fence bit in a Descriptor so that all Descriptors that are posted on the Send queue prior to that Descriptor are completed before the processing can happen on the Descriptor under consideration. Thus, the VI Consumer gets a synchronization mechanism to ensure the contents of registered memory.

COMPLETION OF DESCRIPTORS

The Descriptors need to be completed as soon as the data transfer is completed. The completion of Descriptors is accomplished in two phases. The first phase involves the VI

Provider. Here, the VI Provider updates the Control Segment contents. In addition to this, an entry is generated in the Completion queue if the queue is linked to a Completion queue. The second phase involves the VI Consumer where it dequeues the Descriptor.

COMPLETION OF DESCRIPTORS BY THE VI PROVIDER

The information in the Control Segment of the Descriptor must be updated as soon as the VI NIC has finished processing a Descriptor. The update information includes completion codes, length fields, and Immediate Data.

As soon as the completion indicator is set in the Descriptor, the VI NIC signals that it has finished updating the Descriptor and that the Descriptor has been removed from its internal processing queues. The Status item is the last item to be updated, to ensure that the Descriptor is not removed from the internal processing queues before it is completed.

If a Completion queue is registered for the queue in which this Descriptor was present, the VI NIC adds an entry in the Completion queue. This refers to the completed Descriptor's VI and queue.

COMPLETION OF DESCRIPTORS BY THE VI CONSUMER

There are four ways in which a VI Consumer can synchronize completed Descriptors—by polling a VI Work queue, waiting on a VI Work queue, polling a Completion queue, and waiting on a Completion queue.

The VI Consumer makes polling on a VI Work queue possible by reading the Status field of the Descriptor at the head of the queue. The VI Consumer dequeues the Descriptor as soon as the Done bit is set.

The VI Consumer does polling on a Completion queue by examining the head of the queue. The information pertaining to the Descriptor is written to the Completion queue after the Descriptor gets completed. This information is used by the VI Consumer to trace the appropriate Work queue and then dequeue the head Descriptor.

Waiting on a VI Work queue can also be done by means of a mechanism provided by the Kernel Agent. In this mechanism, the VI NIC is informed that an interrupt must be generated that corresponds to the next completion on a particular Work queue or Completion queue. This interrupt is taken care of by the Kernel Agent, which unblocks the appropriate thread. Even without polling, the thread processes the completion as it would when polled for.

PART

IV

AP

A

THE VARIOUS STATES OF VIRTUAL INTERFACE

In a storage area network implemented with the VI architecture, any data transfer between the devices with VI NIC happens by means of a Virtual Interface. Any system on a SAN requesting the storage devices for some information (bytes of data) causes the creation of a Virtual Interface. It is through a Virtual Interface that the information is retrieved from the storage device. After this, the server passes the information to the system that requested it.

Here the server's VI Consumer is the operating system communication facility and the VI User Agent. The server's VI Provider consists of the VI NIC and the Kernel Agent. For instance, when a request for some information comes to the server, the server's VI Consumer creates a VI. The VI that gets created alternates between the various states until the VI Provider services the VI Consumer's request.

The four states in which VI can exist are Idle, Pending Connect, Connected, and Error. VI is in the Idle state when it is created. It transitions from one state to another, depending on the requests made by the VI Consumer and also on the network events.

IDLE STATE

VI is in this state when it is created. In this state, VI has no Descriptors on its Work queues. A VI can be destroyed only when it is in this state, because it is required that VI not have any Descriptor on its Work queues.

VI in the Idle state transitions to the Pending Connect state when the VI Consumer submits a ConnectRequest to its VI Provider. If this request does not complete within the timeout period specified, VI goes back to the Idle state. Even after VI transitions to the Pending Connect state, if it fails or times out, it goes back to the Idle state.

When VI is in the Idle state, it can receive Descriptors to its Work queues. However, VI does not process the Descriptors until it remains in the Idle state. The Descriptors are processed only when VI transitions to the Connected state or the VI Consumer issues a Disconnect request. On the other hand, if the Descriptors are posted to the Send queue when VI is in the Idle state, they are completed in error, which means that the Descriptors' status is changed to Error and then dequeued.

PENDING CONNECT STATE

VI gets into this state after the VI Consumer submits a connection request to its VI Provider and before the connection is established. The ConnectRequest request is submitted by the VI Consumer while VI is in the Idle state for it to get into this state.

When this request receives a successful response, VI transitions into the Connected state. This happens even when a ConnectAccept request from the VI Provider is successful.

VI transitions to the Idle state when the Connect request is rejected or times out. The same transition happens when the VI Consumer issues a Disconnect request to its VI Provider while VI is in the Pending Connect state. VI also transitions to the Error state if any transport errors or hardware errors are generated from the VI NIC.

Similar to the Idle state, even if Descriptors are posted to the Receive queue, they are not processed if VI is in this state. They are processed only when VI transitions to the Connected state or if the VI Consumer issues a Disconnect request.

If Descriptors are posted to the Send queue of VI that is in the Pending Connect state, VI transitions to the Error state. Because VI is not connected, inbound and outbound traffic cannot be present in this state.

CONNECTED STATE

Connected state is the state in which data flow happens. VI transitions from the Pending Connect state to the Connected state when a ConnectRequest request completes successfully.

VI in this state transitions to the Idle state if a VI Consumer issues a Disconnect request to its VI Provider.

Similar to the Pending Connect state, VI transitions to the Error state in the event of hardware errors.

Descriptors that are posted to the Send and Receive queues of VI in the Connected state are processed normally. All inbound and outbound traffic is also processed normally.

ERROR STATE

VI enters the Error state when an error occurs during normal processing. VI also enters this state when a VI NIC generates an event.

In case VI has a Reliable Delivery or Reliable Reception, some errors that occur when VI is in the Connected state transition it to the Error state. A Disconnect request transitions VI to the Idle state.

If Descriptors are posted to the Receive queue or the Send queue when VI is in the Error state, they are completed in error.

Inbound traffic sent to VI in this state is not accepted. Because the requests posted to the Send queue are completed in error, there is no outbound traffic. If any outbound traffic remains on a queue when VI transitions to the Error state, it is canceled, and the corresponding Descriptors are completed in error.

Figure A.3 illustrates the various states of VI.

A VI that gets created might not successfully transition to the Pending Connect state and then to the Connected state at all times. In other words, the VI Consumer's request might have hindrances while it is being processed and serviced by the VI Provider.

PART

IV

AP

A

ERROR-HANDLING MECHANISMS

There are two types of errors—asynchronous and synchronous. Almost all errors are reported synchronously to the VI Consumer. They are reported either when an operation is attempted or when a Descriptor completes.

The nature of some errors is such that they cannot be reported synchronously. These are asynchronous errors. They cause the processing of the queue to hang, they occur after the completion of a Descriptor, and they occur whenever a network cable gets disconnected.

To handle asynchronous errors, the VI Provider is required to provide a mechanism to deliver them to the VI Consumer. The VI Provider can report different types of asynchronous errors, depending on the connection's reliability level. Errors such as hardware-related issues are reported asynchronously, irrespective of the connection's reliability level. This is because these errors require immediate notification.

Figure A.3
Each VI state transitions to another VI state upon a specific request or event.

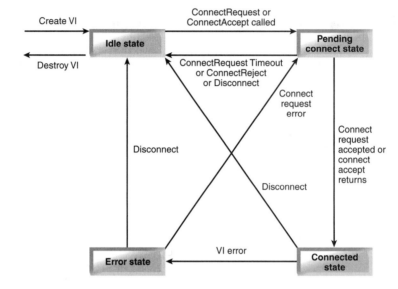

ERROR-HANDLING MECHANISM FOR UNRELIABLE CONNECTIONS

In the case of unreliable conditions where there is a disastrous hardware failure, the asynchronous error-handling mechanism for unreliable connections is called. Severe errors include errors in which the Work queue hangs or the links get lost and errors that arise from VI NIC.

In the case of Unreliable connections, it is assumed that the VI Consumer will implement the appropriate protocol that is necessary to ensure a packet's arrival. Hence, transport-level issues are not reported to the VI Consumer.

ERROR-HANDLING MECHANISM FOR RELIABLE DELIVERY CONNECTIONS

In the case of severe errors, such as Work queue hangs, errors pertaining to the VI NIC, or the loss of link and transport, such as dropped or missed packets, the asynchronous error-handling mechanism for Reliable Delivery Connections is invoked. It is invoked for transport errors after the VI NIC completes one or more Descriptors that have been posted by the VI Consumer.

In case of any error, the VI connection transitions to the Error state. The error-handling mechanism is also invoked, and the VI Consumer takes the required steps as per the error conditions.

ERROR-HANDLING MECHANISM FOR RELIABLE RECEPTION CONNECTIONS

In the case of severe errors, such as Work queue hangs, errors pertaining to the VI NIC, or the loss of link and transport, such as dropped or missed packets, the asynchronous error-handling mechanism for Reliable Reception Connections is invoked. It is invoked after the VI NIC completes exactly one posted Descriptor or none of the posted Descriptors.

In case of any error, the VI connection transitions to the Error state, after which the error-handling mechanism is invoked. Similar to the error-handling mechanism for reliable reception connections, the VI Consumer takes the required steps as per the error conditions.

GUIDELINES FOR THE VI ARCHITECTURE IMPLEMENTERS

Those who will implement the VI architecture need to be aware of certain aspects, such as some of the VI Provider's operations and resources available on any given VI NIC.

Although the VI architecture optimizes the data transfer path, there could be constraints due to some VI Provider operations. This is because of the fact that some VI Provider operations take more time than the process of transferring data, such as buffer registration and deregistration, creating VI, connecting one VI to another, and the transfer of poorly aligned data.

There are a number of requirements for buffer registration, such as kernel transition, locking down physical pages in memory, and manipulating VI NIC Page tables. All these processes take time. Deregistration also takes time.

The VI when created also involves several processes, such as kernel transition, allocating resources that are present in the kernel and the VI NIC, and interacting with the VI NIC. Interaction with the VI NIC is required for a Doorbell to be created and mapped to the VI Consumer's address space.

Whenever a VI needs to be connected to another VI, protocols get executed between the two endpoints. This involves many operations involving both the VI Consumer and the VI Provider. Also, data transfer that is poorly aligned takes a long time to transfer.

A VI NIC supports a finite number of VIs and Completion queues. Owing to overusage of Registration and Deregistration processes, side effects such as the fragmentation of VI NIC tables can happen.

Scalability is another aspect to which the implementers of the VI architecture must pay attention. The interconnect mechanisms need to scale with the number of applications, as well as the number of applications executing within a node. The interconnect mechanism includes the VI NIC, the physical media, and any connection facilitator, such as a switch. The network's throughput must also scale to facilitate the growth in the number of active connections.

PART

IV

AP

A

An Introduction to Available SAN Products

In this appendix

AN OVERVIEW OF SAN PRODUCTS AND SAN SOFTWARE SOLUTIONS

This appendix introduces some SAN products manufactured by different companies, including hardware components and SAN software solutions.

SAN PRODUCTS

A number of hardware components help you set up the SAN infrastructure. These include switches, hubs, and routers.

SWITCHES

Switches are devices that help filter and forward data packets between network segments. Their operation occurs at the data link layer of the Open Systems Interconnect (OSI) reference model.

CAPELLIX 3000 MODULAR SAN SWITCH   The Capellix 3000 Modular SAN switch is manufactured by Gadzoox Networks, Inc. It is the first modular switch introduced for the SAN market. You can construct a robust SAN solution with this switch due to its scalability.

You can implement highly scalable SANs using the Capellix 3000. The modular characteristic of this switch is instrumental in implementing such SANs. When you use this switch, you negate the performance constraints you face when using fixed configurations. This difference in performance occurs because this switch has an integrated 28Gbps switch engine. This engine provides the highest bandwidth of any switch in its class. This negates the hidden cost that would be incurred if fixed configurations were used.

The Capellix 3000 is designed to work with the same Fibre Channel protocol that is supported by all host adapters, RAID controllers, and storage subsystems that use Fibre Channel-Arbitrated Loop (FC-AL). It follows a standards-based loop-switch technology that lets it quickly integrate new and existing SANs.

Here are the features of the Capellix 3000 Modular SAN switch:

- It allows you to scale the number of connections from six to 32 devices.
- It has a Fibre Channel switch engine with a 28Gbps capacity.
- It has a chassis with three slots that is modular in nature.
- It comes with preconfigured SAN management software called Ventana SANtools GX.
- It has the support of native arbitrated loop devices.
- You can connect it to the Network and Storage Management Framework.
- It supports fabric connectivity.
- It has a hot-swappable power supply and fan assembly option.

IBM SAN FIBRE CHANNEL SWITCH   The IBM SAN Fibre Channel switch is a product of IBM Corporation. You can use it to provide native Fibre Channel connectivity to Unix-based servers and Intel-based servers running Windows NT, apart from other servers. You can also interconnect multiple IBM SAN Fibre Channel switches and IBM-compatible switches. This enables the creation of a switched fabric that has hundreds of Fibre Channel ports. This fabric can support large business applications that demand high performance and scalability. It also provides the fault tolerance that is required by several enterprise storage management applications. These include LANless backup, serverless backup, disk and tape pooling, and data sharing. The performance of the switched fabric increases as more switches are added to the fabric.

The IBM SAN Fibre Channel switch does a lot of self-monitoring of SANs. If you use this switch in a SAN, you can be assured that the hosts and storage devices will be registered automatically. It also redirects network traffic automatically when a problem arises in the network.

This switch has two models—2109 Model S08 and 2109 Model S16. Here are the features of the 2109 Model S08:

- It has four shortwave GBICs standard. It also has from one to four additional shortwave or long-wave GBICs.
- The height of a rack-mount type is 43.4mm.
- The height of a tabletop type is 47.2mm.
- The width of the switch is 428.6mm.
- The depth of the switch is 450.0mm.

Here are the features of the 2109 Model S16:

- It has four shortwave GBICs standard. It also has from one to 12 additional shortwave or long-wave GBICs.
- The height of a rack-mount type is 87.3mm.
- The height of a tabletop type is 91.2mm.
- The width of the switch is 428.6mm.
- The depth of the switch is 450.0mm.

7100 EIGHT-PORT FABRIC SWITCH   The 7100 eight-port fabric switch is a product of Vixel Corporation. This switch allows different kinds of clients to connect to it. This is made possible by its auto-sensing capability and ports that configure by themselves. On each port, the switch supports 100MBps performance. When you use this switch in a SAN, you can expect consistent performance due to the 32 frame buffers in every port. You can derive high-availability SAN solutions by cascading or meshing the switches.

This switch offers central SAN connectivity with dedicated bandwidth and port isolation. It can interoperate in a multivendor environment with its fabric- and loop-switching capacity.

PART

IV

AP

B

It allows you to grow a SAN without disturbing the existing infrastructure. Hence, it is very useful in implementing pay-as-you-grow SAN solutions.

The features of the 7100 eight-port fabric switch are as follows:

- The requirement for rack space is reduced considerably by its 1 U form factor.
- It uses third-generation Stealth-3 arbitrated loop technology.
- It provides high scalability with its eight full-speed Fibre Channel GBIC ports.
- It provides 32 frame buffers per port, allowing it to bear a heavy traffic load.
- It has flexible zoning support.
- It has ports that configure by themselves.
- It has auto-sensing capability.

Hubs

Hubs are devices that connect various devices in a network. A hub has multiple ports to which various devices can connect.

Gibraltar Hubs   Gibraltar is a product line of Fibre Channel hubs from Gadzoox Networks, Inc. It includes Gibraltar GS and Gibraltar GL. The Gibraltar hubs come in two versions, one of which has six ports and the other of which has 12 ports. You can use the six-port version if you want to connect to midrange departmental servers. You can use the 12-port version if you want to connect to high-end enterprise servers.

If a port fails, Gibraltar provides reliable data transfer with the help of its Reflex feature. This feature automatically spots the port that has failed and routes the data through some other data path without hindering the network's normal functioning.

You can grow a SAN modularly with this hub. You can be sure of the data integrity, because it is taken care of by a feature called PerfectPort, which is a device that is present in every port that regenerates the signal. It aids in ensuring the integrity of data that is coming into and going out of the hub.

Here are the features of Gibraltar hubs:

- The Reflex feature enables the automatic detection of the failure of any port and makes hot plugging of devices possible.
- It has a PerfectPort feature that amplifies the output signal and enables the addition of more Fibre Channel ports by cascading multiple hubs.
- Management modules monitor, control, and troubleshoot even when the network is down.
- It has two versions. One has six ports, and the other has 12 ports.

8260 Nways Multiprotocol Switching Hub   The 8260 Nways Multiprotocol Switching hub is manufactured by IBM. You can build a high-speed ATM network using this hub, because it is flexible, reliable, and manageable. You can improve network performance with its hot-swappable nature and efficient power-management capacity.

It is highly dependable, because it is based on a backplane that has components that do not fail. In this hub, the critical components can be configured for redundancy. These components include power supplies, controller modules, and management components.

It is designed for high capacity. You can use this hub in any network configuration, because it comes in three sizes, either with ATM or without ATM. Apart from its wide range of media and module types, you can optimize the benefits that you can get from the network by using a wide range of switching alternatives.

Here are the features of the 8260 Nways Multiprotocol Switching hub:

- It has an efficient power and inventory management capacity in that it automatically distributes its load across the available power supplies.
- It has an advanced backplane architecture, so there are no electrical or mechanical components to wear out.
- It has backup and redundancy for all the critical components, so it is highly fault-tolerant.
- It is suited for expansion of ports and shifting to higher-speed technologies such as ATM.
- It allows ATM switching within the hub.
- Network management is efficient, because the distributed management system uses daughter cards to monitor network operations. This is an alternative to using separate management modules that reduces cost of ownership.

VIXEL 2100 ZONING MANAGED HUB   The Vixel 2100 Zoning Managed hub is a product of Vixel Corporation. This hub is hot-pluggable. Hence, the interconnect need not be shut down for either maintenance or reconfiguration. It uses Vixel's hub-on-a-chip architecture with retiming circuitry. You can divide the hub into four full 100MBps Fibre Channel loops or zones.

This hub is inclusive of integrated SNMP management. It also provides you with a number of interfaces for management and control to meet various needs and preferences.

You can access the password-protected embedded Web management interface by using a common Web browser from anywhere. You can do this to perform a variety of jobs, such as monitoring, controlling, and reconfiguring zones and identifying potential problems in the 2100 Zoning Managed hub.

Here are the features of the Vixel 2100 Zoning Managed hub:

- It provides high reliability and performance with its "hub-on-a-chip" architecture.
- From a single hub, it can support four 100MBps Fibre Channel arbitrated loops for a total bandwidth capacity of 400MBps.

PART

IV

AP

B

- To monitor and control the devices on the network, it has an embedded Web management interface that has password protection.
- It allows you to grow the existing SAN with its eight hot-pluggable GBIC ports.
- It provides integrated hub management for implementing SANs with ease.
- By means of isolating Loop Initialization Primitives (LIPs) from applications that are sensitive to delays, implementing zoning ensures maximum stability for each loop segment.

ROUTERS

Routers are components that connect multiple host servers to multiple storage devices.

SAN ROUTER   SAN Router is a part of Pathlight Technology, Inc.'s SAN product family. You can use SAN Router to connect multiple SCSI channels to a Fibre Channel environment and get high performance out of it. It includes fully integrated management and service strategies. You can use it as a standalone or in conjunction with Fibre Channel hubs. It can connect directly to any Fibre Channel switch.

You can use SAN Router in smaller data enterprises as a cost-effective way to make serverless backups. SAN Router can also be used in OEMs as an interconnectivity solution for specific storage devices.

It has a strong engineering base, which is needed for high-end enterprises. You can separate storage traffic from application traffic by using SAN Router in your storage area network. You can perform many more functions, such as serverless backup and delivering data movement.

You can use SAN Router along with SAN management software to maintain and monitor the entire SAN environment. You can also configure SAN Router with two single-ended or differential SCSI ports and one Fibre Channel port. The Fibre Channel port can be a short-wave, long-wave, or optical connection. SAN Router aids in resource sharing and acts as a good platform for value-added functions.

Here are the features of SAN Router:

- It provides a comprehensive solution for SAN connectivity by connecting multiple host servers to multiple storage devices. It uses Fibre Channel and SCSI interfaces to do this.
- It provides transparent performance in that it does not degrade the performance of the SAN in which it is employed. Instead, it provides bandwidths ranging from 40MBps to 120MBps to move data from one interface to another.
- It is scalable and modular in nature. It allows the SAN to grow without any hitches with the help of field-replaceable units and field-installable upgrade options.
- It manages the SAN with the help of Pathlight's SAN management software.

- It shares resources in a very effective manner by implementing Channel Zoning. This also prevents any data corruption resulting from two servers trying to write to the same storage device.

- It provides certain value-added functions apart from providing interconnectivity to your SAN. These functions include routing data across heterogeneous interfaces, saving vital configuration information, and facilitating serverless backup.

HP DOCUMENT ROUTER   HP Document Router is manufactured by Hewlett-Packard. You can use HP Document Router to combine hardware and software for outbound fax, e-mail distribution, local or remote print serving, and intranet publishing into a single multifunctional server appliance. You can use this as a cross-platform network resource to let users "file-print" electronic documents from any application to any output device on the network.

HP Document Router is a better alternative to single-solution products, such as print spoolers and fax servers. This is because it gives you one way to access and manage all the output devices. On the whole, you can enhance an organization's communications by using HP Document Router. It makes this possible by automating and ensuring the delivery of electronic documents.

You can use HP Document Router across various platforms, such as Windows, Unix, AS/400, Macintosh, and mainframe computing platforms. You can use it with any Internet or enterprise application that can print. In addition, you can use it to integrate SAP and Oracle software. If you need to send a document from one platform to another, you need not change the document's format if the destination requires the document to be in a different format.

You can do away with having IT employees configure individual printers and fax software on each client machine. HP Document Router automatically detects and configures printers that are available on the network.

The features of HP Document Router are as follows:

- It has a Web-based configuration.

- It tracks all the jobs on the network through its Web-based interface.

- In case of high-volume throughput across printers, it supports "print farms."

- It automatically detects network printers.

- It is a standalone appliance that supports Plug and Play.

- You can make all the destinations available to any application that can print.

PART
IV
AP
B

SAN SOFTWARE SOLUTIONS

Various software solutions are available to facilitate the management of SANs in terms of data, storage, and hosts on the SAN.

SAN MANAGEMENT SOFTWARE

SAN management software solutions include SAN software that helps you manage the volume of data and protect data. They also help you manage the hardware components present in SANs.

LEGATO NETWORKER 6   Legato NetWorker 6 is produced by Legato Systems, Inc. You can use this solution to provide scalable data protection for your SAN. It has a client/server architecture that has three distinct functions—client, storage node, and server functions. These functions provide the performance needed for managing data on complex networks. Hence, you can also use NetWorker 6 to facilitate heterogeneous enterprise operations, such as serverless backup and library sharing for SANs.

NetWorker does automated media handling, electronic labeling, and media verification, and supports cartridge cleaning. You can add client connections, storage devices, and software nodes through software enablers and make it expand dynamically.

You can use NetWorker with ease, because only a single network server console is required to set up and manage backups and restores. On the whole, NetWorker is an application designed for network backup and recovery.

Here are the features of Legato NetWorker:

- On one Network Edition server, its parallel streaming feature supports a maximum of 32 simultaneous client backup or recovery sessions.
- It has client/server architecture and centralized administration capacity. This enables automated backup for thousands of workstations and servers attached to the network.
- It is highly reliable due to the Legato Network Industry Standard OpenTape Format, which supports data multiplexing for backup and recovery operations.
- You can make systems running Legato NetWorker Network Edition or Power Edition operate with a wide range of tape and optical autochangers. You can do this if you add the appropriate autochanger software module.
- It offers client archive and retrieval services when you add the Legato NetWorker Archive module.
- The number of parallel data streams that can be present in Power Edition is 64 per server or server node and 32 per server or server node for Network Edition.

ATTO ACCELWARE   ATTO AccelWare is a product of ATTO Technology, Inc. You can use this software wherever workgroups share common data that is voluminous in nature. It maintains data integrity across dual platforms. You can let Macintosh and Windows NT workgroup members share data because of ATTO AccelWare's dual-platform capability.

It ensures data integrity for the entire volume of data by controlling access privileges to shared storage. Its design is so robust that you do not need to employ an administrator.

ATTO AccelWare can be installed with ease. You can set up the SAN storage by installing AccelWare Volume Management Software. You can then use ATTO AccelWare Mac if your workstation is Mac-compatible or ATTO AccelWare DP if your workstation is Windows NT-compatible. You can install ATTO AccelWare DP later if you are going to switch from Mac to Windows NT in the future.

It is also easy to use apart from being easy to install. It provides "point and click" usage, easy booting, easy viewing, and easy changing of access settings.

You can use ATTO AccelWare to conveniently manage a project's changing needs without an administrator's help. Its design even considers freelancers, who generally would not be allowed to access all parts of the volume. For this reason, a "no access" option is provided as added security.

Here are the features of ATTO AccelWare:

- It ensures data integrity.

- It provides serial number security.

- It provides multiple access levels with the help of varying access privileges.

- It enables messaging from user to user.

- It provides password protection through on/off switches at each workstation.

- Its control over access privileges to shared resources avoids costly fix-it time.

Virtualization Software Solutions for SANs

A virtualization software solution involves organizing multiple storage devices into logical entities so that storage capacity is managed better and performance is increased. This lets several crucial tasks be performed more efficiently and without any downtime.

VERITAS Volume Manager   VERITAS Volume Manager is a software solution from VERITAS Software Corporation. You can use this software tool to manage storage online in large enterprises and Storage Area Network environments.

VERITAS Volume Manager increases the availability of SAN-based applications by virtualizing the storage resources. Virtualizing storage resources reduces the administrative overhead involved in managing storage devices. Employing VERITAS Volume Manager also prevents disk and hardware failures. It provides the scalability to SANs to help adjust whenever there is a sudden growth of the network in terms of hosts or storage devices.

You can use VERITAS Volume Manager to overcome the physical restrictions enforced by hardware disk devices. The logical volume management layer that VERITAS Volume Manager provides accomplishes this as it spans volumes across multiple spindles.

Here are the features of the VERITAS Volume Manager:

- It enables online storage management, thus allowing data to be accessed even during system maintenance.

- It uses mirroring of storage to ensure high data availability.

PART

IV

AP

B

- It performs automatic relocation of redundant data storage when disks fail without bringing the system down.

- It performs a reverse relocation operation in that it reverts to the original configuration after the failed disk has been replaced.

- It enables fast recovery with the help of Dirty Region Logging (DRL).

- It has tools to monitor performance online so that the I/O bottleneck is reduced.

- It gives you a mirrored data snapshot. This enables online backup of data by means of a backup application such as VERITAS NetBackup.

- It offers the support of Dynamic Multipathing. This helps you access data with ease and also automatically recover the data path over redundant Fibre Channel loops.

SANSYMPHONY   SANsymphony is a product of DataCore Software Corporation. You can use it to convert different disjointed storage units into networked storage pools. You can then allocate storage capacity based on demand to various servers using a simple drag-and-drop interface in a nondisruptive fashion. You can reallocate these virtual storage volumes irrespective of the underlying operating systems. You can assign appropriate privileges and make the volumes sharable between cooperating servers.

When you use SANsymphony to manage storage pools, you can easily expand storage capacity, because you can add disk capacity without disrupting application servers. You don't have to perform any expensive reconfiguration, because SANsymphony makes the storage resource behave like an integrated disk volume to the OS.

In nearly all application environments that use SANsymphony, there is a substantial improvement in performance of disk arrays and JBODs due to SANsymphony's software caching. Direct disk access is minimized due to the storage domain servers, because they increase cache availability along the data retrieval path.

SANsymphony provides a feature called Point-in-Time Snapshot, which allows you to create a view of logical volumes in a network storage pool without occupying cycles on the application server. This can be used to permit two application servers to access the same set of data at the same time. Thus, any online processing continues without getting disrupted.

Here are the features of SANsymphony:

- It allows storage to expand with ease.

- It enables shared storage pools across a network.

- It has a simple drag-and-drop interface.

- It enables LANless backups.

- With the help of its built-in protocol bridging, it allows Fibre Channel disk arrays to be added to storage domain servers without disrupting the existing external storage, such as SSA and SCSI.

- It allows you to customize the availability of storage devices to various applications, depending on their demanding nature.

APPENDIX

FREQUENTLY ASKED QUESTIONS

Q   **What are storage area networks all about?**

A   Storage area networks (SANs) provide a new technique of connecting servers to storage devices. SANs offer advantages such as increased performance, storage capacity, scalability, and management to connect a number of servers and disks. On a large scale, Fibre Channel products, along with hubs, switches, and management software, are being used in the implementation of SANs.

Q   **What is Fibre Channel?**

A   Fibre Channel is an interface that is employed in applications that require high speed, such as storage. Current implementations of Fibre Channel provide speed in the range of 1GB (200MBps full duplex), and further improvements are expected in the future. The types of Fibre Channel topologies are point-to-point, arbitrated loop, and fabric. The two most widely employed topologies in SANs are fabric and arbitrated loop. Fibre Channel enables high-speed data transfers. Fibre Channel connections can extend up to 10 km. Fibre Channel has facilitated new storage applications such as disaster recovery, clustering, and sharing storage resources. An additional feature is networking scalability and flexibility in the server-to-storage scenario.

Q   **What is Fibre Channel-Arbitrated Loop (FC-AL)?**

A   Arbitrated loop is one of the topologies of Fibre Channel. In arbitrated loop, up to 126 devices with one fabric (switch) can be connected to the loop segment through a loop hub. In a situation where devices need to send data, the devices need to arbitrate for gaining access to the loop, because the loop is a shared transport. Fibre Channel ensures data integrity with the set of commands it provides.

Q   **Is it possible to directly connect two nodes?**

A   It is possible to connect two or more Fibre Channel nodes. In a single FC-AL topology, only 127 nodes are allowed to be active at one time because of addressing issues. If you cable FC-AL through a central hub, higher availability can be ensured in a Fibre Channel SAN. Switched Fibre Channel can support 16 million node addresses.

Q   **What is a Fibre Channel fabric?**

A   One or more Fibre Channel switches in a single configuration defines a fabric. Fabric switches can provide 100MBps per port; therefore, the aggregate bandwidth can actually be increased by adding devices to a switch. Fabric switches can provide services to assist in the registration of devices and the identification of targets (disks) by servers. Storage networks can be extended for large enterprises by connecting multiple fabric switches. Fabrics are a highly scalable architecture, because the addressing scheme used for fabrics supports up to 15 million devices.

Q   **Why do I need to use storage area networks?**

A   With the increasing volume of data that needs to be accessed today, the conventional method of connecting servers and storage devices does not serve the purpose. The parallel interface, Small Computer System Interface (SCSI), has limitations in terms of speed, distance (up to only 25 meters), and the number of attached storage devices due to the parallel cabling employed. SCSI cannot be employed to provide support for up to terabytes of data.

Another point to be considered is that in these server-to-storage connections, the server alone has all the control over its attached storage. With the technology moving from server-centric to data-centric applications, it becomes necessary to have a suitable means of accessing shared data resources. Storage area networks permit the sharing of storage resources as well as server clustering, high-speed access to storage, LANless tape backups, and other applications that are required for mission-critical enterprise networks.

Q   **What is a Gigabit Interface Converter (GBIC)?**

A   Gigabit Interface Converter (GBIC) is a type of removable transceiver that is commonly employed in Fibre Channel hubs, switches, and HBAs. The purpose of a transceiver is to convert one form of signaling into another, such as fiber-optic signals into electrical signals. GBICs are a critical component of high-speed data transport because the lack of quality signaling results in no data integrity.

Q   **Are LAN technologies such as Ethernet being replaced by Fibre Channel?**

A   Fibre Channel is mainly employed in storage area networks that are based on the serial SCSI-3 protocol, even though Fibre Channel can support LAN protocols such as IP. An FC-based SAN works as a separate network and is highly recommended for high-speed block transfers of data to or from the disk. SANs offload LANs for user traffic and eliminates the bottleneck issue between the servers and storage devices.

Q   **Is it possible to employ SANs in a LAN or WAN environment?**

A   SANs work in conjunction with LAN, WAN, and MAN environments to offer improved performance and functionality as a network layer that exits behind the server layer. In a tiered client/server architecture, Fibre Channel SANs work toward enhancing performance by offloading the servers in the architecture. SANs not only offer a platform for server clustering in the market but also facilitate advanced management features such as mirroring and high-speed remote backup.

PART

IV

AP

C

Q   **Is it possible to use both hubs and switches in a storage area network environment?**

A   Yes, it is possible. Configurations can mix fabric switches and loop hubs in a single SAN, because it is possible to balance bandwidth requirements with per-port costs. Switches can support arbitrated loop devices via Fabric Loop Ports (FL_Ports). Multiple storage devices can be supported using fabric switches for high-speed backbones with fan-out of arbitrated loop hubs at a reasonable price.

Q   **In what kinds of applications are loop hubs suitably deployed?**

A   Multiple loop hub products can be used in a variety of applications. Small, single-vendor configurations generally use unmanaged hubs. In mission-critical environments that cannot tolerate downtime and that require instant notification of major events, managed hubs are used. Zoning managed hubs such as the Vixel 2100 are used in tape backup and other applications that require segmentation for specific operations. In some applications that require high bandwidth per device or long (10 km) links, instead of a loop, which is a shared 100MBps transport, fabric switches are used. You need to keep in mind that in storage applications, arbitrated loop hubs offer more than the required bandwidth and device population for efficient performance.

Q   **In what kinds of situations can I employ fabric switches?**

A   Fabric switches can be employed in high-bandwidth applications (full-motion video). Loop hubs support only 126 devices, so fabric switches are suitable in configurations that require more than that. Fabric switches are commonly used for long links (up to 10 km) in campus and disaster-recovery installations because of the advantage that each port in a fabric switch can drive a bandwidth of 100MBps without affecting the other ports. Fabric switches are also used for disruption-sensitive applications such as tape backup, because these switches can isolate the effect of loop initializations for attached loop devices.

Q   **Can Fibre Channel be implemented only with fiber-optic cables?**

A   Fibre Channel is not limited to working only with fiber-optic cables. It also supports copper cabling and active and passive copper.

Q   **How can SAN management be categorized?**

A   In mission-critical applications, SAN management is a crucial factor. Management software can be split into different categories: management of switches, hubs, and HBAs (storage network management); the location and utilization of disk resources (storage resource management); data placement; tape backup; RAID and volume management (storage management); and management of LAN, WAN, and storage network resources (systems management).

Certain management software products offer storage network management of intelligent hubs and switches. The advantage is that the user gains visibility to the SAN transport from a single screen. In addition to the integrity features that are engineered into certain hub and switch products, the management software might also be able to practically monitor the SAN transport and aid in minimizing downtime. You can make decisions regarding capacity planning and the optimal utilization of SAN resources by using the performance monitoring facilities.

Q **How can Fibre Channel be used to implement disaster recovery?**

A Fibre Channel can provide links between devices that are located as far as 10 km from each other. Fibre Channel's support for long connections, along with the SCSI-3 protocol application, assists in disaster recovery. In a disaster recovery configuration, the production site is generally set up in a dual-path topology. SANs, at the production site, can make use of switches or hubs or both, based on the bandwidth and other needs. You can utilize Fibre Channel switches to isolate the long links from the production site to the disaster recovery location. This isolation process enables off-loading the disaster recovery traffic from the switch segments or local loop. The disaster recovery site can also be designed to provide an extra level of data security for the mirroring functions by supporting redundant data paths. In the case of hierarchical storage management (HSM), the disaster recovery site also uses a tape backup system.

Q **What is the first step in implementing or deploying SANs?**

A Before you implement any new technology, you might want to look at the operational and business issues that the technology is expected to resolve. In relation to SANs, you need to keep in mind that backup and scalability issues need to be resolved. You should also consider the cause of any problems in your environment.

Q **What should be done to eliminate the downtime in a SAN environment?**

A Two main building blocks help you design your SAN to achieve high availability—management software and redundant data paths. Loop hub products that support auto-recovery functionality can isolate problem nodes. At the same time, the information that a problem has been rectified is passed on to the management software. If the problems are identified and resolved quickly, the overall mean time to repair is reduced.

Another important factor that helps you work toward high availability is redundant data paths. For example, consider the usage of redundant switches, which provide the server with not only a primary path but also a backup path to the storage. If a switch or link malfunctions, the backup path diverts the traffic. Using loop hubs can also build redundant configurations, because loop hubs offer path fail-over. In full redundancy, all the components, such as power supplies and cabling, can be replicated; therefore, this is preferred over the dual power supplies method.

PART

IV

AP

C

Q **Is it possible to bridge and route between Fibre Channel and Ethernet protocols?**

A It is possible to bridge the Fibre Channel protocol to the Ethernet protocol. In terms of routing between the two, Fibre Channel/Ethernet routers are currently unavailable. The feasible solution would be to load a PC node with both a Fibre Channel adapter card and an Ethernet network interface card (NIC) so that the computer on its own works as a Fibre Channel router.

Q **Compare Fibre Channel SAN and the parallel SCSI connectivity currently used.**

A Because native Fibre Channel disk drives can support 10Mbps I/O, the storage applications move the SCSI data directly to the channel, thereby making maximum use of Fibre Channel's gigabaud bandwidth. Fibre Channel also offers higher speed than SCSI and can support both fiber-optic and copper cabling. Fibre Channel is a better choice than parallel SCSI because of its ability to map IP. Fibre Channel's IP ensures improved data management and increased data access, because it allows networked storage devices to access multiple nodes or servers.

Q **What do SANs offer in terms of natural applications, and to what extent do SANs enable advanced management features?**

A SANs offer an open, extensible platform to enable storage access in data-intensive environments such as data warehousing, OLTP, server clustering, and storage management applications. Fibre Channel SANs ease the process of backup and remote mirroring, distributed HSM, and fault-tolerant data access. The storage devices can be connected up to a distance of 10 km by using Fibre Channel. The remote storage locations can support features such as disk mirroring for disaster recovery applications.

Q **What is the maximum native I/O transfer rate of a Fibre Channel SAN?**

A Currently, Fibre Channel can support 133MB, 266MB, 532MB, and 1.0625GB bandwidths (each value is double the previous). The goal is to develop a 4GB Fibre Channel specification.

Q **How do I build a fully redundant SAN?**

A You need to cable two fully independent, redundant loops to ensure full redundancy in Fibre Channel SANs. With this cabling method, two independent data paths are equipped with fully redundant hardware. This is achieved by the dual ports that many disk arrays and disk drives offer (for a high-availability environment). Higher-availability port bypass functionality is offered to each loop by wiring each loop through a hub.

Q   **What is the importance of hubs in SANs?**

A   Similar to the purpose of Ethernet hubs in LAN environments, Fibre Channel hubs offer fault tolerance in SAN environments. In Fibre Channel-Arbitrated Loop, each node behaves like a repeater for the remaining nodes on the loop. However, if even one node fails, the entire loop fails. Therefore, hubs create fault isolation in Fibre Channel SANs. The bypass functionality of a hub's port ensures that a problem port is automatically bypassed, with many faults avoided. It is possible for stations to be added to or removed from the loop without causing severe loop problems. You can build redundancies into hubs so that they can be used in enterprise systems that do not work with unplanned downtime.

Q   **Are SANs limited in terms of interoperability?**

A   In earlier developed SANs, the different components offered by many vendors faced the problem of interoperability. This does not mean that SANs lack interoperability, because the future holds promise that this interoperability issue will become less of a problem between hubs, switches, and HBAs in the market.

Q   **Is Fibre Channel the only protocol that works well with SANs?**

A   Earlier, Fibre Channel seemed to be the most suitable communications link in SANs, because Fibre Channel could offer SANs with the speed and distance required. Currently, SANs are generally implemented with the arbitrated loops and switched topologies of Fibre Channel, but future development shows signs of SCSI over IP to be applied in SANs.

PART

IV

AP

C

GLOSSARY

8b/10b encoding   An encoding scheme that transmits data in the form of bytes (1 byte equals 8 bits) to a 10-bit format. This scheme, developed by IBM, is used to encode and decode Fibre Channel data transmissions. This method is defined in the FC-1 layer.

ACK frame   Acknowledgment frame. Used to control end-to-end data flow. This frame is sent by the destination to verify the receipt of the data transmission in a Class 1 or Class 2 connection.

adapter   A hardware unit (circuit assembly) that aggregates I/O units and communications links to a system bus. It helps transmit data between the system bus and external links. There are different kinds of adapters, such as I/O adapters, Host Bus Adapters (HBAs), and FC adapters.

address   A formatted number specifying the network location of a device, node, or any other component on a network. See *SCSI address* and *FC-AL address*.

address identifier   A 24-bit number that forms a part of the frame header in an FC communication. It indicates the source (S-ID) and destination (D-ID) addresses.

analog signal   An electrical signal that has a continuous nature. It varies in frequency, phase, or amplitude to denote changes in the transmission.

ANSI   American National Standards Institute. A standards organization that fosters the development of technology standards in the U.S.

arbitrated loop   An FC topology that enables the interconnection of two to 126 devices in a single serial loop circuit. It supports all classes of service and is controlled by arbitration. The topology guarantees in-order delivery of frames.

arbitration   A method wherein the devices on the loop contend and gain temporary access to communicate over the loop.

ARP   Address Resolution Protocol. A function that is used to translate an IP address to an Ethernet address.

ATM   Asynchronous Transfer Mode. A high-speed packet-switching transport that is used for data transmission over LANs or WANs. It lets nodes transmit simultaneously with an any-to-any connection where a fixed-length unit of data is transmitted.

attenuation   A loss of power due to transmission communication devices and media.

backup   Creating a copy of data that can be used to restore the system in case the original data is corrupted or lost.

bandwidth   The transmission capacity of a medium (cable, link, and so on) in terms of the range of frequencies that can be sent through the circuit in a given length of time. This is usually measured in Mbps or Gbps.

bridge   A device used to connect two or more devices or networks and forward packets between them by reading and filtering data packets and frames. A bridge is usually used to connect dissimilar media and signaling systems. The FC 4/2 bridge is an example of a bridge that is used to connect dissimilar media. See also *router*.

callback   A scheme used in event-driven programs whereby a function or handler is registered (callback handler) and is called or invoked asynchronously when a specified event occurs.

cascade   A method of connecting one hub or switch to another hub or switch. This lets you increase the number of ports or the distance of an arbitrated loop. The maximum number of levels to which you can cascade depends on your product.

channel   A point-to-point link that is used mainly to transport data from one port to another.

CIM   Common Information Model. A management structure that enables the management of disparate devices through a central application.

class of service   The type of service provided by the FC topology in terms of the delivery scheme to be followed. Different classes have different sets of specified delivery characteristics and attributes.

Class-1   A class providing a dedicated connection between two ports. It requires an acknowledgment for every frame activated.

Class-2   A class providing no dedicated connection between two ports. It uses a frame-switching service to deliver the frames. It needs an acknowledgment for every frame delivered.

Class-3   A class providing datagram service between two ports (or multicast service between multicast originators and recipients). It requires no acknowledgment of frames delivered.

Class-4   A class providing a connection between ports. It uses a fraction of the available bandwidth (through a fractional bandwidth virtual circuit). It requires an acknowledgment of frames delivered.

Class-6   A class providing a unidivisional dedicated connection that uses multicast service. It requires an acknowledgment of frames delivered. Used mainly in areas such as video broadcasting.

Class-F   A class providing connectionless service between E-ports. Predominantly used for coordination and configuration of the fabric.

client   A software program (or, in general, a node) that is used to contact the server and obtain data.

cluster   A type of parallel or distributed system that interconnects a set of devices or servers and lets it be used as a single unified device or server. It helps provide load balancing and automatic failures.

PART

IV

AP

D

coaxial cable   A cable or medium used for high-speed transmissions. It consists of two channels—one that carries the signal and one that acts as the ground and prevents noise from affecting the signal. Both channels run along the same axis (one enclosed by the other)—hence the name coaxial.

communication memory   Any region of memory that is registered with the VI Provider in order to store and manage Descriptors and communication buffers.

community   A grouping (relationship) between an SNMP agent and a number of SNMP managers that defines authentication, access control, proxy characteristics, and so on.

completion queue   A queue that contains information about all the completed Descriptors. This is of great use in creating a single point of completion notification for multiple work queues.

control segment   The first component of a Descriptor. It contains information about the type of operations to be performed by the VI NIC, the location of the next Descriptor or the work queue, and so on.

controller   A component that is attached to the system topology. It includes a request/response identification mechanism (RAID controller).

Copper cables   Cables, whose core is made of copper wires, used to connect SAN devices and servers. These cables support high-speed transfers and are extremely cheap when compared to fiber optic cables.

CRC   Cyclic Redundancy Check. An error-correcting code used in FC. It is a number derived from the block of data to be transmitted. By recalculating the number, the receiver can confirm whether there were any transmission errors.

credit   The maximum number of receive buffers that an F_Port can provide to its attached N_Port. This numeric value lets the N_Port transmit frames without overshooting the limit.

daisy-chaining   A concept that lets you expand the number of ports by interconnecting the interconnect devices, such as switches and hubs.

DAS   Direct Attached Storage. A type of storage topology wherein the storage device is directly attached to the server or host.

Data center   Also known as datacenter. A centralized repository of storage that includes the central data processing facility of an organization, the network of the facility, and human resources that manage the data repository.

data payload   (Also called payload.) The actual amount of data that can be carried in one packet. The actual amount excludes any header and control information.

data storage   The holding of storage in an electromagnetic form for access by computer processors. This storage could be in a number of forms—primary, secondary, or tertiary storage. The devices that hold this data are known as storage media.

datagram   A service that lets data be sent to multiple devices attached to the fabric.

default zone   A component that contains all the devices that do not form a part of the zones in the active zone set.

Descriptor   A structure that describes a data movement request to VI NIC. It is comprised of different segments, such as the control segment, address segment, and data segment.

digital signal   A signal that uses discrete steps to depict information.

Disaster Recovery   The capability of a system to respond to interruptions in services to restore all the critical functions of the business. The tasks that are used to accomplish the restoration are also known as the disaster recovery plan.

disk mirroring   A technique that is used to write data to different disks using the same controller. This is basically used to ensure fault tolerance.

disk pooling   A SAN concept that lets multiple hosts access storage devices and therefore enables data sharing across hosts and systems.

Doorbell   A mechanism that is used to notify the VI NIC of a Descriptor being posted to a work queue. Only an operating system should be able to establish a Doorbell and allow the VI NIC to identify the VI that posted the Descriptor to the work queue.

Ethernet   A type of widely used LAN which is connected over coaxial or twisted pair cables. Some examples of Ethernet connections are 10BASE-T and 100BASE-T connections.

E_Port   Expansion port. A port on a switch that is used for interswitch connections. This port enables the cascading of switches and helps you build redundant, high-availability topologies.

ESCON   Enterprise System Connection. An IBM technology that is predominantly used to connect storage devices to mainframes over fiber-optic cables.

F_Port   Fabric port. Used to attach N_Port to a switch fabric.

fabric   A kind of topology in SANs that uses a crosspoint switched network. It contains one or more elements, such as switches or directors, that take care of frame routing and therefore relieve the devices that are connected to it of management tasks. In this topology, N_Ports are connected to F_Ports on a switch.

fabric login   A process used by N_Ports to determine whether a fabric is present and to initialize the link settings before communication with other N_Ports is attempted.

FC-0   The bottom layer of the FC-Physical standard. Represents the characteristics of the physical medium and interface.

FC-1   The middle level of the FC-Physical standard. Controls 53/106 encoding and decoding.

PART

IV

AP

D

FC-2   Handles the framing and protocol frame format, ordered set usage, and so on. It is the top level of the FC-Physical standard and defines the rules for signaling protocol, sequence, and exchanges.

FC-3   Handles common services such as striping definition that are used by N_Ports. This layer is part of the upper layer in the Fibre Channel architecture.

FC-4   The top layer in the Fibre Channel standard and a part of the upper layers of the architecture. Provides mapping of the lower layers to upper-level protocols.

FC-AL address   Refers to the automatically assigned 8-bit device address, on a private FC-AL loop, when loop initialization occurs.

FC-CT   Fibre Channel Common Transport protocol.

FCIA   Fibre Channel Industry Association.

FC-PH   Fibre Channel Physical and signaling standard. It contains mapping to the three layers (FC-0, FC-1, and FC-2) and further indicates specifications for media types and transmission speeds.

fiber-optic cable   Used for high-speed transmission over large distances. It consists of thin dielectric material, such as glass, through which data is transmitted in light pulses.

Fibre Channel   A generalized transport mechanism that has no native protocol for data delivery. It uses existing protocols, such as SCSI, and transports them in frames. The frames are decoded at the other end to get the real message.

Fibre Channel-Arbitrated Loop (FC-AL)   Refers to a generalized workgroup topology where media access is processed through arbitration. This topology can support a maximum of 126 devices without using fabric protocols.

FICON   Fibre Connection. A technology that is used to connect S/390 systems to provide a parallel enterprise server.

frame   A collection of bits that defines the data and its control information. It is the smallest unit of data transfer.

full duplex   A method that enables simultaneous transmission and reception of data over a single link.

gateway   A device or node on the network that enables the interconnection of two different, incompatible networks.

GBIC   Gigabit Interface Converter. A removable component that is used to link Fibre Channel and Gigabit Ethernet transport.

Gbps   Gigabits per second.

GBps   Gigabytes per second.

half duplex   A two-way communication system that enables only single-sided conversation. At any given point in time, only one party of the conversation can talk.

handshake   The process of two modems or ports (end nodes) agreeing to the method of data transmission in a given connection.

HBA   Host Bus Adapter. A circuit-assembled interface between that system bus and Fibre Channel.

HIPPI   High-Performance Parallel Interface. Provides an advanced interface that enables data transfer rates in the range of 80Mbps.

HSM   Hierarchical Storage Management. A software- and hardware-based system that manages data storage by moving data between the different disks or other storage resources.

hub   A device that connects to a specific node and enables transmission between all the connected nodes. It provides automatic initialization and removal of the nodes in a Fibre Channel-Arbitrated Loop topology.

in-band   The management of the information between the management agent and the host.

initiator   A server or workstation that starts the transaction between tape drives and disk drives.

JBOD   Just a Bunch Of Disks. A set of disks clubbed together and configured as a single segment or node in the loop.

K28.5   A 10-bit special character that denotes the beginning of a Fibre Channel command.

kernel agent   A part of the operating system that is needed by the VI Architecture. It includes the role of the device driver for the VI NIC. It has the kernel software that is required to register communication memory and manage VI processes.

L_Port   Loop port. Supports Arbitrated Loop protocol. Lets you connect F_Ports and N_Ports as a loop-capable port.

LAN   Local Area Network. A group of computers and other devices in a limited area that are connected over a communication link. The link enables the different devices and computers to communicate with each other.

latency   The minimum amount of time it takes a network device to transfer or forward a frame. The higher the latency, the slower the transmission.

link   1. The connection between nodes in a topology, along with the associated transmitters and receivers. 2. A full-duplex channel that is present between two network fabric elements. These elements could be nodes, routers, or switches.

LIP   Loop Initialization Process. The sequence that allows the ports that join a loop to obtain an AL_PA address. It is also used to indicate loop failures and to reset a node.

long-wave hub   A type of hub used in Fibre Channel Arbitrated Loop topologies to connect over long distances. It uses long-wave lasers and fiber-optic cables to transmit over long distances.

loop topology   A closed-circuit topology in which each node is connected to two neighboring nodes. The bandwidth in this topology is shared among the nodes.

LUN   Logical Unit Number or Logical Unit. The physical disk drive that can be addressed as a single entity. It can map to a portion of a disk or pool multiple disks to be referenced as a single address.

MAN   Metropolitan Area Networks. A network that interconnects computers and other devices across an area larger than LANs but smaller than WANs. This term is used to refer to the interconnection of several smaller LANs within a specified geographical limit. It is sometimes also referred to as *campus networks*.

management station   A device (typically a computer) that is used to host the management software.

Mbps   Megabits per second.

MBps   Megabytes per second.

memory handle   A programmatic construct that is created by the VI Kernel Agent when a process registers communication memory. It represents the authorization of a process to specify a memory region to the VI NIC.

memory protection attribute   The access right granted to VIs and to memory regions for Remote Direct Memory Access (RDMA).

memory protection tag   A unique identifier that is associated with VI and the memory region to define VI's access permissions to a memory region. It is generated by the VI Provider to be used by the VI Consumer.

memory region   A region of a process's virtual address space that is registered as communication memory, allowing the VI NIC to access it directly. Its size is not defined.

memory registration   The process of creating a memory region. The result of this process is a memory handle, which the VI process needs to provide with any virtual address within the memory region.

message   A unit of data interchange that is defined by the application.

message latency   The amount of time from the initiation of a message from a source until the recipient is notified that the complete message is present in its memory.

message overhead   The amount of time that is needed to initiate transmission of a message, inform the recipient of the message's availability, and process the data involved in moving data from the source to the destination.

metadata   Data that is associated with other objects or data. It contains information about the characteristics of the object or data it points to.

MIA   Media Interface Adapter. A device that lets you connect fiber-optic-based devices to copper-based devices or adapters.

MIB   Management Information Base. An SNMP structure that contains all configuration and device information and is used for device management.

mirroring   See *disk mirroring*.

modulation   The process of encoding a given signal (analog or digital) to a different waveform. It is performed to adapt the signal to a different frequency range.

MTBF   Mean Time Between Failures. The time difference between two failures. It is a measure of a device's longevity.

MTU   Maximum Transmission Unit. The length of the largest frame that might be sent on a physical medium.

multicast   A transmission system that lets you send broadcasts to multiple N_Ports on a fabric. The broadcast may be restricted to only a subset of N_Ports on the fabric.

multiplex   A method to deliver a single transmission to multiple devices. It also can coalesce data from multiple destinations to a single transmission medium.

N_Port   Node port. Refers to the hardware port in a Fibre Channel connection that enables data communication over the fabric.

NAS   Network Attached Storage. A storage topology in which the storage devices are connected to the network directly.

NDMP   Network Data Management Protocol. A network-based protocol that lets you communicate without OS dependencies for performing centralized backups.

network fabric   The set of routers, switches, connectors, and cables that connects a set of nodes in a network.

NIC   Network Interface Controller. A device that provides an electromechanical attachment of a computer to a network. It helps with copying data from memory to the network medium, transmitting, and copying data from the medium back to memory.

NIC handle   A programmatic construct that represents the authorization to do communication operations by using a local VI NIC.

node   1. A hardware device in a fabric or loop that enables the transmission of data over the network. It can support more than one port. 2. A processing location in computer networks. It could be a computer attached to one or more links of a network.

OFC   Open Fibre Control. A safety method used to ensure that high-intensity laser signals are not used for transmission when there is a break in the fiber cable.

PART

IV

AP

Operating System   Often abbreviated as *OS*. Is a program that controls all other programs in a computer. It manages the sharing of the internal memory among the different applications. It also manages the input/output operations and provides parallel processing.

ordered set   A set of low-level link functions that is used to manage frame transport and media access. It includes frame delimiters and primitive signals and is made up of four 10-bit characters. It always starts with a K28.5 special character.

OS independent   Also known as operating system independent. It is a term commonly used to address solutions or programs that are compatible on any operating system. These solutions typically use an abstraction layer that hides the operating system from the rest of the solution or program.

out-band signaling   A signaling mechanism that separates the transmission of data signals and management information. It is usually used to provide an alternative method to transmit management information outside the fabric (usually over the Ethernet).

outstanding   The state of the Descriptor after it has been posted on a Work queue and before it is completed. It is the time interval between when a process posts a Descriptor to a Work queue and the Descriptor is completed.

packet   A unit of data interchange between nodes that has data segments that are transmitted in an ordered stream. It might be divided further into smaller units called cells and transmitted. But the order in which it is transmitted is preserved so that the smaller units get back to the form of the same packet at the destination node.

point-to-point   A type of connection in which a dedicated connection is established between the communicating nodes or devices.

port   A hardware component within a node that enables data communication over Fibre Channel.

post   The act of placing a Descriptor on a VI Work queue.

primitive signal   A type of ordered set that is sent to indicate the status of the devices. It is used for buffer-to-buffer control and helps maintain byte and word synchronization.

protocol   A formal set of rules that is defined to govern data transmission conventions such as timing control, error control, and so on.

QoS   Quality of Service. The metrics that predict behavior, the speed with which data is transmitted, and the latency associated with a given network.

RAID   Redundant Array of Inexpensive Disks. A method of combining multiple disk modules into a single logical unit.

RAID-0   A disk configuration that uses striping and three or more disk modules. This RAID level provides no redundancy.

RAID-1   A disk configuration that uses an equal number of mirrored disks and data disks and provides complete redundancy.

RAID-3   A disk configuration that uses disk striping and a dedicated parity module but provides no mirroring.

RAID-5   A disk configuration that uses disk striping and stores parity information in a distributed method across all the disk modules. This provides for a truly high-availability configuration.

RDMA   Remote Direct Memory Access. An operation of a Descriptor that involves moving data in a local scatter-gather list directly to or from a memory region on a remote node.

receive queue   One of the two queues that are associated with a VI. It has Descriptors that have information about where the incoming data needs to be placed.

redundancy   A term used to refer to duplicated network paths or devices. Redundancy is used in SANs to provide fault-tolerant and high-availability configurations.

repeater   A device that has a circuit with a recovered clock, which is used to regenerate and amplify the signal received and then retransmit it.

router   A device that is used to forward packets in a network between one device and another. It is also used to forward packets from one network to another. It can decide the best possible path to be followed on the basis of certain metrics, which is why it is also known as an intelligent router.

SAN   Storage Area Network. A server-to-storage network that offers high scalability, availability, and manageability. It can offer gigabit speed connectivity with a comprehensive fault tolerance system and low ownership costs.

scatter-gather list   A valid list of the mapping of logical to physical addresses that will be written to for a particular transfer. This is useful to ensure that the data at various locations can be copied or moved sequentially.

SCSI   Small Computer System Interface. An ANSI standard electronic parallel interface that is used to connect I/O hardware devices to systems.

SCSI Address   Refers to the address assigned to each SCSI device either in a loop or as a part of the switched SAN network.

send queue   One of the two queues that are associated with a VI. It has Descriptors that have information about the data to be transmitted.

sequence   A group of frames transmitted from one N_Port to another. All transmissions in a sequence are unidirectional.

server   A computer that attends to the requests of other computers—usually remote, client computers. These computers generally have centralized data storage capacity and stress I/O connectivity to serve the requests.

SES   SCSI Enclosure Services. A part of SCSI protocol that is used to monitor the physical status of the enclosed devices.

SNMP   Simple Network Management Protocol. A protocol that is designed to let you obtain management information from devices. It has a set of commands that let you get status and parameter information from devices.

SONET   Synchronous Optical Network. A standard that is used to map payloads on an optical network.

spatial reuse   A concept that enables an increase in the aggregate bandwidth by allowing simultaneous traffic to be transmitted over a bus.

SSA   Serial Storage Architecture. A high-speed loop interface that provides high-speed point-to-point connections, especially to storage devices.

star topology   A type of topology in which the physical configuration is connected to a central hub that handles all the communication.

striping   A RAID technique that maps consecutive ranges of virtual data addresses to array members in a cyclic fashion to enable writing a file to multiple disks.

switch   A component that provides multiple simultaneous connections between devices and enables the use of full bandwidth.

System Area Network   A network that interconnects nodes in a distributed computer system. It is characteristic of high bandwidth and low latency.

TCP/IP   Transmission Control Protocol/Internet Protocol. A set of communication protocols that are used to connect hosts on the Internet. IP is used to move packets of data from node to node. TCP is used to verify the correct delivery of data from client to server.

Topology   A terminology used to refer to the physical or logical arrangement of the different nodes in a network.

trap message   An SNMP procedure that is used by SNMP agents to notify the SNMP management station of certain events.

TTL   Time To Live. An attribute that determines how long an entry can reside in the cache before it expires.

tunneling   A technique that is used to connect two hosts over a different network.

Unicast   A routing mechanism that identifies an optimal path between any two switches in a fabric.

user agent   A software component that makes an operating system communication facility use a specific VI Provider.

VI   Virtual Interface. A mechanism by which a VI Consumer directly accesses a VI Provider in order to do data transfer operations.

VI address   A VI's logical name.

VI Consumer A software process that consists of an application, an OS communication facility, and VI User Agent. It uses a virtual interface to communicate.

VI NIC address The logical network address that corresponds to the VI NIC, which is assigned by the OS. It lets processes identify a remote node in a network corresponding to its VI NIC attachment to the network.

VI Provider A set of components that instantiates a Virtual Interface.

VM Virtual Memory. The address space that is available to a process running in a system with a memory management unit.

WAN Wide Area Network. It is an extension of a network that is connected over telecommunication links. The network is typically spread across geographies.

WDM Wavelength Division Multiplexer. A type of multiplexer that provides multiple wavelengths to be combined and transported over a single cable. This technology lets up to 80 (or even more) separate wavelengths be multiplexed into a single stream that can be sent over a single fiber-optic cable.

Work queue A set of Descriptors that are to be processed by a VI NIC. A VI has two Work queues—the Send queue and the Receive queue.

workstation A computer used for applications that require moderate computing capability and comparatively high graphics quality.

write-back cache A caching method in which modifications to the data in the cache are not copied to the cache source until absolutely necessary. This ensures that the number of write operations to the main memory is reduced.

WWN World Wide Name. A registered unique 64-bit identifier that is used to refer to nodes and ports in a fabric.

zone A component that has a set of devices that can access each other through port-to-port connections. It ensures that only devices that are a part of it are permitted to communicate with each other.

zone set A component that is used to group zones. It lets you activate and deactivate a set of zones together. However, only one zone set can be active at any given point in time.

zoning A feature that enables grouping of multiple ports to form a separate virtual private SAN. It is the process of logically segmenting the network according to the relationships between the entities.

PART
IV

AP
D

INDEX

Hey, you've got enough worries.

Don't let IT training be one of them.

Get on the fast track to IT training at InformIT,
your total Information Technology training network.

 | **www.informit.com** |

■ Hundreds of timely articles on dozens of topics ■ Discounts on IT books from all our publishing partners, including Que Publishing ■ Free, unabridged books from the InformIT Free Library ■ "Expert Q&A"—our live, online chat with IT experts ■ Faster, easier certification and training from our Web- or classroom-based training programs ■ Current IT news ■ Software downloads ■ Career-enhancing resources